Divested

Divested

Inequality in the Age of Finance

KEN-HOU LIN
MEGAN TOBIAS NEELY

OXFORD
UNIVERSITY PRESS

Oxford University Press is a department of the University of Oxford. It furthers
the University's objective of excellence in research, scholarship, and education
by publishing worldwide. Oxford is a registered trade mark of Oxford University
Press in the UK and certain other countries.

Published in the United States of America by Oxford University Press
198 Madison Avenue, New York, NY 10016, United States of America.

© Oxford University Press 2020

CIP data is on file at the Library of Congress
ISBN 978–0–19–063831–3

9 8 7 6 5 4 3 2 1

Printed by Sheridan Books, Inc., United States of America

CONTENTS

Introduction

FINANCE HAS BECOME AN essential fabric of contemporary American life. From how we afford our educations, buy homes, or run businesses, to how we plan for retirement and so much more, finance governs our everyday lives. How did this come to be, and what are the consequences for inequality in American society? This is the question at the heart of *Divested*. In the process of answering it we explore a range of related questions: How did finance become the most lucrative of all businesses? How has it transformed US corporations? When did every household decision become an investment decision? Most importantly, how has finance shaped the distribution of resources among Americans?

These days, finance is so fundamental to our everyday lives that it is difficult to imagine a world without it. But until the 1970s, the financial sector accounted for a mere 15 percent of all corporate profits in the US economy. Back then, most of what the financial sector did was simple credit intermediation and risk management: banks took deposits from households and corporations and loaned those funds to homebuyers and business. They issued and collected checks to facilitate payment. For important or paying customers, they provided space in their vaults to safeguard valuable items. Insurance companies received premiums from their customers and paid out when a costly incident occurred.

By 2002, the financial sector had tripled, coming to account for 43 percent of all the corporate profits generated in the US economy. These profits grew alongside increasingly complex intermediations such as securitization, derivatives trading, and fund management, most of which take place not between individuals or companies, but between financial institutions (Turner 2015). What the financial sector *does* has become opaque to the public even as its functions have become crucial to every level of the economy. The decisions made by households, corporations, and states are all guided by financial markets whose workings are, to most, utterly inscrutable.

And as American finance expanded, inequality soared. Capital's share of national income rose alongside compensation for corporate executives and those working on Wall Street. Meanwhile, among full-time workers, the Gini index (a measure of earnings inequality) increased 26 percent, and mass layoffs became a common business practice instead of a last resort. All these developments amplified wealth inequality, with the top 0.1 percent of US households coming to own more than 20 percent of the entire nation's wealth—a distribution that rivals the dominance of the robber barons of the Gilded Age (Saez and Zucman 2016). When the financial crisis of 2008 temporarily narrowed the wealth divide, monetary policies adopted to address it quickly resuscitated the banks and secured the affluent's assets but left employment tenuous and wages stagnant.

The past four decades of American history have therefore been marked by two interconnected, transformative developments: the financialization of the US economy and the surge in inequality across US society. This book shows that *one cannot be understood without the other*. Indeed, the rise of finance is one fundamental *cause* of the heightened inequality in the contemporary United States. The most damaging consequence of the contemporary financial system is not simply recurrent financial crises, but a widening social divide between the haves and have-nots. To understand contemporary finance is to understand contemporary inequality.

We are not the first to claim that the rise of the US financial sector engendered inequality. In the fall of 2011, protesters occupied Zuccotti Park, only blocks from the New York Stock Exchange, calling attention to the stark disparity in wealth between Wall Street and Main Street. Occupy Wall Street protesters initially demanded the arrest of financiers responsible for the 2008 crisis, a tightening of Wall Street regulation, a ban on high-frequency trading, and an investigation into political corruption. As the movement grew, the protesters' demands became more ambitious. The movement's well-known slogan—"We are the 99%"—called on the American public to reclaim power and resources from "the 1%," that small group of financial and political elites who control the vast majority of American capital. Protesters attributed stark inequality to a revolving door between New York and Washington, or between finance and politics, tipping the balance of political power in the favor of organized corporate interests, allowing ruling elites to prosper while working- and middle-class Americans flounder.

Occupy protestors were initially ignored by the mainstream media, yet they garnered international attention as they took on the problem of inequality and the extreme wealth of the "1%" on Wall Street. The movement began with a small encampment in a public park in September 2011. Within weeks, it had spread across the country and around the world. The mobilizations peaked on October 15, when organizers tallied 950 participating cities in more than 80 countries around the world. Major European capitals, such as Rome and Madrid, had crowds estimated at 200,000 to 500,000 people, and more than 70,000 protesters turned out for nationwide actions in the United States. Despite facing criticism for their leaderless, democratic approach and evolving demands, the protesters' central message condemning inequality spread far and wide.[1]

Perhaps the most successful outcome of the Occupy movement is that it underlined Wall Street's role in widening economic inequality between the 99 percent and 1 percent. In his 2012 State of the Union address, President Barack Obama emphasized that a "deficit of trust between Main Street and Wall Street" warranted the Dodd-Frank Wall Street Reform and Consumer Protection Act of 2010. Pundits including economist Paul Krugman publicly shared the sentiments espoused by Occupy protesters, arguing that the industry responsible for the Great Recession must pay for the damages caused by its greed and excess. Democrats and Republicans alike came to recognize that economic inequality was a paramount concern, and populism arose as the winning ideology in the 2016 presidential election. Still, amid scathing critiques and powerful political movements, the money to be had in financial services swelled and inequality continued to expand.

Of course, the overall connection between finance and inequality feels intuitive. Exactly *how* finance drives inequality, however, remains obscure. This is in part because finance is an all-encompassing term used for a diverse, interconnected web of activities—many of which cannot be adequately explained by even its handsomely paid practitioners. Financial activity is not restricted to individuals participating in banking and investment to make purchases or manage their wealth; large organizations including firms, nonprofits, and governments fund their operations through finance. The providers and consumers of these services are just as diverse, including community banks and credit unions that serve local ventures, global conglomerates that simultaneously operate in retail and investment banking, boutique funds that specialize in niche markets, and nonbank financial institutions such as insurance firms, payday lending, and corporations' financial arms. All these financial producers and consumers have different agendas, incentives, resources, and constraints. Furthermore, with money constantly changing hands, contemporary finance conceals how resources are transferred from the have-nots to the haves.

Likewise, inequality can refer to a variety of uneven distributions. Economists Thomas Piketty and Emmanuel Saez (2006) brought top income concentration to the fore in discussions of inequality, documenting that the share of national income earned by the top-percentile families increased from less than 10 percent in the late 1970s to more than 20 percent in recent years. This New Gilded Age also features expanding wealth inequality, declining share of income for labor, stagnating median wage growth, diminishing employment security, persisting gender and racial wage gaps, booming student debts, and lingering pessimism and mistrust.

Because of these intricacies, studies on this topic often touch only fragments of the connections between finance and inequality. Building on previous scholarship, this book intends to provide a more comprehensive, synthetic account of how financialization has led to greater inequality in the United States. Using a wide variety of evidence, we document the ascendance of finance on Wall Street, Main Street, and in households, documenting how it has exacerbated economic inequalities.

Divested shows that what warrants concern is not the egos or testosterone levels of financial professionals but why even law-abiding bankers and fund managers may directly or indirectly put many American families in harm's way. While we sympathize with the populist view that the excessive earnings on Wall Street are indefensible, we suspect the connection between finance and inequality runs wider and deeper than excessive greed and reckless behavior. Policies targeting a specific set of high-earners, such as earnings caps or progressive taxes, are necessary but insufficient to address the issue of rising inequality. Furthermore, we disagree with populist claims that financial professionals are inherently "evil" or particularly flawed; like many others, they strive for success and believe wholeheartedly in their own hard work and deservedness. Some cheat to get ahead and others cheat so they do not fall behind, to be sure, yet most people in finance believe that they follow the "rules," outperform other market actors, and fittingly reap the rewards of their skilled labor.

Divested argues that the rise of finance represents a paradigmatic, regressive shift in how American society organizes economic resources. In this process, finance reshapes the economy in three principal ways. First, it creates excessive intermediaries that extract resources from society without providing commensurate economic benefit. New financial instruments are invented to serve "unmet" demands, but most of these serve only financial institutions. The process is facilitated by the concentration of market power, the rising political influence of financial power-holders, and the private intermediation of public policies. As a result, financial firms and their elite workers accrue unprecedented amounts of resources.

Second, finance loosens the codependence between capital and labor, weakening the demand for labor and workers' bargaining power. When firms outside the financial sector shift their resources and attention from their core business to financial arms, they exclude workers from the revenue-generating process and diminish workers' worth and leverage. Furthermore, as ever more resources are channeled toward lending, speculative trading, and shareholder payoffs, employment growth slows, particularly for mid- and low-level workers. Consequently, labor's share of income reduces while executive compensation skyrockets. As earnings disparities widen, the relationship between employer and employee at all but the top levels worsens.

Third, finance undermines existing social institutions such as labor unions and large corporations that used to buffer economic risks by providing employment security and reliable health and retirement benefits. The disappearance of these safeguards transfers uncertainties from organizations to families, further elevating the need for financial services. An increasing number of American families come to rely on debt to get by and financial assets to secure retirement. These financial products not only channel more resources to the financial sector but are invariably regressive: poor households pay the highest interests and fees, while rich households have the most resources to gain from financial market volatility.

By analyzing the ascendance of finance and how it has promoted and preyed upon economic disparities, this book rejects the idea that rising inequality in the United States is in any way "natural" or irreversible. We show, instead, how the trajectory of economic development, as well as the widening gap between the rich and the poor, have emerged from a series of political negotiations and institutional changes at the global, national, industrial, and firm levels. We illustrate this point throughout the book.

Reasonable people might argue that even if the rise of finance led to higher inequality, finance may have nonetheless increased the efficiency of capital allocation and led to faster economic growth. But the evidence indicates otherwise. As the United States financialized, economic growth slowed. Investment in plants, stores, machines, computers, and, most importantly, workers declined. Meanwhile, firms' overall profits stagnated (Lin 2016; Moosa 2017; Tomaskovic-Devey, Lin, and Meyers 2015), leading firms to contribute fewer taxes to the government's revenue.

Writing a book means making choices not only about what to write, but what *not* to write. We do not discuss in great detail the causes and consequences of the 2008 global financial crisis. Considerable research and journalism have explored these topics. Instead, we examine how decades of structural shifts fueled the crisis and amplified its ramifications. We focus on the developments in the United States because of its arguably unique position in the global financial landscape. However, it should be noted that parallel and associated developments have been observed in a number of other countries. These developments are referenced throughout the book and discussed in the concluding chapter.

We also do not claim that the rise of finance is the sole cause of upward-trending inequality. Concurrent developments such as globalization, techno-logical advancement, deunionization, changing employment relationships, educational disparities, and shifting political landscapes all play their part in widened inequality—and they have been extensively explored in previous scholarship.[2] We argue that financialization is *fundamental* to understanding contemporary inequality because it promotes and complements all these other inequality-inducing developments.

Before moving forward, we must reiterate that this book is deeply indebted to past and contemporaneous scholarship on related topics, from sociology to economics, finance, political science, management, and history. We strive to bridge these disciplines and connect the subfields within. We hope our attempt provides a more unified account of the links between financializa-tion and inequality, humbly aware that we have omitted numerous impor-tant contributions to this topic due to the inherent limitations presented by any book's first and last pages. As such, we take no credit for any idea that sounds even remotely familiar and encourage the readers to explore the rich literature that has emerged in the past decade.

Organization of the Book

The first chapter defines what finance is and what we mean by financiali-zation, a concept introduced long before the 2008 financial crisis that has since gained popularity in both academic and public discussion. We argue that finance, while having served an important function in many societies, has become too much of a good thing in the United States, citing evidence demonstrating its extraordinary growth in and beyond the last quarter of the 20th century. A brief historical account identifies the political and institu-tional roots of financialization, from the Bretton Woods Agreement to the political reorientation in the 1980s, underscoring that the shift was not a nat-ural development of a capitalist economy but a historical product contingent on a wide variety of events.

Moving forward, we turn to the issue of inequality. Why does inequality matter? How has inequality deepened in recent decades? The distribution of market income has become extremely uneven over the past four decades, but social policies never catch up to this trend. The majority of workers have not seen real growth in their earnings; as capital income outpaces labor income, *owners* take increasingly more than *doers*. The majority of Americans have not benefited from the economic growth of the late 20th century, and a significant portion face shrinking economic prospects. We provide a synopsis of the existing explanations for rising inequality and identify some of their shortcomings before outlining the contours of our investigation into the connection between financialization and inequality.

Chapter 3 considers how the financial sector has evolved through tremendous changes since the 1980s. We argue that the expanding profits and ballooning compensation in finance are not driven by this sector's contributions to the economy, but by the concentration of market power, the entanglement of finance into politics, and the private intermediation of public policies. We also show that most of the income absorbed by finance has been captured by a limited set of elite workers, particularly white men. Their colleagues who are women and racial minority men, on the other hand, have gained relatively less. Even *within* the ranks of finance, the industry's success has led to wider class, gender, and racial divides.

All industries strive to advance their interests, so, as Chapter 4 asks, why hasn't the rest of the economy pushed back? In short, many nonfinancial corporations have actually become financialized. As finance became a profitable venture in the 1970s, many large corporations expanded their involvement in financial markets as lenders and traders. The emerging dominance of the shareholder-value model also imported the logics and practices of Wall Street to Main Street. These developments created a small number of winners—such as fund managers and CEOs—with devastating consequences for working Americans in the forms of wage and employment stagnation.

Among the many socioeconomic transformations connected to the growth of finance, perhaps none is as widely experienced as rising household debt. Chapter 5 describes the origin, distribution, and consequences of household debt, including the ways that the expansion of credit has benefited the rich and disadvantaged the poor. At the turn of the 20th century, credit began to be conceived as a remedy of social illnesses. Since then, bolstering access to credit has become a main goal of the government. We argue that the problem of inequality has been misconstrued as a problem of illiquidity and that expanding access to credit has been a cause of, not a solution to, economic divides. Over the past three decades, affluent households have captured most of the opportunities associated with household credit, while middle-class families carry heavier debt burdens and low-income households remain largely unable to borrow except in the most usurious circumstances.

One person's debt is another's wealth. In Chapter 6, we explore this other side of the coin: how financialization has transformed wealth accumulation and inequality in the United States. Financial assets, particularly stocks, are now key vehicles through which American families preserve and multiply their wealth. Nevertheless, stock ownership remains highly uneven. Not only do wealthy families control most of the stock market, there is also a considerable racial divide in who invests in the stock market. Instead of serving as the great leveler, the stock market mostly rewards the "haves" and the financial professionals who serve them. Access to the stock market is restricted to the wealthiest and whitest, alongside privileged workers and baby boomers with retirement accounts. Accordingly, the constant tension between capital and labor has opened economic fault lines between privileged and marginalized workers and between older and younger generations.

In 2007–2008, the tremendous financial expansion suffered an enormous blow: the total value of the US stock market halved, profits of the large banks tanked, and once-abundant streams of credit suddenly dried up. The economy seemed to grind to a halt as the haphazard foundations of so much wealth were revealed. In Chapter 7, we review the outcomes of this reckoning, focusing on major developments since the 2008 financial crisis. Policy and legal responses have accomplished much in terms of boosting liquidity, reducing systematic risk, and penalizing fraudulent activities, yet we argue that most of these policies were designed to *restore* rather than *reform* the financial order. Consequently, economic inequality continued to expand in the aftermath of the financial crisis.

Divested focuses on the United States, but the trends and problems it explores are global. In the conclusion, we turn to developments around the world, showing that the connections between financialization and inequality are endemic to the developed world. As a given country becomes more financialized, top income's share of income surges, financial professionals and wealthy families benefit, labor's share of income declines, and employment destabilizes. We close the book with a remark on the policy implications of our analysis. Financial reform must not continue to stabilize and preserve financial sectors, but to reprioritize the stability and preservation of society.

CHAPTER 1 | The Great Reversal

THE WORD "FINANCE" CONJURES up flashy images of towering skyscrapers, crowded trading floors, sophisticated mathematical models, lightning-fast computer servers, and serious, manic men in well-tailored suits. Finance is not, however, uniquely modern. From at least ancient Sumer to the Greek, Roman, and Chinese empires and beyond, finance has been a key element of societies. At its simplest, finance is simply a *social contract* that establishes trust and mobilizes economic resources among parties to facilitate production or consumption.

Consider the ancient Sumerian city of Uruk, where archaeologists unearthed tokens resembling lambs, cows, dogs, bread loaves, oil jars, honey, and clothing in sealed clay vessels. These tokens are believed to represent a crude form of a futures contract: a promise to deliver certain goods at a fixed price in the future. Financial historian William Goetzmann (2016) argues that it is no accident finance emerged in one of the first true cities: as residents of Uruk began to interact with an expanding array of fellow inhabitants plying different trades, personal agreements became infeasible. Handshakes (or their ancient equivalents) were replaced with formal contracts devised to facilitate economic cooperation.

Among the various forms of financial activities developed in early civilizations, many are still impactful to modern societies. The financial technologies of early Islam derived from mathematic toolkits used in pre-Islamic, ancient Middle Eastern civilizations (Burke 2009). Central banking, limited liability investments, and business corporations arose in the Roman Empire, while commercial loans, real estate development, and sovereign debt appeared throughout ancient China. Later, as intercontinental trade became prevalent, the Hindu-Arabic numeral system facilitated commerce from Spain to India to China by allowing traders to mail promissory notes (*suftaja*) and payment orders (*ruq'a*). Finance is a basic form of social organization that arises, both in situ and through a range of human interactions and cultural exchanges that span human history.

Arguably, finance is also indispensable for a prosperous society. Economists Robert King and Ross Levin (1993) have, for instance, tied the size of financial intermediaries, the decentralized allocation of credit, and the amount of credit available for private firms to faster economic growth and capital accumulation across 80 countries in the years between 1960 and 1989. In the United States, similar evidence suggests that relaxing intrastate bank branch restrictions in the 1980s was associated with increased local economic growth (Jayaratne and Strahan 1996).

Economist John Kay (2015) has established a set of four important functions broadly served by finance in modern societies. First, and most basically, via payment systems such as credit cards, wire transfers, and direct deposits, finance facilitates economic transactions. Second, finance puts idle resources to effective uses by matching investors with additional capital to entrepreneurs, organizations, and consumers who can leverage that capital in productive ventures. Third, it allows people to manage personal resources across their lifetimes and across generations through saving and borrowing. Finally, finance helps both families and businesses cope with uncertainties with risk-management tools such as insurance and derivatives. Looking at it this way, we might note that a society without finance is not only inconvenient, but also fragmented, inefficient, nearsighted, and vulnerable.

If finance is both fundamental to and ubiquitous in human society, what does it mean when we say the American economy has become *financialized*? We define financialization as *the wide-ranging reversal of the role of finance from a secondary, supportive activity to a principal driver of the economy.* Instead of serving the economy, finance now imposes its own logics, preferences, and practices throughout the economy as well as other parts of the society. While facilitating transaction, finance draws income away from consumers and revenue away from the producers and merchants. Rather than channeling capital to constructive uses, sophisticated maneuvers extract resources and redirect wealth without consideration for long-term consequences. And, counter to its roles of smoothing economic fluctuations and managing uncertainties, finance generates mistrust and intensifies precariousness among American families.

We contend that financialization in the United States manifested in three interdependent processes, all of which accelerated after the late 1970s. The first is the rising dominance of the financial sector over US society. Figure 1.1 presents the profits of the financial sector as a percentage of all corporate profits in the United States. The trend is clear: prior to 1980, the financial sector, on average, earned around 15 percent of all corporate profits. That share expanded steadily in the mid-1980s, rose to more than a third of all corporate profits in the early 1990, and declined during the economic boom of 1990s. It would hit a historic high of 43 percent in 2002. The financial crisis of 2008 temporarily cropped finance's share of corporate profits to only 10 percent of all corporate profits, and yet the financial sector rebounded. Financial institutions' rising profits have meant a surge in compensation for financial workers, who on average earn 70 percent more than workers in other industries (Philippon and Reshef 2012; Tomaskovic-Devey and Lin 2011).

The rise of finance not only manifested in economic measures but in cultural and political terms. Today, the American financial sector influences how states govern markets, how top executives manage their firms, how society measures individual success, and even how we evaluate the economy's

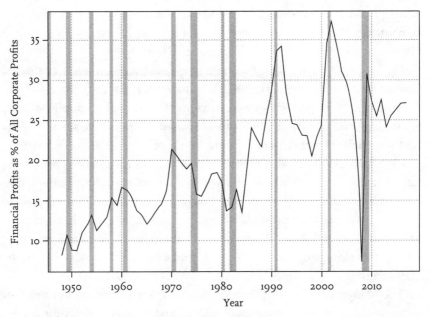

FIGURE 1.1 FINANCIAL SECTOR PROFITS AS PERCENTAGE OF ALL CORPORATE PROFITS
NOTE: Corporate profits with inventory valuation adjustment. Financial sector includes the Federal Reserve banks and industries such as credit intermediation and related activities; securities, commodity contracts, and other financial investments and related activities; insurance carriers and related activities; funds, trusts, and other financial vehicles; and bank and other holding companies. SOURCE: Bureau of Economic Analysis, National Economic Account, Table 6.16.

performance (Davis 2009; Fligstein 2001; Fligstein and Shin 2007). An expert in finance becomes an expert in *everything*—even politics. The number of government officials affiliated with Wall Street rose over time in both Democratic and Republican administrations.

In the private sector, finance became the most common route to the top echelon of management. More than a third of Fortune 100 chief executives arrived in their corner offices with a strong financial background (Fligstein 1993), often as chief financial officers or on Wall Street. The entrenched influence of finance helps to account for why the financial sector's dominance remained robust in the aftermath of the 2008 financial meltdown, despite mounting political pressure and constant challenges from civil society.

A second process in the financialization of the US economy has been the increasing participation of the nonfinance firms in financial markets. This participation takes both passive and active forms. The triumph of the shareholder-value model—a belief that the only interest a firm should pursue is that of its shareholders—has submitted US firms to the wills of financial markets. While corporate managers in most of the 20th century largely focused on how to increase sales to maintain the growth and stability of their firms, the competency of executives today is measured by their ability to boost the company's stock price, even at the cost of stability and growth (Davis 2010; Lazonick and O'Sullivan 2000; Useem 1993).

Figure 1.2 illustrates dividends and stock buybacks—when a company buys its shares from the marketplace to reduce its outstanding shares—paid by nonfinancial corporations as percentages of their total profits. That is, it shows how much of corporate earnings is used to reward the stock market and shareholders rather than funding future operation.[1] Again, the 1980s emerges as a pivotal decade. Before that decade, US corporations tended to pay their shareholders around a third of their annual earnings, retaining the rest for reserves, capital investments, and other uses. After 1980, the profits used to boost stock prices escalated sharply, peaking at more than 100 percent in the late 1980s. In other words, for many years, corporate America depleted its savings or sold assets to pay financial investors *more* than what they earned.

The economic boom of the 1990s reduced the proportion but not the amount of outgoing profits to shareholders, and the share of payout would rise again. But in the 1990s, stock buybacks became another main channel through which corporations distributed their resources to shareholders (Lazonick and O'Sullivan 2000). Since that decade, the net issuance of corporate stock has been consistently negative, meaning that public corporations now pay more to shareholders than they receive from issuing stocks. Thus,

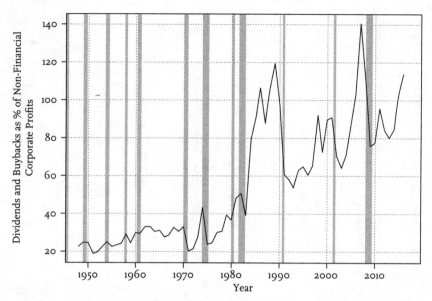

FIGURE 1.2 DIVIDENDS AND STOCK BUYBACKS AS PERCENTAGE OF NONFINANCIAL
CORPORATE PROFITS

NOTE: Financial payments are calculated as the sum of dividends (NCBDPAA027N) and stock repurchases (NCBCEBA027N) paid by nonfinancial corporations. Nonfinancial corporate profits are calculated with inventory valuation adjustment. The sum of financial payments can exceed profits since stock repurchase is considered an expense, not a component of profits. SOURCE: Federal Reserve Bank of St. Louis, Federal Reserve Economic Data; Bureau of Economic Analysis, National Economic Account, Table 6.16.

it is now more accurate to say that the financial market raises funds from public corporations rather than the other way around. Since 2000, almost all corporate profits have gone straight to the stock market, leaving fewer and fewer resources for companies' expansion, savings, and development.

On top of the siphoning of corporate funds into the stock market and shareholder payouts, many nonfinancial corporations assumed active roles in financial markets as lenders and speculators in their own right. They issued credit cards and loans to other companies. Figure 1.3 documents these interests and dividends: beginning in the 1970s, we see a significant proportion of corporate income stemming from lending to households and businesses trading in financial markets. The steep decline in the early 2000s suggests firms now depend less on earnings through financial channels, but their absolute interest income did not fall until the 2008 crisis, and their total financial asset holdings have continued to increase (see Figure 2.6). Consequently, it is hard to tell whether the importance of financial income to nonfinancial companies will rebound as the Federal Reserve starts to adjust interest rates.

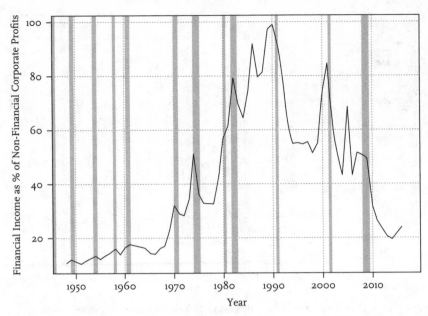

FIGURE 1.3 INTERESTS AND DIVIDENDS RECEIVED AS PERCENTAGE OF NONFINANCIAL
CORPORATE PROFITS

NOTE: The trend is calculated as the sum of interests received (NCBIREA027N) and
dividends received (NCBDREA027N) by nonfinancial corporations over nonfinancial corporate profits with inventory valuation adjustment. SOURCE: Federal Reserve Bank of St. Louis,
Federal Reserve Economic Data; Bureau of Economic Analysis, National Economic Account,
Table 6.16.

The third process at play in what we call the financialization of America
is US households' increasing consumption of financial products. Drops in
public support programs, stagnating wages, and bleak retirement prospects
have pushed families to embrace various financial products at different
stages of their lives. Figure 1.4 presents total household debt as a percentage
of personal disposable income in the United States. Before 1980, household
debt was about 65 percent of disposable income. The absence of wage growth
since the 1980s, though, prompted low- and middle-income households to
borrow more, taking on debt to finance not only luxuries but day-to-day
needs. In 2007, the debt-to-earnings ratio for US households had flipped
on its head: Americans now had 132 percent as much debt as income. The
rise was driven by mortgages, credit cards, and student loans, guided by the
belief that credit could be a solution for economic inequality. If a college education could mean higher earnings, for instance, taking out a student loan
was seen as a good investment.

This is partially why the rapid expansion of debt disproportionately
impacts women and racial minority men: lending agencies target these

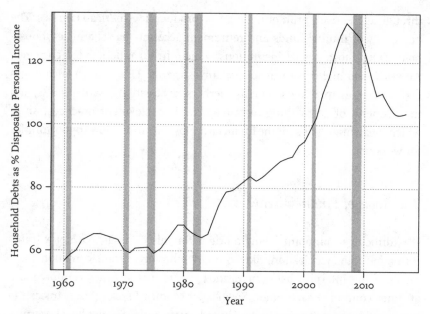

FIGURE 1.4 HOUSEHOLD DEBT AS PERCENTAGE OF PERSONAL DISPOSABLE INCOME
NOTE: The trend is calculated as the Credit Market Instruments by households and non-
profit organizations (CMDEBT) over disposable personal income (A067RC1A027NBEA).
SOURCE: Federal Reserve Bank of St. Louis, Federal Reserve Economic Data.

vulnerable populations for their high-interest products, selling potential customers on the transformative potential of debt (Roberts 2013; Rugh and Massey 2010; Wyly et al. 2009). Meanwhile, young adults have become increasingly indebted from student loans, which have ballooned from close to $10,000 per borrowing graduate in 1993 to more than $35,000 in 2015 (Sparshott 2015), and real wages are, in many sectors, declining (they haven't kept up with even very modest inflation).

In addition to debt, financialization transformed household *wealth*. It has become unfashionable, if not imprudent, to just put savings in the bank. Everyday people are instead encouraged to invest in multifarious financial products, from stocks and bonds to mutual and exchange-traded funds. We are taught that it is best to learn how to harness the power of passive income (Fridman 2016)—or at least find ways to increase the value of our homes.

These processes—the rising dominance of the financial sector in the US economy, the increasing participation of nonfinancial corporations in financial markets, and the growing consumption of financial products among households—reinforced and fueled one another over time. Both the financial and nonfinancial sectors have profited from household debt and wealth through aggressively promoting financial products to American families. The popularity of mutual funds and retirement accounts has channeled household savings to financial institutions, which, in turn, demanded corporate America yield higher returns to stock investments. This tension encourages corporate reorganizations such as mergers, acquisitions, and spinoffs, and the adoption of cost-cutting technology and employment practices, all of which mean huge gains for the financial sector but diminishing opportunities for workers.

The Roots of Financialization

It is difficult to pinpoint a single origin for this dramatic, complex transformation. Financialization, like so many other great transformations, is a result of the interplay between various events that at times reinforce and at times contradict each other. Sociologist Monica Prasad (2012) traces the history of credit expansion in the United States back to agricultural overproduction in the late 19th and early 20th centuries, a situation that prompted the government to promote consumption and stimulate growth with both guarantees and tax incentives. While Prasad provides a compelling account of how finance has long been leveraged by the state as a solution to economic problems, we focus on postwar developments, particularly the rise and demise of the Bretton Woods system, the capitalism crisis of the 1970s, and the subsequent reorientation of US government and business. We agree with Prasad that earlier developments predisposed the United States to a credit-centered policy model in the 20th century. Yet the rise of finance cannot be adequately understood without considering the global monetary system that emerged after World War II.

The Bretton Woods System

The establishment of the Bretton Woods Agreement of 1944 provided the foundation for today's global financial system. As the end of World War II neared, 730 delegates from all 44 Allied nations gathered at the Mount Washington Hotel in Bretton Woods, a remote town in New Hampshire, to outline the postwar international monetary and financial order. Spurred by the need to fund postwar reconstruction and remove barriers to international trade, the delegates convened to prevent a recurrence of the monetary chaos and economic warfare that had emerged during the interwar period.

In those years, protectionism surged, the Great Depression arose, and the gold standard collapsed. It could not happen again.

Two opposing visions divided the conference: on the one hand, the UK head of delegates, John Maynard Keynes, proposed the establishment of an International Clearing Union that would serve as the international central bank for all national central banks. This bank would issue a supranational currency, the *bancor*, to regulate currency exchange and protect debtor countries' interests by discouraging trade imbalances. On the other hand, US delegate Harry Dexter White, representing what was then the largest exporter and creditor country in the world, insisted on maintaining the dominance of dollar and the value of his country's tremendous gold reserves, which amounted to three-quarters of all central bank gold in the world at that time.

The conflict between the old and new powers resulted in the Bretton Woods Agreement and the establishment of the International Monetary Fund (IMF), which reflected Keynes's supranational institution in form but attended to White's call for the preservation of the United States' interests in substance. Instead of creating an independent, supranational reserve currency, member nations agreed to peg their currencies to the US dollar and maintain fixed exchange rates. The United States, in turn, upheld the interwar gold standard by fixing the US dollar to gold. As a result, the US dollar became the global reserve currency that backed all other currencies.

The IMF was established as a lender of last resort, which would provide emergency funds for member nations by pooling gold and national currencies based on assigned quotas. However, the IMF does not regulate trade imbalance between countries, as Keynes proposed. Furthermore, rather than operating with a one-state, one-vote governance model, the IMF allocates voting rights to governments based on the size of their contributions. This measure effectively gave the United States veto power over any decision.

The relatively conservative path taken in Bretton Woods proved inadequate to answer the monetary needs of post–World War II reconstruction efforts. The responsibility to maintain the monetary order and prevent social unrest fell on the United States, the only country with sufficient economic resources to assume this role. The aid was executed by simultaneously expanding imports of foreign goods and creating long-term loans and grants, such as the Marshall Plan, which provided over $12 billion for European countries to rebuild communities and industries (Kunz 1997).

The United States' support for Europe, and later Japan, was not purely altruistic. Once the war reached its end, the United States moved quickly to counter the Soviet Union's imposing threat to its dominance and acted from its immense interest in deterring the spread of communist influence in Europe and Asia. Economic intervention was considered critical if the US-led coalition was to persevere.

The dollar has since become the United States' largest export. It remains, even today, more globally popular than any other American product. The tremendous outflow of dollars through aids and trades, combined with its military dominance, made the United States into other countries' ideal trade partner. After all, the dollar held "real value" for its believers and could be reliably converted to gold, appeasing its doubters.

Clearly, control of the international reserve currency has tremendous benefits. As economist Barry Eichengreen (2010: 3) stated: "It costs only a few cents for the Bureau of Engraving and Printing to produce a $100 bill, but other countries had to pony up $100 of actual goods in order to obtain one." Being able to purchase and borrow with its own currency allowed the US government and, to some extent, American consumers to obtain foreign goods at a lower cost. The US government was also able to "tax" other countries by printing more dollars but maintaining the same exchange rates with other currencies.

The Bretton Woods system was established on the promise that the Federal Reserve would honor the gold standard at $35 per ounce and on Allies' confidence that the United States could maintain its economic might. However, as West Germany and Japan recovered from the war in 1950s, the United States began to lose its manufacturing monopoly in the global market. This economic decline was compounded by the costly Vietnam War and the US government's willingness to maintain trade imbalances with Europe and Japan as rewards for their allegiance (Stein 2011). All these developments weakened global confidence in the American dollar. In 1960, the London gold price rose to $40 per ounce, meaning that traders could purchase gold at a lower cost from the US Treasury and resell it in other countries to make a profit. European countries and Japan now faced a dilemma that would resurface among other export-oriented economies in the future: their economic growth depended on the US deficits. However, the more dollars were in circulation, the less value they had in the open market. To hedge the risk, some countries began to increase their gold reserves and, in the following decade, reduce their dependence on the dollar.

That attack on US gold reserve was dramatized in a 1964 international blockbuster: a gold dealer named Auric Goldfinger attempted to bomb the gold reserve at Fort Knox, Kentucky, to reduce its gold supply, but the conspiracy was sabotaged by a British agent named James Bond (rewarded with a White House lunch with the US president). Outside movie theaters, the US gold reserve continued to dwindle. Worried that their dollar reserves would lose value in the near future, countries such Switzerland and France had begun to sell their dollar reserves back—for US gold. In 1965 alone, the French navy was sent across the Atlantic to pick up $150 million worth of gold. By 1966, non-US central banks held $14 billion worth of gold, while the United States had only $13.2 billion in gold reserves. The fixed exchange rate between dollar and gold was becoming as fanciful as any spy movie.

Thus, in 1971, President Nixon revoked the $35 per ounce of gold exchange rate set back at Bretton Woods. The US government had to address the unprecedented, multifaceted threat of a global dollar run, inflation, and unemployment. The unilateral announcement formally concluded the Bretton Woods system, and the dollar's value against gold took a dive. Inflation rose. Yet the global primacy of the dollar endured, because the Nixon administration persuaded Saudi Arabia and other oil-producing countries in the Middle East to value their oil export in dollars and purchase US debt securities with their surplus. In exchange, the US government would protect these countries with both financial and military aid.

Since most industrialized countries did not produce sufficient petroleum for their own consumption, this agreement maintained the global demand for the dollar and protected its value from a true nosedive. In other words, the "petrodollar" system replaced gold—a universally valued but not particularly useful commodity—with oil, a necessity for all industrialized economies. The need for crude oil led countries in Asia and Europe to further develop economic and monetary policies that targeted the United States as their main export market. It also provided the US government a new source of funding for its deficit spending over the coming decades. Just as the dollar was about to lose its reserve status, it was rescued by a strong global military presence and a willingness to maintain trade deficits.

The export of dollars also created a global market for dollar-denominated financial products such as treasury securities; agency, municipal, and corporate bonds; and mortgage-backed securities. These purchases channeled foreign capital to every corner of the US economy and significantly expanded the provision of credit. That said, the benefits came with consequences. Since the reserve currency status made imports artificially cheap, it undermined the United States' industrial competitiveness in both domestic and international markets. Furthermore, the petrodollar system delayed, but did not resolve, the dollar crisis. As trade deficits increased, the US government had to either prop up the demand for dollars through other mechanisms or accept a sharp devaluation of its currency that would increase exports but worsen its citizens' economic well-being.

The Capitalism Crisis of the 1970s

Scholars commonly mark the 1970s as the onset of US financialization, when the decline of industrial production was accompanied by expanding financial activities (Boyer 2000; Magdoff and Sweezy 1987). However, interpretations of the relationship between these two indicators diverge. Sociologist Giovanni Arrighi (1994) describes financial expansion as a recurring phase in a capitalist economy. In his view, US capitalism in the 1970s, much like Genoese, Dutch, and British economies in the past centuries, came to a stage of maturity, during which investment in production failed to yield sufficient returns, and capitalists turned to finance to maintain and expand profits. Post-Keynesian economists James Crotty and Gerald Epstein, on the other hand, focus on the emerging tension between the "rentiers" class—financial institutions and owners of financial assets—and the rest of the economy (Crotty 2003; Epstein and Jayadev 2005). From this perspective, financialization represents the transfer of resources to the rentier class from the entrepreneurs and workers who actually create economic value. Thus, the expansion of financial activities is not a result but a driver of industrial decline. We see evidence for both claims.

As the Bretton Woods system reached its end in the 1960s, a series of related developments began to throw US capitalism into question and challenged the interest of the business elites in particular. The rise of union and consumer power resulted in a series of social reforms (Dewey 1998; Dunlap and Mertig 1991; Gottlieb 2005); the passage of the National Environmental Policy Act, the Occupational Safety and Health Act, and the Consumer Product Safety Act all created new federal agencies to regulate corporate activities and profits.

There were also external threats to US capitalism. In addition to the devaluation of the dollar and the emergence of manufacturing competitors, the United States was beginning to lose its grip over its international trade balance in the late 1960s. In 1971, it faced its first merchandise trade deficit since the depression of 1893. The Arab oil embargo against developed economies came in 1973, and the subsequent surge in oil prices sharply increased the cost of manufacturing and transportation (Miller and Tomaskovic-Devey 1983), which meant lower domestic profits and curtailed global markets (though the threat was later partially neutralized with the petrodollar agreement).

The sense of crisis deepened during the "stagflation" of the 1970s, a period of simultaneous recession and high inflation. Under the leadership of Paul Volcker, the Federal Reserve fought inflation by rapidly tightening the supply of money with high federal funds rate in the early 1980s. The inflation rate fell from 11.27 percent in 1979 to 3.21 percent in 1983, but the policy also led to a recession (GDP growth declined from 3.15 percent annually in 1979 to 1.98 percent in 1983) and deteriorated employment in the United States (whose unemployment rate increased from 5.6 percent to 10.8 percent in the same period) and other dollar-linked economies.

These challenges elicited a rapid mobilization and reorganization of the business sector (Akard 1992). In a confidential memorandum to the US Chamber of Commerce, future Supreme Court Justice Lewis Powell (1971) asserted that "no thoughtful person can question that the American economic system is under broad attack." This attack, he argued, came not only from extremists on the left, but also from "perfectly respectable elements of society: from the college campus, the pulpit, the media, the intellectual and literary journals, the arts and sciences, and from politicians." Powell urged business elites to prioritize these challenges and counterattack in all possible social-political arenas. For instance, when it came to the college campus, Powell suggested the Chamber of Commerce establish "a staff of highly qualified scholars in the social sciences who do believe in the system" and "a staff of speakers of the highest competency." The Chamber should provide incentives for these scholars to publish in scholarly journals and popular and intellectual magazines, as "one of the keys to the success of the liberal and leftist faculty members has been their passion for 'publication' and 'lecturing.'"

Businesses also mobilized to influence public policy directly. Political scientists Jacob Hacker and Paul Pierson (2011) note that public affairs officers, lobbyists, and political action committees (PACs) associated with corporations proliferated during this time. For example, the number of firms with registered lobbyists in Washington, DC, grew from 175 in 1971 to 2,445 by 1982. Similarly, from 1976 to 1980, corporate-funded PACs grew from fewer than 300 to more than 1,200. Both the influential Heritage Foundation and the Cato Institute were founded, sponsored respectively by Joseph Coors of the Coors Brewing Company and Charles Koch of Koch Industries. These organizations relentlessly pushed back all the reforms made in the early 1970s and provided the infrastructure for the emergence of a neoliberal consensus in the 1980s (Neustadtl and Clawson 1988).

Another crucial development in the 1970s was the reform of the US retirement system, which brought a large portion of household savings into financial markets. Workers of earlier generations had generally obtained their retirement income through corporate pension plans, which depended heavily on their employers' financial health. Declining profitability put a great deal of financial stress on small firms, which were forced to either renounce their pension plans or face bankruptcy. The resulting retirement reform, designed to disperse risks, led to an outflow of retirement funds into financial markets via investment companies (Gourevitch and Shinn 2007).

In sum, the economic turmoil of the 1970s marked the end of US postwar prosperity and spurred various collective actions. From the business mobilization against regulation to the Federal Reserve prioritizing inflation over unemployment and the transformation of the retirement system, all these developments planted seeds for the financialization of the US economy.

Political Reorientation

The business mobilization of the late 1970s proved fruitful for corporations in the 1980s, as political opinion shifted to favor corporate over public interests. This ideological transition was spearheaded by Ronald Reagan, a charismatic speaker who campaigned for a "free enterprise" system. His presidential administration embarked on various initiatives to eliminate constraints on corporate ventures. Even the postwar Keynesian economic model (the legitimacy of which was undermined during stagflation) was officially ousted in his inaugural address: "Government is not the solution to our problem; government *is* the problem." Reagan's political agenda sprang from neoliberal ideology, the idea that markets (and other social spheres) function best, even self-regulating, with minimal government intervention.

While Reagan's Democratic predecessor, Jimmy Carter, advocated frugality, Reagan solved the problem of slow economic growth with deficit spending. The national debt skyrocketed 168.2 percent in eight years through an influx of foreign capital, particularly from Organization of Petroleum Exporting Countries (OPEC) and Japan, which also provided consumer and corporate credit to feed US household and corporate consumption and investment. However, debt-led prosperity can only be sustained with a continuous inflow of foreign capital; maintaining the "competitiveness" of US financial institutions in international capital markets became a national priority.

The ascendance of the belief in "free enterprise," the need to maintain the dollar's status in the post–Bretton Woods era, and the debt-led economy together opened an unprecedented political opportunity to undo all the financial restrictions set in place during the New Deal era. The deregulation of the financial industry began to unfold in the 1980s and sped up in the subsequent decades. It first blurred the boundary between commercial banks and savings and loan associations, then the line between commercial and investment banks, and, finally, the firewall between banking and other financial activities. As the Financial Services Authority was established in the United Kingdom to minimize regulation and reclaim London as the center of global finance, the US government seemed stuck: it would have to follow suit, consolidating an ever-more powerful financial sector under the control of a handful of firms. All these policies were driven by the belief that the market is efficient and self-regulating, as well as by the implicit understanding that the growth and stability of the US economy required a financial sector that attracted sufficient international capital and exercised global influence (Tomaskovic-Devey and Lin 2011).

To be clear, financial deregulation wasn't without pushback. The speed of deregulation was much slower than Reagan had hoped, and the Competitive Equality Banking Act of 1987 actually reaffirmed a restriction preventing commercial banks from selling insurance, real estate, and securities underwriting (Scheer 2010). Yet Reagan's desire for minimizing financial regulation was eventually fulfilled by the Clinton administration, when the technically verboten 1998 merger of Citibank and Travelers insurance was celebrated by media as a "bold" move to update an antiquated financial system. The US Congress quickly issued a post hoc Glass-Steagall waiver for the newly formed Citigroup and, within a year, passed the Financial Services Modernization Act of 1999, which wiped out any of the measure's remaining regulations.

It is tempting to attribute the policy changes and the financialization of the US economy to political orchestration by a conniving financial sector, but this account would be incomplete without emphasizing other important developments. Sociologist Greta Krippner (2011) argues that the market-oriented shift, for instance, should not be considered a mere result of business interest's influence in politics, but also as consistent with government officials' desire to obscure the role of policy in the allocation of credit during political turmoil. Similarly, the deregulation of interest rates was welcomed by middle-class consumers, eager to protect their savings against inflation. The continuing, market-based reform of retirement plans also fueled the financial sector. After the Revenue Act of 1978 officially allowed the use of salary reductions for contributions to defined-contribution retirement plans (which require employers and employees to contribute to retirement accounts), these began to replace defined-benefit plans (plans that guarantee certain amount of income after retirement) as the most popular retirement benefit among large corporations. This development, too, channeled a tremendous amount of resources into the financial services industry (Cobb 2015).

Among these concurrent developments, the dynamics of the business sector are most relevant here. As corporate America launched a counterattack against the progressive political movement, it was undergoing its own series of internal transitions. The declining profitability of firms and the economic uncertainties that arose in the 1970s undermined the traditional, manager-centered governance model. Agency theory arose, attributing the failure of corporate America to the misalignment of interests between managers and the shareholders (Dobbin and Jung 2010; Fama and Jensen 1983; Fligstein 2001). In this view, managers were mistakenly rewarded for the *size* of their firms and therefore had tremendous interest in pursuing stability and ex-pansion over efficiency. Accordingly, firms' profitability dropped and share prices suffered.

All this opened space for new, alternative models of corporate govern-ance. Agency theory contended that, to realign ownership and control, firms should maintain an independent board of directors to oversee managerial decisions, use debt rather than equity financing, specialize in only the most profitable activities,[2] and compensate managers with stocks. Agency theorists even argued that management should be subject to external control: their performance needed to be evaluated based on the stock price, and managers should be replaced if the stock underperformed. The triumph of agency theory, along with the emergence of large retirement fund institutions, led to a broad-based adoption of the motto "Maxima Shareholder Valorem" among US firms. These beliefs have been inscribed into almost all corporate finance textbooks used in college courses and business schools, spreading as scien-tific truth to generations of aspiring executives (Cardao-Pito 2017).

Overall, this historical account shows that the financialization of the US economy cannot be viewed as solely driven by the financial sector's interests or as a mature stage of capitalist economy. The Bretton Woods Agreement initiated an enduring, systematic dependency on the dollar, which was sus-tained by international trade in crude oil and export-oriented emerging economies. This led to a constant inflow of funds to the US financial system and pressure for the government to flex its dominance in the global market. Business mobilization that had begun in the 1960s steered policymakers away from the state-centered Keynesian economic model to the market-based, neoliberal mentality so often attributed to "Reagan Republicans." This reorientation fueled financial deregulation in the 1980s and the 1990s as well as the rising political preference for the use of monetary, rather than fiscal, policies to address economic stagnation. These developments also reflected the state's twin aims of protecting middle-class households' savings and promoting consumption.

The 2008 financial crisis and its aftermath have left many questioning whether financialization will—or even *can*—continue in the United States. On its surface, the crisis certainly drew attention to the oversized role of finance in the US economy, and it at least initially reversed the trend of domestic deregulation. The realization of just how interconnected the global economy is has also encouraged national governments to coordinate their reforms. Some nonfinancial firms, such as GE, have since spun off their financial operations to avoid heightened scrutiny. For a moment, the era of big finance seemed to be coming to an end.

Still, determining whether financialization has run its course eventually depends on its institutional roots. The global financial order appears largely intact a decade later. If anything, the crisis reaffirmed the dollar's status as a global currency, as the Federal Reserve served as lender of last resort for major foreign banks who ran out of dollars (Tooze 2018). For lack of a better alternative, many countries still peg their currencies to the dollar or use it as their main reserve, especially those emerging countries that target the United States as their main export market or are facing their own domestic economic and political fragilities. Many institutional investors purchase US securities for safety, even with the understanding that the dollar is likely overvalued—a trend only worsened by the US government's loose, borderline inflationary, monetary policy and continued deficit spending.

The continued demand for dollars and associated securities permitted the Federal Reserve to curb the credit shortage with a massive supply of money. The strength of the dollar also allowed the Obama and Trump administrations to boost the economy through further deficit spending. These policies were executed on the basis of a decades-long belief that a profitable financial sector is crucial to economic growth, even though the sector's relentless pursuit of profit precipitated the global financial crisis. While such policies prevented a complete collapse of the global economy, as we will consider in Chapter 7, it is also clear that they did more to restore than reform the financial order.

Summary

What is finance and what is financialization? While ubiquitous, these terms are rarely clearly defined. We argue that finance should be understood as a social contract that mobilizes economic resources to promote production and consumption. Across societies and throughout human history, finance has played an important role in facilitating economic prosperity. However, finance can be "too much of a good thing" when it reduces rather than promotes production and disrupts rather than stabilizes consumption. When finance's role changes from a servant to the master of the economy, we refer to this reversal as financialization.

Financialization has been a defining feature of the US economy since the 1980s. The income transferred to the financial sector grew dramatically in the last quarter of the 20th century. Even nonfinancial corporations shifted their attention toward financial markets, depleting their resources to pay for dividends and stock buybacks, while profiting from lending and other financial activities. At the same time, American families have incurred a rising amount of debt to cope with economic uncertainties and leverage socioeconomic mobility. These developments created a feedback loop as finance became the dominant organizing principle of America's political, business, and cultural spheres.

The rise of financialization was the result of a series of historical events. The Bretton Woods system outlined the post–World War II international monetary order, designating the dollar as the global reserve currency. The Cold War subsequently enshrined the United States as *the* locomotive of the capitalist world, and the United States deliberately maintained a trade deficit with its allies to export dollars and boost their reconstruction. The Bretton Woods system began to crumble in the 1960s, as the United States lost its monopoly in the global manufacturing market. The continuing trade imbalance, the deterioration of the US gold reserve, and the Vietnam War–driven fiscal crisis all contributed to its eventual demise during the Nixon administration. Yet the status of dollar endured, partly because crude oil was traded in dollars and partly because there was no readily apparent, competitive reserve currency. This precarious primacy set the stage for a dramatic turn toward financialization.

The crisis of 1970s motivated a series of business mobilizations aiming to counter the progressive movements in the 1960s. A new distrust in the state-centered Keynesian model that guided much of the policies since the New Deal rose (Avent-Holt 2012), and the uncertain macro environment led banks to start creating financial products in regulatory gray areas. The financial sector made persuasive claims for deregulation. The Federal Reserve's decision to prioritize monetary order over employment in the midst of stagflation favored financial activities by raising interest rates and bringing in foreign investments. Soon, even nonfinancial firms hopped on this gravy train, expanding into financial markets through lending and speculation.

Together, these developments came to a head in the 1980s, as Reagan took over the White House. As the administration leveraged the primacy of dollar for debt-led growth, the Keynesian model was displaced by market idealism. The state, which needed to maintain the dollar's status even without gold backing, promoted the financial sector by eliminating all the restrictions set in place during the Great Depression (symbolized by the death of Glass-Steagall) and encouraging corporate and bank consolidation. In hindsight, this would all look like an unwittingly built house of cards.

Taking place along financialization has been a sharp growth of economic inequality. Later in this book, we will explore how finance has transformed American life and made it more unequal, but first, we need to consider the very idea of inequality. Why does inequality matter, beyond simple notions of fairness? How has inequality risen over time? What explains who wins and who loses? In the process of exploring these questions, we will also propose a unified account of how financialization became a fundamental cause of rising inequality in the United States.

CHAPTER 2 | The Social Question

This, then, is the social question of today: how are the economic institutions of society, in which so much power and privilege are concentrated, and which are essential to the well-being of all, to be organized and conducted so that their benefits may be justly shared by all members of society?

—IRA HOWERTH (1906, in the *American Journal of Sociology*)

The outstanding faults of the economic society in which we live are its failure to provide for full employment and its arbitrary and inequitable distribution of wealth and incomes.

—JOHN MAYNARD KEYNES (1936, *The General Theory*)

HUMAN SOCIETIES ARE FULL of inequality of all kinds. Some people are granted dignity, and some are despised. Some are more intelligent based on a set of standards, while some are viewed as dull. Some have much better physical or mental health than their peers. Some are considered more attractive. Some command while others obey. All these inequalities together translate to different life experiences: some people live with comfort and fulfillment, while some suffer and struggle to get by.

Inequality in the form of unequal access to economic resources has become the most pressing social issue of our time. Economic inequality is important because it is, in a sort of flow-chart view of the world, a fundamental inequality from which many others stem. Economic inequality determines who has access to tangible goods and services such as food, housing, transportation, education, and healthcare. It also grants some people less tangible but widely valued resources such as respect, power, security, opportunity, autonomy, dignity, and happiness (Alderson and Katz-Gerro 2016; Firebaugh and Schroeder 2009; Lamont 2002; Oishi and Kesebir 2015; Wilkinson 2005). Indeed, economic inequality goes far beyond the unequal distribution of resources. It has wide-ranging social and psychological implications for individuals and entire communities.

Concerns about the just distribution of economic resources are, perhaps, as old as time. In *King Lear*, Shakespeare contemplated how the absolute concentration of power and wealth could be corrosive even to the haves, with his dethroned king regretting his past and calling for redistribution:

> Oh, I have ta'en
> Too little care of this! Take physic, pomp.
> Expose thyself to feel what wretches feel,
> That thou mayst shake the superflux to them
> And show the heavens more just.

In the *Wealth of Nations*, Adam Smith (1776) wrote:

> No society can surely be flourishing and happy, of which the far greater part of the members are poor and miserable. It is but equity, besides, that they who feed, clothe, and lodge the whole body of the people, should have such a share of the produce of their own labour as to be themselves tolerably well fed, clothed, and lodged.

Worries about economic divides intensified in the 19th century. As the Industrial Revolution stimulated rapid economic growth, it created human calamities such as massive poverty, hunger, and social upheaval. "The Social Question"—why our current socioeconomic system fails to provide economic security and human dignity for the majority—has been a perennial one, always asked and never quite answered in every industrialized society.

Thus, the fact of inequality (and its rise in the United States and other developed countries) is established. What that inequality *means*, however, spurs furious debate. Some dismiss rising inequality in the United States as a non-issue and insist that its poor still enjoy a decent standard of living compared to many in other countries. Others believe that inequality is unimportant so long as there is strong mobility—sufficient opportunity for a person to improve her economic standing. And some argue that inequality *is* American because it represents the vibrancy and dynamism of a capitalist economy, in which people have the freedom to fulfill their economic potential.

Harvard economist Gregory Mankiw presents a sophisticated version of these views in the widely read essay "Defending the One Percent" (2013). He argues that inequality only becomes worrisome when the rewards do not reflect people's contributions and therefore fail to optimize economic growth.

This is not the case for contemporary America, in Mankiw's opinion, where innovative entrepreneurs such as Steve Jobs and Steven Spielberg offer products with wide appeal and receive high compensation for their unique talents and efforts.

But how valid are these claims? Contrary to the myth of the American dream, absolute intergenerational mobility—the difference between parents' and children's economic status, generally with children doing better than their parents at the same age—has been declining in the United States (Chetty et al. 2017). While about 90 percent of children born in 1940 had greater economic success than their parents, that is true for only about 50 percent of the cohort born in the 1980s. Cross-national studies have shown that the correlation between inequality and relative mobility is negative: as the rungs of the economic ladder grow further apart, parental economic standing becomes more predictive of children's life chances (Andrews and Leigh 2009; Krueger 2012; OECD 2011).

Comparing social mobility in the United States with its northern neighbor, Canada, we see that Canadian sons born at the bottom of the economic ladder are less likely to stay at the bottom than are their American counterparts, and Canadian sons born into the top 10 percent of households are less likely to remain at the very top than are American sons with the same fortune (Corak 2013). The difference is, in part, because affluent American parents are able to obtain better education for their children via more spending in property taxes (they can move to districts with better schools and higher tax bases) and college tuition. In Canada, however, educational expenses are much lower and so there is less advantage conferred by simply being rich (Jerrim and Macmillan 2015).

Second, opinions like Mankiw's equate *income* with *economic contribution*. These theories understand contemporary inequality as mainly driven by individual differences in productivity. Mankiw uses entrepreneurs such as Jobs and Spielberg as examples of how talent and hard work lead to economic success. Yet he refrains from naming any executives or financial professionals whose economic contributions are difficult to observe. While there is no doubt that firms are willing to pay more for productive CEOs, whether highly paid CEOs are in fact more productive is another question. Indeed, plenty of evidence has shown that millionaire CEOs do not outperform their lower-paid counterparts. Their expensive compensation packages, in fact, hurt a firm's bottom line without providing shareholders better returns (Brick, Palmon, and Wald 2006; Cooper, Gulen, and Rau 2016; Core, Holthausen, and Larcker 1999; Hill, Lopez, and Reitenga 2016). To put things in perspective, Albert Einstein made only about 10 times as much as an average worker did in 1933, while the top CEOs today make 300 times as much as their employees.[1] One should certainly hope that their productivity warrants their earnings.

The belief that income reflects productivity—a combination of talent and effort—translates to a perception that those with less income must not be as talented or hardworking as those with more. This mentality crystalized in an infamous 2014 tweet from Donald Trump: "Money was never a big motivation for me, except as a way to keep score." For Trump, born into an upper-class family, money is not a basic necessity (he has plenty), but it is a symbol of *moral superiority*. Yet money is a terrible way to keep score, since the competitors in this tournament rarely take money from each other; they are taking resources from people who need them to survive.

Similar beliefs confuse profitability as legitimacy and price as value. The success of entrepreneurs used to be measured by the quality of their products, how they treated their workers, their efforts toward community building, and their charitable contributions. Now CEOs' accomplishments are largely measured by the financial value they create for themselves and stockholders. The *Forbes* list of the wealthiest billionaires is widely circulated every year. Do you recall ever hearing about the year's most generous philanthropists?

Another unspoken idea behind "inequality is good" (or at least the neutral result of fair competition) is that humans are solely motivated by economic gains. Advocates for inequality often suggest, as Mankiw did, that in an egalitarian utopia in which material resources were equally distributed, there would be no reason for work at all. We have already pointed out that economic concerns are important to nearly every aspect of an American's daily life, but so are a variety of other factors such as social status, friendship, loyalty, affection, ethics, and self-fulfillment. This view ignores that many caregivers (particularly mothers) make great economic contributions without receiving any monetary compensation (Folbre 2001). The naive assumption that we should consider only one dimension of social life is convenient for economic modeling but detrimental to our understanding of society.

Then there is the opinion that even the poor in America still enjoy a far better standard of living. This is simply misguided. The fact is, the poor in the United States face *exceptional* hardship compared to their counterparts in many other countries. A 2016 US Department of Agriculture report indicated that 12.7 percent of American households did not have a stable supply of food, and 5 percent were marked as having "very low" food security (Coleman-Jensen et al. 2016). The pandemic of hunger has been particularly serious among American children, 14.5 million of whom did not have food security in 2015. That's a full 20 percent of children at risk of hunger on any given day in one of the world's richest countries. In a 2013 Gallup World Poll (OECD 2014: Figure 1.7), more than 20 percent of American families reported that they could not afford the food they need, which exceeded industrialized peer countries Canada (11.5 percent), France (10 percent), and Germany (4.6 percent).

Comparing the poor in the United States with those in the most impoverished societies confounds between- and within-country inequalities. While global economic disparities are persistent and troubling, assessing economic standing in absolute terms fails to recognize that poverty is always a relative measure for within-society comparison. That is, the poor are never poor because they cannot afford certain goods or services, but because the lack of resources disenfranchises them from fully participating in the society in which they live (Townsend 1979).

Another popular claim is that inequality promotes economic growth and that, as long as there is growth, the rising tide will (eventually) lift all boats. The proponents of this view follow the logic that the more unequal a society is, the more incentives there are for its members to invest in their skills and maximize their contributions to the economy. In this view, widening inequality is a product of a liberalized market and can be taken as a marker of a robust capitalist economy. This perspective assumes there is a trade-off between the pursuits of equality and growth. Prioritizing the former over the latter will make everyone worse off.

Opponents of this view counter that heightened inequality undermines general access to education and healthcare as well as causes social and political unrests, all of which impede economic growth. For example, a study of developed countries finds that a significant gap between low-income households and the remainder of the population yields less economic growth, potentially reflecting a human capital deficit among low-income families who lack sufficient resource to invest in education (Cingano 2014). While existing studies find mixed results on the relationship between inequality and growth (Banerjee and Duflo 2003; Benabou 1996; Forbes 2000; Ostry, Berg, and Tsangarides 2014), it is evident that most American families have experienced little income gain since the level of inequality began to take off.

A certain level of inequality *may* promote innovation, investment, and hard work, but a growing body of research indicates that, like finance, inequality can be too much of a good thing. A significant social cleavage between the haves and have-nots could reduce the motivations of both to seek advancements, since there is little possibility to climb the social ladder. Moreover, too much inequality could worsen social and health problems such as physical and mental illness, drug use, imprisonment, obesity, violence, and teenage pregnancies, again to the detriment of economic growth (Wilkinson and Pickett 2011).[2] A study that followed more than 17,000 British men over 10 years found that working-class men were more likely to die from heart diseases, and attributed the mortality difference to extensive stress (Marmot et al. 1978). In the United States, widening economic inequality is also associated with poorer health (Subramanian and Kawachi 2006), and lower levels of happiness among middle- and lower-income Americans (Hout 2016).

Inequality also promotes social unrest, because those at the margins of the economy have less to lose and more to gain for committing crimes (Imrohoroglu, Merlo, and Rupert 2001; Kang 2015). Other social consequences of economic inequality in the United States include greater disparities in marriage rates and educational attainment, residential segregation, and declines in social cohesion and trust (Cherlin 2014; Costa and Kahn 2003; Mayer 2001; Neckerman and Torche 2007).

In a big-picture view, heightened inequality is even detrimental to democracy. It expands the influence of the rich and reduces the participation of the poor. In the United States, when preferences differ across income levels, policies tend to address the interests of the wealthy and do not attend to the interests of low-income constituents (Gilens 2005). It is also no news that large campaign contributions grant greater access to politicians. While it is unclear whether more money actually helps win an election (Cockburn 2016), having more money gives affluent individuals exclusive opportunities to steer policies, especially those related to the distribution of resources.

Among the definitive answers this book cannot provide, a fundamental one is whether the current, increasingly unequal allocation of resources will help the United States better prosper in the long run and how to account for social costs that arise even when inequality promotes economic growth. What we can do, however, is show that the status quo is far from the simple result of market efficiency; it results from a specific set of institutional changes that benefit some and harm others.

Inequality Trends

Perhaps the most well-known trend since the 1980s has been the concentration of income among top earners (Piketty 2014; Piketty and Saez 2006). Between 1980 and 2014, the top 1 percent's share of pretax national income doubled, from 10.7 to 20.2 percent. This growth has been driven by the working rich such as corporate executives, lawyers, and financiers, as well as by those who live off of income made from investment returns. The growth at the very top is even more striking: the top 0.1 percent's share of national income quintupled, from around 1 to 5 percent.

Setting aside the super-rich, how the rest of the population divides the remaining economic resources also warrants consideration (Autor 2014). The most common measure for economic inequality is the Gini coefficient, invented by Italian statistician and sociologist Corrado Gini in 1912. The Gini coefficient ranges from 0, when all members of the society have identical income or wealth, to 1, when one person or household receives all the income or owns all the wealth.

Figure 2.1 presents US income inequality measured by the Gini coefficient before and after taxes and transfers.[3] The distribution of market income has grown more uneven since the 1970s, from 0.41 to 0.51. While the level of inequality is lower after accounting for taxes and transfers, redistributive policies are infrequently updated, leading to a parallel upward trend, rising from 0.32 to 0.40. The weakness of the redistributive policies in the

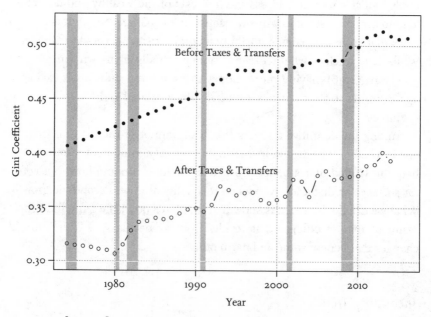

FIGURE 2.1 INCOME INEQUALITY BEFORE AND AFTER TAXES AND TRANSFERS
NOTE: The Gini coefficient is calculated at the household level adjusted for household size. Countries include OECD nations and Russia. We prioritize the measure of inequality based on the 2012 income definition over the prior definition. When both are unavailable, we interpolate the missing values with observed Gini. SOURCE: OECD Stat.

United States makes its level of inequality much higher than most advanced economies and only lower than less developed countries such as Chile, Mexico, Turkey, and Russia.

Another way to look at the distribution of earnings is to examine how the wage growth has varied by demographic backgrounds. Figure 2.2 contrasts the inflation-adjusted growth of average wages in 1980–1985 and in 2010–2015 by gender, race, and education level. There is still a wage gap between women and men, but, in general, women have made substantial progress, ranging from a wage increase of 33 percent for college-educated white women to about 7 percent for black women with a college degree. Men's trajectories, in contrast, have diverged greatly by their level of education: for men with at least a college degree, average wages increased 24 percent among whites and 23 percent among black men. For men without a college degree, wages dropped by 8.2 percent among whites and 1 percent among black men. Education has become a decisive factor for

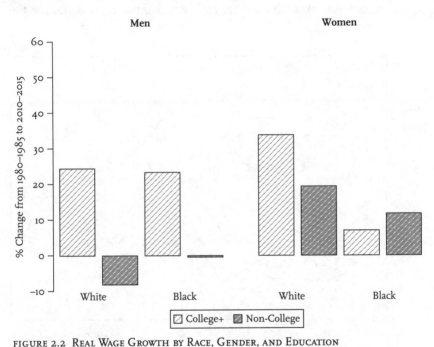

FIGURE 2.2 REAL WAGE GROWTH BY RACE, GENDER, AND EDUCATION

NOTE: Estimates include non-Hispanic black and white private-sector employees aged 25–65. Wage is calculated as annual earnings divided by the product of usual work hours per week and the number of weeks worked and inflation adjusted by the consumer price index published by the Bureau of Labor Statistics. College+ refers to those with at least a college degree, while noncollege includes those with some college experience or an associate degree.
SOURCE: Bureau of Labor Statistics, Current Population Survey Annual Social and Economic Supplement.

men's economic well-being. Those without college degrees are left out of wage growth.

There also have been substantial changes occurring in how earnings are allocated throughout the workforce. Figure 2.3 illustrates inflation-adjusted trends at various percentiles of the wage distribution between 1980 and 2016. Only those workers in the top quarter experienced some degree of wage growth. For more than half of the workforce, wages stagnated, or even dropped, during this period. A downward trend in the 1980s and early 1990s saw many workers receiving 5 to 10 percent less in hourly wages than they had in 1980. The trends rebounded in the late 1990s but have plateaued since then.

Those top earners did see major gains between the mid-1990s and mid-2000s: workers at the 90th percentile of the wage distribution made 31 percent more per hour in 2016 than in 1980, and the 95th percentile's wages increased by 46 percent. But in the same period, the GDP increased more than 170 percent when accounting for inflation. In other words, even the most privileged workers did not see their wages grow in proportion to the

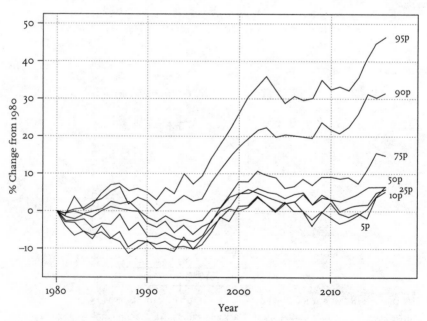

FIGURE 2.3 WIDENING WAGE DISTRIBUTION

NOTE: Estimates include all private-sector employees aged 25–65. Wage is calculated as annual earnings divided by the product of usual work hours per week and the number of weeks worked and inflation adjusted by the consumer price index published by the Bureau of Labor Statistics. SOURCE: Bureau of Labor Statistics, Current Population Survey Annual Social and Economic Supplement.

overall economy. The difference cannot be explained by employment benefits or rising healthcare costs, which stably constituted between 11 and 13 percent of the total compensation in this period.[4]

The destination was capital. Figure 2.4 presents the share of capital income as a percentage of all private income before taxes and transfers.[5] It reveals a rise from under 40 percent to over 46 percent over 30 years. Each recession since the 1980s triggered a jump. And this trend was concurrent with a surge in women's labor force participation from 43 to almost 60 percent and as an average full-time workweek increased from 39.42 to 41.58 hours. More Americans are working, and they are working longer hours. Yet their share of national income has decreased over time.

The rising inequality since the 1970s has been driven by wage growth among the highest earners and the increasing transfer of income from workers to employers. There has been enormous economic progress at the national level, yet few American workers today have enjoyed its full benefit. Many—notably low- and median-wage workers and white and black men without college degrees—have fared significantly worse. In the United States, the rising tide lifted the yachts but flipped the boats.

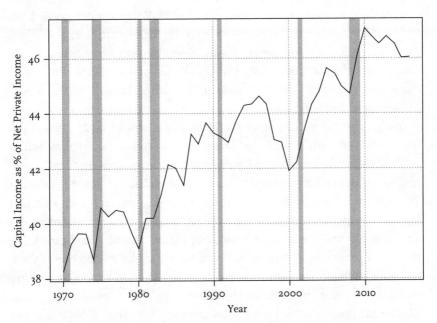

FIGURE 2.4 Capital's Share as Percentage of All Private Income

NOTE: Calculated as private-sector gross operating surplus over the sum of compensation and private-sector gross operating surplus. SOURCE: Bureau of Economic Analysis, National Economic Account, GDP by Industry Series.

> Caution in handling generally accepted opinions that claim to explain
> whole trends of history is especially important for the historian of
> modern times, because the last century has produced an abundance of
> ideologies that pretend to be keys to history but are actually nothing but
> desperate efforts to escape responsibility.
>
> —HANNAH ARENDT (1973)

Mainstream economists contend that the allocation of economic resources is largely determined by supply and demand in the markets. Rising inequality, in this view, reflects a weakened demand for labor and a divergence in workers' productivity. Economists Claudia Goldin and Lawrence Katz (2009) argue that the deceleration in the expansion of the education system and rapid technological advancement starting in the 1980s created a mismatch between the supply and demand for skilled labor. Naturally, wages rose for better-educated workers and fell for the rest. Economist David Autor (2003; 2013) also shows that, as repetitive, routinized tasks such as record-keeping and assembly are taken over by automation technology, the demand for low-skilled labor has dropped, and with it, their wages.

This trend intensified with international trade. With imported goods from China and other developing countries flooding the marketplace, workers in competing, domestic industries saw their employment security and wages drop (Acemoglu et al. 2014; Autor, Dorn, and Hanson 2013). Trade agreements made cheap foreign labor accessible to US firms, kicking off the much-maligned trend of "offshoring." Corporations began to subcontract production to foreign companies and move profitable plants abroad, with only design, marketing, and distribution units retained in the United States (Davis 2016).

This is a broadly convincing explanation for rising inequality. Many people readily accept the skill-centered account as *the* explanation for the widening divide in contemporary America. Business owners frequently complain that they cannot find workers with the right set of skills to fill their labor needs. The clear solution seems to be promoting higher education and expanding vocational programs, preferably through individual borrowing. Yet if there is a skills shortage, shouldn't employers be incentivized to provide training that equips workers with the most-needed skills? The popularity of on-the-job training programs has been declining among US firms. The rhetoric and reality seem mismatched.

Peter Cappelli (2012), a professor of management, attends to this last fact, arguing that there is not an education shortage but a training deficiency among American firms. Compared to other economic agents, individual employers know best which skills they need, and they should be most capable of transferring these particular skills to their workers. More and more employers, however, are reluctant to provide the necessary on-the-job training to their employees or to offer higher wages for workers to develop these skills outside the company. The skill-shortage claim is convenient only because it allows companies to offload the vocational trainings to universities and public-funded programs home and abroad.

In addition, the skill-based account of inequality tends to portray technological advancement and globalization as exogenous forces—meaning they took place outside of anyone's control—and therefore assign workers the responsibility to adjust. It fails to acknowledge that these developments did not unfold in a vacuum. That is, what technology should be developed and what trade agreement needs to be signed are always political decisions that reflect existing interests and power differentials.

Consider that battery-powered cars were introduced to the United States as early as the 1990s, but only rose in actual adoption in the 2010s. Strong opposition from the oil and gas industry, with their obvious interest in propping up gasoline consumption, kept car companies from fully investing in the new technology or shifting their production to electric. In a firm, managers often decide what technology to develop or purchase and how the production process should be designed, and that creates demands for specific technology. Innovation is not an organic process, but one biased toward the preferences of the managerial class. Going back further, sociologist Caroline Hanley (2014) finds that a primary goal of the development and implementation of computer technologies at General Electric in the 1950s was the prevention of unionization among the company's service workers. In this process, the managerial workers redefined themselves as the core workforce and came to view clerical workers, many of who were women, as nonproductive and disposable.

Likewise, many trade deals are negotiated with multinational companies' profits in mind. Such deals frequently bring immediate benefits to specific firms and damages to broader swathes of workers, small domestic firms, and even sovereign rights. The North American Free Trade Agreement (NAFTA) was signed by the Canadian, Mexican, and US governments in 1994, ostensibly to promote trade in agriculture, textiles, and automobile manufacturing by removing certain trade tariffs among the signatories. Chapter 11 of NAFTA, for instance, allows investors doing business in other countries to legally challenge public-welfare or economic regulations on the basis that governmental intervention may hurt their investment outlooks. While these "investor-state" provisions do not allow foreign investors to upend national laws, Chapter 11 allows foreign investors to extract large payouts from governments. Thus, the prospect of future litigation may deter participating countries from implementing regulations. As journalist William Greider (2001) notes, "The most disturbing aspect of Chapter 11 . . . [is] its expansive new definition of property rights—far beyond the established terms in US jurisprudence and with a potential to override established rights in domestic law."

NAFTA negotiators understood Chapter 11 as providing a system of checks and balances to curb sovereign rights in international trade. As principal deputy general counsel for the US trade representative, Daniel Price led the US negotiations and is generally credited for crafting the Chapter 11 investor-state provisions. Price later explained to an academic audience: "NAFTA checks the excesses of unilateral sovereignty. . . . The parties did not stumble into this. This was a carefully crafted definition" (quoted in Greider 2001). Shortly after negotiating NAFTA, Price went into the private sector. As a trade attorney at Powell Goldstein, he initiated the first Chapter 11 lawsuit against Mexico. In 2002, Price was appointed by George W. Bush to the Panel of Arbitrators of the International Centre for Settlement of Investment Disputes. At the same time, Price was representing private corporations in high-profile lawsuits against Canada and Mexico. In the early 2000s, Price brought suit against Mexico on behalf of Fireman's Fund Insurance (owned by Munich-based Allianz) while simultaneously lobbying the US government to serve Allianz's interest (Eberhardt and Olivet 2012).

A more recent example of corporate interest influencing trade deals is the Trans-Pacific Partnership (TPP), a trade agreement among 12 countries in the Americas, Asia, and South Pacific. The TPP was designed to promote transnational trade by reducing tariffs among partnering countries and opening up financial markets to investors. Multinational corporations rallied behind the agreement, lobbying in support of aspects of the deal that aligned with their interest. Nike, Google, Hollywood studios, and pharmaceutical companies were among its corporate champions (Ho 2013).

Cross-national studies indicate that the impacts of technological change and globalization are not uniform but moderated by public policies and labor-market institutions (Alderson and Nielsen 2002; Kristal 2013; Lee, Nielsen, and Alderson 2007). In many European countries, worker representatives actively participate in trade negotiation and serve on the boards that oversee corporate decision-making. The compensation for workers in these countries tends to be arranged collectively at the sectoral or industry level, which guarantees a decent standard of living for workers and a more equitable sharing of business income.

In contrast, organized labor in the United States has experienced significant erosion in numerical as well as political terms. In the 1960s, around
a third of private-sector workers were union members, and national labor
coalitions such as AFL-CIO and United Automobile Workers were promi-
nent actors involved in setting industrial and labor policies (Avent-Holt 2018;
Freeman and Medoff 1992; Rosenfeld 2014; Stein 2010). Both the share and
the number of unionized workers in the private sector dropped rapidly in
the late 1970s and have been in steady decline since. Now, as more states
adopt antiunion legislation, such as "right to work" statues, unions protect
only one in every 20 private sector workers.[6] Labor unions still exercise some
degree of political influence, but their roles in setting the national agenda or
firm compensation practices are marginal at best.

Unions are critical labor market institutions that help balance power
between capital and labor and compress the distribution of wages among
workers vertically as well as horizontally. A strong labor union ensures that
executive pay is held in check with other workers' wages (Shin 2014). As
democratic organizations, unions also tend to advocate for compensation
systems that promote solidarity and commitment. Accordingly, the wages in
a unionized workplace are weighted by the principles of equity and seniority,
which reduce various forms of discrimination (Rosenfeld and Kleykamp
2009; 2012; Lin, Bondurant, and Messamore 2018).

Not only union members suffer when labor union power wanes. It also
undermines nonunion workers' wages and well-being. When labor unions
had a significant presence in the United States, they bargained for higher
compensation and better working conditions, and that compelled nonunion
firms to improve their employment terms to compete for workers or avert
the threat of unionization (Leicht 1989). Sociologists Bruce Western and Jake
Rosenfeld (2011) find that wage inequality is lower among nonunion workers
in highly unionized regions and industries, suggesting that unions help institutionalize norms for fair pay that benefit all workers.

The disintegration of labor organizations has been compounded with an
embrace of market-oriented employment practices such as performance pay
and employment outsourcing (Kalleberg 2011), which weakened workers'
collective bargaining capacity and widened inequality. Performance or incentive pay refers to a compensation plan in which a significant portion
of workers' earnings is determined by the outcome of the tasks they perform. It has gained popularity since the 1982 recession for its supposed efficiency: the system rewards workers based on their merits and minimizes pay
discrimination unrelated to productivity. From the employer's perspective,

performance-based compensation or promotion reduces supervisory costs and prevents the free-rider problem.

Performance pay may be a sensible approach for rewarding workers who perform certain "easy to count" activities such as sales and piecework, but it is difficult to implement properly in most situations. To ensure an objective "performance" metric, many plans focus on immediate, quantifiable outcomes, which discourages workers from the important but hard-to-measure economic tasks that rely on the cooperation of different workers. Individual efforts are often difficult to evaluate, and subjective judgment, along with biases, often creeps into the determination of merits and compensation (Castilla and Stephen 2010; Roth 2006).

Taken to the extreme, performance pay creates a Darwinian workplace by curving individual performance. Jack Welch pioneered this method at General Electric in the 1980s, believing that the firm could achieve success only by rewarding the most productive workers and culling the rest. Similar ranking systems have since been adopted by companies such as Microsoft, Expedia, Yahoo, and Facebook. These commonly resulted in increased conflict among workers, strained relationships between employees and management, and reduced collaboration and worker morale.

In addition to performance pay, contract and temporary staffing became common practices. Rather than hiring relatively more expensive employees, many firms now opt to subcontract certain functions or "rent" workers from temporary staffing agencies in the unit of person-hour. The proportion of workers employed by these help agencies has grown fivefold, from under 0.6 percent of the US workforce in the early 1980s to almost 3 percent in the 2000s (Autor 2003), and the share of employers using such "off-roll" workers increased from 0.5 percent in 1990 to 5.4 percent in 2000 (Cappelli and Keller 2013). These workers, often women and minority men, tend to perform supportive tasks that do not accumulate human capital (that is, they are not learning skills recognized for career advancement), and they receive lower wages and benefits than rank-and-file employees.

These new work arrangements are particularly detrimental to low- and middle-skilled workers, who used to find entry-level positions in large firms and leverage the internal labor market for upward mobility as they gained skills and insider knowledge. When considering the changes in firm-size wage premium—the difference in compensation between large and small enterprises—over the last 30 years, we see that large firms in the United States were once equalizing institutions. They paid low-level employees more wages as an investment in their workforce. Newer, market-oriented practices adopted by these firms have reduced these wages, leading to higher inequality (Cobb and Lin 2017). The outsourcing of middle- and low-skilled tasks also creates "rich" firms and "poor" firms. The former generate handsome profits to be shared among a smaller number of employees, while the latter compete to provide low-cost services such as catering, cleaning, staffing, and customer support (Song et al. 2018).

A common theme across these market-oriented employment practices is that they transfer economic uncertainties from firms to workers. Traditionally, firms smoothed unforeseen economic downturns by utilizing cash reserves or subsidizing troubled units with profits made in others. Today, performance pay and employment outsourcing directly expose workers to the uncertainties in markets. Some workers surely benefit from having their earnings tied to performance during economic booms or gain additional opportunities from new employment practices, but individual workers tend to have less resource to cope with economic uncertainties, so these trends make their livelihood more vulnerable than ever before.

The dispersion of risk undermines workers' collective bargaining power relative to that of management. Rather than uniting workers who share the same interest, performance pay pits workers against each other. Accordingly, within-workplace categorical distinctions shifted from employers and employees to "productive" and "unproductive" workers. Subcontracting and temporary staffing inserted a group of second-class citizens with little claim over compensation-setting, workplace policies, and working conditions (Tomaskovic-Devey and Avent-Holt 2019). Their precarious status separates them from permanent employees and effectively prevents all workers from forming a strong front to negotiate with management.

Taken together, the rising inequality in the United States is not a "natural" result of apolitical technological advancement and globalization. Economic inequality is not a necessary price we need to pay for economic growth. Instead, the widening economic divide reflects a deeper transformation of how the economy is organized and how resources are distributed. It feels tidy to attribute the prevalence of new employment practices or inequality in general to changing social norms and excessive "corporate greed," yet such an account leaves the question of what socioeconomic conditions promote "corporate greed" but constrain "labor greed" unexplored.

The Rise of Finance as a Fundamental Cause of Inequality

The rise of finance expanded the level of inequality since the 1980s through three interrelated processes. First, it generated new intermediations that extract national resources from the productive sector and households to the financial sector without providing commensurate economic benefits. Second, it undermined the postwar accord between capital and labor by reorienting corporations toward financial markets and undermining the direct dependence on labor. Third, it created a new risk regime that transfers economic uncertainties from firm to individuals, which in turn increases the household demands for financial services.

Economic Rents

In the previous chapter, we showed that the financial sector's share of total corporate profits surged from around 15 percent to as high as 43 percent in 2001 (Figure 1.1), even though the sector employed only 6 percent of the US workforce. Where do all these profits come from? Most of the revenue for banks used to be generated by lending out deposits. By paying depositors lower interest rates than they charged borrowers, banks made profits in the "spread" between the rates. This business model began to change in the 1980s as banks expanded into trading and a host of fee-based services such as securitization, wealth management, mortgage and loan processing, service charges on deposit accounts (e.g., overdraft fees), card services, underwriting, mergers and acquisitions, financial advising, and market-making (e.g., IPOs [initial public offerings]). Altogether, these comprise the services that generate noninterest revenue.

Figure 2.5 presents noninterest revenue as a percentage of commercial banks' total revenue. Noninterest income constituted less than 10 percent of all revenue in the early 1980s, but its importance escalated and its share of income rose to more than 35 percent in the early 2000s. In other words, more than a third of all the bank revenue—particularly large banks' revenue—is generated today by nontraditional banking activities. For example, JPMorgan Chase earned $52 billion in interest income but almost $94 billion in noninterest income right before the 2008 financial crisis. Half was from activities such as investment banking and venture capital, and a quarter from trading. In 2007, Bank of America earned about 47 percent of its total income from noninterest sources, including deposit fees and credit card services.

The ascendance of the new banking model led to a significant transfer of national resources into the financial sector in terms of not only corporate profits but also its elite employees' compensation. Related industries, such as legal services and accounting, also benefitted from the boom. However, whether these noninterest activities actually created value commensurate to their costs has been questioned, particularly when the sector has been

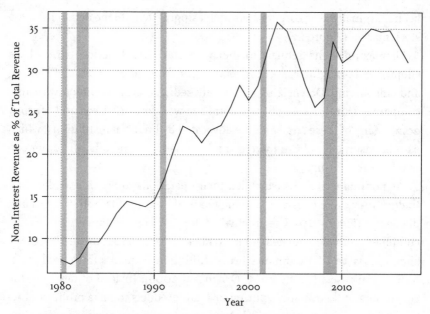

FIGURE 2.5 NONINTEREST REVENUE AS PERCENTAGE OF TOTAL REVENUE AMONG FDIC BANKS

NOTE: The sample includes all FDIC-insured commercial banks. SOURCE: Federal Deposit Insurance Corporation Historical Statistics on Banking, Table CB04.

dominated by only a handful of banks. Some argue that these earnings represent economic rents—excessive returns without corresponding benefits. In the next chapter, we trace the evolution of banks and other financial institutions and discuss the consequences for inequality.

The Capital-Labor Accord

Besides extracting resources from the economy into the financial sector, financialization undermined the capital-labor accord by orienting nonfinancial firms toward financial markets. The capital-labor accord refers to an agreement and a set of production relations institutionalized in the late 1930s (Bowles, Gordon, and Weisskopf 1986; 2015; Gordon 2002). The accord assigned managers full control over enterprise decision-making, and, in exchange, workers were promised real compensation growth linked to productivity, improved working conditions, and a high degree of job security. This agreement was reinforced by New Deal labor reforms such as unemployment insurance, collective bargaining rights, maximum work hours, and minimum wages. As a result, for most of the 20th century, labor was considered a crucial driver for American prosperity. Its role, however, has been marginalized as corporations increasingly attend to the demands of the stock market (Figure 1.2).

To maximize the returns to their shareholders, American firms have adopted wide-ranging cost-cutting strategies, from automation to offshoring and outsourcing. Downsizing and benefit reductions are common ways that companies trim the cost of their domestic workforce (Briscoe and Murphy 2012). Many of these strategies are advocated by financial institutions, which earn handsome fees from mergers and acquisitions, spinoffs, and other corporate restructuring.

As nonfinancial firms expanded their operations to become lenders and traders, they came to earn a growing share of their profits from interest and dividends (Figure 1.3). The intensified foreign competition in the 1970s, combined with deregulated interest rates in the 1980s, drove this diversion, with large US nonfinance firms shifting investments from production to financial assets (Crotty 2003; Orhangazi 2008). Instead of targeting the consumers of their manufacturing or retail products to raise profits and reward workers, these firms extended their financial arms into leasing, lending, and mortgage markets to raise profits and reward shareholders.

Figure 2.6 shows the amount of financial assets owned by US corporations as a percentage of their total assets. Financial assets here consist of Treasury, state, and municipal bonds, mortgages, business loans, and other financial securities. In theory, financial holding is countercyclical, meaning that firms hold more financial assets during economic contractions and then invest these savings in productive assets during economic booms. However, there has been a secular upsurge in financial holding since the 1980s, from about 35 percent of their total assets to more than half. Even when we remove financial corporations from the picture, we see a rise in financial holding from under 15 percent to more than 30 percent in the aftermath of the recession. Again, as American corporations shift their focus from productive to financial activities, purchasing financial instruments instead of stores, plants, and machinery, labor no longer represents a crucial component in the generation of profits, and the workers who perform productive tasks are devalued.

In addition to marginalizing labor, the rise of finance pushed economic uncertainties traditionally pooled at the firm level downward to individuals. Prior to the 1980s, large American corporations often operated in multiple product markets, hedging the risk of an unforeseen downturn in any particular market. Lasting employment contracts afforded workers promotion opportunities, health, pension, and other benefits, unaffected by the risks the company absorbed. Since the 1980s, fund managers have instead pressured conglomerates to specialize only in their most profitable activities,

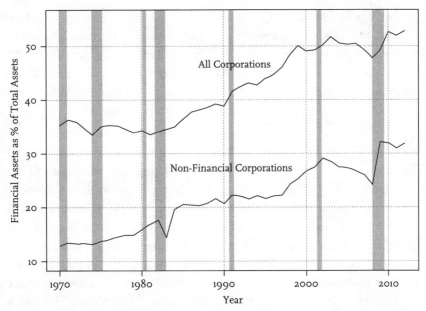

FIGURE 2.6 FINANCIAL ASSETS AS PERCENTAGE OF TOTAL CORPORATE ASSETS

NOTE: Financial assets include investments in governmental obligations, tax-exempt securities, loans to shareholders, mortgage and real estate loans, and other investments but do not include cash and cash equivalence. Financial corporations include credit intermediation, securities, commodities, and other financial investments, insurance carriers, other financial vehicles and investment companies, and holding companies. SOURCE: Internal Revenue Service Corporation Complete Report, Table 6: "Returns of Active Corporations."

pooling risk at the fund level, not at the firm level. Consequently, American firms have become far more vulnerable to sudden economic downturns. To cope with that increased risk, financial professionals advised corporations to reconfigure their employment relationships from permanent arrangements to ones that emphasize flexibility—the firm's flexibility, not the employees'. Workers began to be viewed as independent agents rather than members or stakeholders of the firm. As more and more firms adopt contingent employment arrangements, workers are promised low minimum hours but are required to be available whenever they are summoned (Deery and Mahony 1994; Golden 2015; Lambert 2008; McMenamin 2007; Mills 2004).

The compensation principle shifted, too, from a fair-wage model that sustains long-term employment relationships to a contingent model that ties wages and employment to profits (meaning more workers are involved in productivity pay schemes than they realize; should their portion of the company lag in profits, their job, not just their compensation, is on the line). Retirement benefits also transformed from guarantees of financial security to ones dependent on the performance of financial markets (Cobb 2015). Of course, this principle mostly benefits high-wage workers who can afford the fluctuations. Many low-wage workers, not knowing how many hours they will work and how much pay they will receive, are forced to borrow to meet their short-term needs (Morduch and Schneider 2017). Later in the book, we detail the financial turn among nonfinancial firms and discuss how it reduced employment and increased inequality among workers.

Atomized Risk Regime

The dispersion of economic risks and the widening labor market divide are reflected in the growing consumption of financial products at the household level. As defined-contribution plans gradually replaced defined-benefit pensions as the default benefit in the private sector, mutual funds and retirement accounts flourished. This new retirement system allows workers to carry benefits over as they move across different employers (helpful when jobs are ever-more precarious), but it ties their economic prospects to the fluctuation of financial markets. Families became responsible for making investment decisions and securing retirement funds for themselves.

Retirement in the United States, thus, is no longer an age but a financial status. Many middle-class families have had to cash out their retirement accounts to cover emergency expenses. Many others fear that they cannot afford to exit the workforce when the time comes. And these are the *lucky* ones. About half of American workers have neither defined-benefit nor defined-contribution plans; that rate declines to a third among millennials.[7] Affluent families, who allocate an increasing proportion of their wealth to financial assets, benefit, since they have sufficient resources to buffer downturns and can gain substantially from financialization. Still, the only sure winners are financial advisors and fund managers, who charge a percentage of these savings annually, without having to pay out when there are great losses.

The expansion of credit is supposed to narrow consumption inequality across households and smooth volatility across the life course. Instead, it, too, adds to economic uncertainty. The debate about whether Americans borrow too much obscures the reality that the consequences of debt vary dramatically across the economic spectrum (as well as by race and gender). The abundance of credit provides affluent families the opportunity to invest or meet short-term financial needs at low cost. At the same time, middle-income households carry increasingly heavy debt burdens, curtailing their ability to invest and save, and low-income households are either denied credit or face enormously high rates that go beyond preventing savings to imprison the impoverished in a cycle of debt payments. More and more Americans are in the last category: unable to service their obligations (that is, to pay the bills on their debts), many families have become insolvent, owning less than they owe. The credit market has been revealed as a regressive system of redistribution benefiting the rich and devastating the poor.

In this atomized risk regime, financial failure is attributed to a personal lack of morality or sophistication. Everyday workers are urged to educate themselves about the market, enhancing their financial literacy. "Financial inclusion" has become the buzzword of the day. Financial self-help like the perennial best-seller *Rich Dad, Poor Dad* and *Secrets of the Millionaire Mind* fly off the shelves (Fridman 2016), while entire governmental agencies and public outreach programs are established to promote the "savvy" use of financial products. We will take a closer look at how debt and the financialization of wealth exacerbate inequality in two subsequent chapters.

Summary

Inarguably, the level of inequality in the United States has increased dramatically in the past four decades. The argument is about what the fact of rising inequality *means*. We discuss how some popular beliefs about inequality are mistaken: higher levels of inequality tend to lead to lower, not higher, social mobility. The idea that income measures one's productivity is an assumption, not a fact. And America's poor fare much worse than their counterparts in other wealthy countries, with hunger a constant threat to a fifth of American children.

Whether inequality promotes economic growth among industrialized societies is undecided. Its defendants often speak with more conviction than evidence. In the meantime, a growing body of studies indicates that inequality has a variety of adverse effects, including spreading illness, boosting crime rates, and eroding social cohesion and trust, which undermines democracy. Even if inequality did promote economic growth, is the price too high?

Trends in inequality have been quite staggering over the past few decades. Piketty and Saez brought top income concentration to the fore, paying attention to the tremendous gains made by those at the very top of the income distribution. Yet the widening economic divide is not only between the 1 and the 99 percent. The Gini coefficient of market income distribution in the United States has grown by about 20 percent since the 1970s without commensurate rises in redistributive policies. That has meant a parallel surge in the after-taxes-and-transfers distribution.

Inequality, of course, impacts people differently depending on their race and gender. While women in general have made substantial gains in their wages, thanks to the ongoing feminist movement, men without college degrees have seen a significant erosion of their wages, particularly among whites. Distribution-wise, we find that more than half of the workforce faced wage stagnation between 1980 and 2016, when financialization took off. Only those in the top quarter of the wage distribution experienced growth, and even gains lagged far behind the national economic growth. This is because workers' share of national income has been declining, from above 60 to below 54 percent, and there is a significant divergence regarding how this smaller share of pie is distributed among workers.

Mainstream economics contends that these developments were driven by the rising demand for skilled labor and the weakening demand for manual and routine work, in part due to globalization and technological advancement. Yet this account largely overlooks political processes, such as curtailing labor union power, and institutional practices, such as market-oriented employment arrangements, which exacerbate the impacts of macro developments (see also Galbraith 2012).

Financialization has motivated or complemented many of these inequality-inducing developments through three interwoven processes: the extraction of economic rents from the nonfinancial economy for the benefit of the financial sector, the demise of the capital-labor accord, and the dispersion of economic risks from the state and organizations to families. In the next four chapters, we examine the inequality consequences of how financialization unfolded on Wall Street, Main Street, and residential streets.

CHAPTER 3 | Finance Ascends

IN THE AFTERMATH OF the 2008 financial crisis, much of the discussion on financial reform was dedicated to reducing the instability of the financial system. That instability has three main, mutually reinforcing sources. First, large banks, along with some other financial institutions, are "too big to fail." That is, their sheer size guarantees that the failure of one would lead to the collapse of all. Often, they are also "too big to manage," meaning that the top executives have limited knowledge about the specific operation of individual divisions and the actual financial risks to which their companies are exposed.

The second source of instability comes from the tremendous level of debt held by these financial institutions. Before the financial crisis, the capital-to-asset requirement for major banks was as low as 3 percent. In other words, for every $100 banks spent, only $3 needed to come from their own pocket. The other $97 were other people's money, whether it came from depositors or creditors. Moreover, the 3 percent requirement was risk-weighted, meaning that banks could pile up their assets without raising more equity, so long as these assets were deemed "risk-free." Thus, it was not unusual for banks to operate with a leverage ratio of more than 35. Like walking on a tightrope, the extreme levels of debt made these financial institutions vulnerable to economic turbulence.

The third ingredient in this recipe for disaster is systemic. An overwhelming majority of today's financial dealings take place between financial institutions (Turner 2015). The dense network of transactions chains the fate of one institution to the others', often without the parties involved being aware. Any house on fire, whether a mansion or a shack, has a good chance of burning down the whole city.

The first two diagnoses come with clear prescriptions. Financial conglomerates need to be better managed and compartmentalized, if not broken up altogether, to avoid some reckless activities from bringing down the whole system (and to the annihilation of household savings). Capital requirements should be tightened, and financial institutions should be required to hold additional liquidity to hedge against an emergency. Versions of these reforms have been implemented since the Dodd-Frank Wall Street Reform and Consumer Protection Act.

The issue of interdependence, however, is more difficult to treat.

While it is certainly important to minimize the instability of financial markets and prevent another finance-driven economic crisis, the emphasis on stability overlooks the fact that the financial sector could harm the US economy and undermine middle- and working-class Americans even in the *absence* of financial crisis. Indeed, since the late 1970s, the United States has seen a proliferation of financial activities. Complex transactions such as leveraged buyouts, asset-backed securities, and derivatives trading have allowed for an unprecedented amount of money to change hands and generated extraordinary profits for the deal-makers. However, it is not clear at all how much these costly "ingenuities" promoted economic growth.

To understand how we came to this point, we first examine the evolution of the financial sector, particularly the banking industry, since the 1980s; the timing and magnitude of the income transfer from the rest of the economy to the financial sector; and inequality within the financial sector. Neither ingenuity nor skill were the primary cause of extraordinary profit and compensation in the financial sector. What we observe is an emerging redistributive system that transferred resources from Main Street to Wall Street.

The Transformation of Finance in the United States

Prior to the 1980s, the US financial sector was rather feudalistic; each financial institution served its own constituency and territory. Aiming to level the playing field between national banks (chartered by the federal government) and community banks (chartered by states), the McFadden Act of 1927 subjected national banks to state branching regulations, which limited their growth (Jayaratne and Strahan 1997). To prevent a recurrence of the large-scale banking crisis that set up the Great Depression, the Banking Act of 1933 (Glass-Steagall) prohibited Federal Reserve member banks from dealing, selling, or investing in nongovernmental securities and investment banks from taking deposits. As a result, JPMorgan decided to focus on commercial banking, and some of its employees left to form Morgan Stanley. The Bank Holding Company Act of 1956 put banks under the supervision of the Federal Reserve and prohibited them from acquiring out-of-state banks or engaging in nonbanking activities such as manufacturing, transportation, and insurance.

The combination of geographical and operational restrictions created a highly compartmentalized but deeply embedded financial sector, in which the pursuit of profits was balanced with the maintenance of personal rapport (Polanyi 2001). Commercial banks accepted deposits from and made loans to households and businesses in their home or neighboring counties. Most of their profits came from the difference between the interests they paid and charged. Since these banks managed household deposits, their operation was closely monitored by federal and state agencies. To make sound loan decisions, commercial bankers were required to have extensive knowledge about local industries and, perhaps more importantly, the reputation of their borrowers. It was in these bankers' interest to promote community development because their earnings depended on the prosperity of the local economy.

Investment banks in New York and other major cities, meanwhile, facilitated the issuance and transaction of stocks, bonds, and a variety of financial securities. Unlike commercial banks that served ordinary Americans and local businesses, investment banks worked as both financial advisors to and middlemen between wealthy individuals and large national companies. They profited not from making loans but from taking a cut of each transaction. Since market-making required these firms to hold certain inventory, they also made profits from the difference between the buying and selling prices of securities. Similar to community banks, investment banks' success depended not only on the services they provided but also on the trust and friendships they cultivated with their affluent and corporate customers. Because these bankers did not handle the money of ordinary citizens, their activities were only loosely restrained by regulatory agencies such as the Securities and Exchange Commission (SEC).

Other significant financial institutions included mutual banks and credit unions, which had promoted savings and provided credits, respectively, to middle- and low-income households. Unlike commercial banks, these institutions were owned by members who either resided in the same area or belonged to the same organization. They were, therefore, committed to collective interest. Since the early 20th century, savings and loan associations (S & Ls) had been the primary mortgage providers for American households. To promote homeownership in particular, a series of policies were set in place to strengthen S & Ls' role. For example, the Federal Home Loan Banks were established in 1932 to provide liquidity to S & Ls. When competition from commercial banks intensified in the 1960s, S & Ls were allowed to pay slightly higher interest rates on their deposits to attract more savings. Manufacturers such as General Motors and General Electric and retailers such as J.C. Penny also created financing arms to provide direct credit to their customers. Since these financial arms did not take deposits, their de facto lending activities were tolerated by the regulatory agencies.

The logic behind this compartmentalization was that it would promote stability and prevent excessive financial power. And it did: between 1942 and 1980, bank failure was virtually nonexistent, averaging 5.4 banks per year in the whole country. However, some regulations led to inefficiency. The geographical restriction prevented banks from expanding and taking advantage of economies of scale. It also shielded banks from competition and left many businesses and households ill-served when their local banks were poorly managed or outright discriminatory. Moreover, national corporations often required interstate banking services, which were costly because of tight regulation. The separation of commercial and investment banking prohibited commercial banks from seeking higher returns for their deposits and investment banks from attracting funds from households; in theory, both led to the financial system's suboptimal performance. Nevertheless, whether these financial institutions reached their optimal levels of efficiency was of secondary concern to this generation of policymakers and regulators scarred by the 1931–1932 banking panics. No one wanted another Great Depression.

The compartmentalization began to unravel after 30 years of stability. Until this point, the post–World War II banking sector had grown at a steady pace. The return of veterans and the dominance of US firms in the global market provided abundant opportunities for banks to prosper. Their share of corporate profits doubled in the 1950s, rising from 8.8 to 16.6 percent (Figure 1.1).

Two developments in the early 1960s threatened this upward trend. First, the intensified competition for deposits from thrift institutions, such as credit unions and S & Ls, forced banks to increase their interest payments and therefore increase the cost of their funds. Second, the emergence of the commercial paper market—an uncollateralized security issued by firms with excellent credit ratings—allowed corporations to trade cash flow directly with one another to meet their short-term needs. This development reduced the profits that banks gained from corporate finance.

Profitability returned in the latter half of the 1960s, as the Federal Reserve extended interest rate ceilings to thrift institutions, limiting competition for deposits. In the meantime, large commercial banks began to reorganize themselves by establishing single-bank holding companies, legal entities that allowed them to issue commercial paper that was not subject to the Fed's interest caps. These banks increased their overseas subsidiaries and branches into countries where there were no interest ceilings and reserve requirements: the number of banks with foreign branches grew from seven in 1955 to 79 in 1970, and the number of foreign branches increased from 115 to 532 (Houpt 1999).

This period of prosperity was brief. To avoid gold depletion (recall this imminent threat in the 1960s, as discussed in Chapter 1's section on Bretton Woods), the Treasury Department hiked short-term interest rates on governmental securities. Aimed at persuading domestic firms and foreign governments to maintain their dollar reserves, this policy destabilized the business model of the banks, particularly for thrift institutions. Mutual banks and S & Ls accepted mostly deposits with short maturity but held long-term mortgage loans that paid fixed interest. Stagflation in the 1970s worsened the situation. The lack of economic growth severely reduced the demand for credit and, therefore, banks' lending activities. High inflation discouraged savings, the main source of banks' reserves, and reduced the value of existing loans, which constituted most of banks' assets.

Some fund managers saw this as an opportunity to tap into the large pool of money they had no access to previously. Money market mutual funds, which tracked the market rate and lured middle-class families' savings by promising some stability amid high inflation, ballooned. This new financial product, uninsured by the Federal Deposit Insurance Corporation (FDIC), paid several percentage points higher interest than the ceiling, and it gained popularity throughout the 1970s. Foreseeing the impending collapse of the Bretton Woods system and the dollar's international standing, multinational corporations began ferrying their funds overseas and exchanging dollars for foreign currencies.

All these developments drained household and business savings from traditional banks. Figure 3.1 presents the private deposits as a percentage of total assets among the US commercial banks between 1934 and 1980. The proportion of assets funded by private deposits reached its highest point after the conclusion of World War II. There was a gradual decline in the following two decades, partially driven by the competition from thrift institutions and corporate disintermediation. The sea change, however, took place in the late 1960s and 1970s, with the proportion of assets funded by private deposits dropping from 72.4 percent in 1968 to 57.9 percent (pre–Great Depression levels) in 1977.

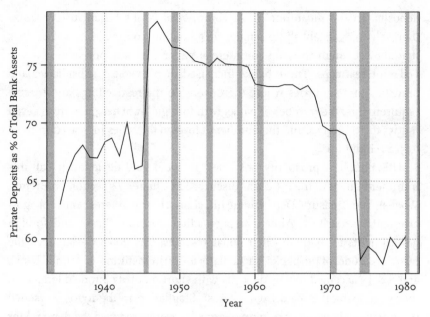

FIGURE 3.1 PRIVATE DEPOSITS AS PERCENTAGE OF TOTAL BANK ASSETS, 1934–1980
NOTE: The sample includes all FDIC-insured commercial banks. Private deposit refers to the deposits of individuals, partnerships, and corporations. SOURCE: Federal Deposit Insurance Corporation Historical Statistics on Banking, Tables CB09 and CB15.

Since banks were not allowed to attract deposits through higher interest rates, they began to provide perks such as free toasters (which could cost more than $100 after adjusting for inflation) or signing bonuses for new customers. Automated teller machines (ATMs) came into fashion, advertised for their convenience. New products, such as negotiable order of withdrawal, or NOW, accounts, money market accounts, and real estate investment trusts (REIT), were promoted to boost bank revenue. To compensate for their losses in private deposits, commercial banks began to borrow heavily from other, more expensive, sources.

The 1970s banking crisis, it must be remembered, unfolded in an era of ideological transition. The Keynesian economics that dominated postwar policies started to lose legitimacy by failing to explain—let alone effectively solve—long-lasting stagflation. In the meantime, the relentless business mobilization that began in the 1960s meant that no one was willing to waste this opportunity to advocate for a "free market" system in which the expansion of liberty promised the preservation of life and the pursuit of happiness. There had been proposals to deregulate the financial sector as early as the Eisenhower administration (Hester 2008), but it was the combination of economic turmoil and political reorientation in the 1970s that made these proposals appealing.

Maine was the first to break. Interstate and intrastate branching restrictions began to loosen when Maine, in 1978, allowed an out-of-state bank-holding company to operate in its territory. Many states followed suit, and, by 1990, almost all had allowed out-of-state banks to operate or acquire in-state banks. The interstate banking system was recognized as the "new reality" in the Riegle-Neal Interstate Banking and Branching Act of 1992, which allowed bank-holding companies to acquire banks in any state or merge banks located in different states into a single network.

The first major nationwide financial deregulation also came in 1978, when the Supreme Court ruled in *Marquette National Bank of Minneapolis v. First of Omaha Service Corporation* that national banks could charge interest rates according to the ceiling set by their home state. This ruling allowed national banks to offer credit cards to anyone in the United States and export high interest rates from unregulated to regulated states. Consequently, Citibank, Wells Fargo, and other national banks moved their credit card operations to South Dakota and Delaware, states willing to repeal interest caps to attract corporations. To protect state-chartered banks from competition, more restrictive states began to loosen or abolish their interest caps. The demise of antiusury laws opened the gates, and a series of high-interest consumer financial products flooded through.

The second and perhaps most pivotal deregulation was the Depository Institutions Deregulation and Monetary Control Act of 1980, in which Congress repealed a set of banking regulations that had been in place since the Banking Act of 1933. This allowed banks to merge, phased out regulatory control over interest paid on savings accounts (Regulation Q), granted credit unions and S & Ls the right to offer checking accounts, raised the coverage of deposit insurance, and effectively permitted banks to pay interest for even on-demand deposits. Along with the Garn–St. Germain Depository Institutions Act of 1982, this act weakened the distinction between commercial banks and thrift institutions. To avoid thrift institutions from switching to federal charters, some states such as Texas and California adopted even more liberal rules regarding thrifts' investment activities.

This brave new world brought immediate problems. The deregulation of interest rates across deposit-taking institutions severely weakened S & Ls because most of their portfolios were still fixed-income, low-yielding mortgages and their expertise in other lending markets was limited. The situation worsened as the federal housing credit programs established in the Johnson administration came to capture a growing share of mortgage markets and as commercial banks greatly increased residential lending via adjustable-rate mortgages.

The S & Ls' threats were compounded by pervasive financial fraud. The industry was operating under the governmental guarantee that insolvency would be addressed with public funding. "Bankruptcy for profit" became a winning strategy for deceitful owners and executives, incentivizing the looting of their own thrifts and dumping broken balance sheets on the public (Akerlof et al. 1993; Black 2013). Banks inflated the net worth of their acquisitions through fraudulent accounting, exploiting the interest spread between long- and short-term bonds, and issuing irresponsible, nonrecourse loans to earn origination fees and high interests, knowing full well that these loans would default in a few years. As a result, a third of S & Ls failed in the 1980s and 1990s. A traditionally community-based mortgage system withered.

The deregulation of interest rates and intensified competition also reduced the profitability of banks' traditional deposit-loan model, which was further squeezed by the emergence of nonbank lenders (Chapter 4). Many banks failed to adjust to the competitive environment and closed in the 1980s. Over 1,000 institutions were closely monitored by the FDIC by 1986, and over 700 banks failed in 1988. To lure customers from competitors, banks often lowered their lending standards and provided attractive services concealing a variety of "gotcha" fees. Account fees for maintenance, transfer, overdraft, and minimum balance flourished in the 1980s, becoming an important source of revenue for the banks. On top of high interest rates, credit cards came with fees for late payment and balance transfers. These charges, disproportionate to their actual costs, have been largely paid by middle- and lower-income households with less liquidity. Furthermore, commercial banks expanded their products to include mutual fund, trust, investment advising, leasing, insurance, consulting, appraisals, and security brokerage services.

In addition to legislative loosening, supervision and enforcement lagged. Agencies such as the Federal Reserve and the Securities and Exchange Commission pulled back from their oversight roles. Believing that markets were self-correcting and that bankers had a vested interest in protecting the financial system, regulators seemed to have Panglossian optimism about how these new developments would help "manage risks" and "serve unmet demands." The Federal Reserve even reinterpreted the Glass-Steagall restrictions several times to legitimize illegal activities such as firms' simultaneous operation in investment, insurance, and banking industries. Eventually, the Financial Services Modernization Act of 1999, passed in response to the merger of Citicorp and Travelers Insurance Company, repealed the Glass-Steagall Act and allowed this joint operation. It was now legal for a single financial institution to operate in almost all financial markets. Banks promised that they could self-regulate. Specific personnel were designated to manage the risks across different operations to ensure full compliance with existing regulations. These chief risk officers proliferated in the first decade of the 21st century; instead of *reducing* risk, however, these professionals used various new derivatives to *justify* the risks bank took to maximize returns (Pernell, Jung, and Dobbin 2017).

As financial institutions consolidated, personal relationships (even though they were often discriminatory) and commitment to customers (once critical to successful banking) were lost. Banks became far less embedded in the communities they served, free to relentlessly pursue profits without considering the consequences. The new owners of these subsidiaries rarely have extensive knowledge about the customers they serve, let alone any genuine interest in seeing them prosper.

The Deregulation-Profit Paradox

"It is demonstrable," said he, "that things cannot be otherwise than as they are; for as all things have been created for some end, they must necessarily be created for the best end. Observe, for instance, the nose is formed for spectacles, therefore we wear spectacles. The legs are visibly designed for stockings, accordingly we wear stockings . . . and they, who assert that everything is right, do not express themselves correctly; they should say that everything is best."

—VOLTAIRE, *Candide, ou l'Optimisme*

The most paradoxical outcome of deregulation may be the fast-climbing profits of the financial sector. In theory, one would expect deregulation to have heightened competition among firms and thus attenuated industry's earnings, as firms were forced to either lower the price or provide better and more costly services to gain market share. This has not been the case. The financial industry's national profit share increased from 15 to more than 40 percent in the decades following deregulation. The trend is even more puzzling when we consider the economies of scale and the rapid advancement of information technology, which significantly reduced the costs of most banking activities and supposedly undermined incumbent advantages.

An obvious explanation for this paradox, at least before 2008, was that deregulation made the financial sector more productive. As restriction after restriction was removed, financial institutions became able to make greater contributions to the economy and therefore receive higher rewards. After all, if the customers or their representatives are willing to pay banks large sums of money, they must consider the services or products they receive "worth it." One could also recount all the financial innovations since the late 1970s and explain how they changed our economic lives for the better. Without mass-market credit cards, consumers would have to carry cash around and could not obtain the goods they need when they need them. Without leveraged buyouts, it would be difficult to liberate poorly managed firms from the hands of incompetent executives and put valuable assets in good use. Without derivatives, farmers, airlines, and other businesses would be exposed to economic volatilities deterring them from investment. Without subprime and adjustable-rate mortgages, a large segment of Americans could never become homeowners and have stable and productive family lives.

The only problem is that the promotion of these financial services rarely has the welfare of consumers, workers, farmers, businesses, or homeowners in mind. Rather, these ventures' profitability *depends* on the harm they bring. Most revenue for mass-market credit card issuers comes from interest payments. The longer the card users carry their balances, the more these firms profit. Furthermore, management funds that take over other enterprises often fail to enhance the performance of these firms (Appelbaum and Batt 2014). In many cases, the managed businesses and their workers are sacrificed to line the pockets of fund managers. Most derivatives are not used by farmers and businesses to hedge risks, but by traders to place bets against one another. Since many traders have limited knowledge about the underlying assets, derivatives' prices do more to conceal than reveal the associated risks. Subprime and adjustable mortgages operate under the assumption that their consumers will be able, over time, to afford higher or varying interest payments—but if that were the case, why wouldn't the borrowers be able to obtain prime, fixed-rate mortgages?

Financial economist Thomas Philippon (2015), among others, questions whether the financial industry has become more efficient due to deregulation and the proliferation of new products, technologies, and industrial consolidation. The evidence says no. The profit in finance is largely driven by the quantity of intermediation. That is, even with all the "innovations" in finance, how much customers pay for financial services has remained stagnant since 1900. The unit cost averages around 1.87 percent (and was significantly higher in the 1980s and the 1990s). If these new developments have indeed lowered the operating cost of finance, the difference has clearly been pocketed by financial professionals.

We argue that these innovations did not create extraordinary profits for the financial sector, but rather an emerging system allowed the financial sector to extract resources from other industries and households with new products that provide few commensurate benefits. This system builds upon three interrelated developments: the concentration of market power, the deepening of political involvement, and the private intermediation of public services.

Concentrated Market Power

The banking sector's market power began to consolidate in the 1980s, following an unprecedented level of mergers and the emergence of regional bank compacts (Amel and Jacowski 1989). The Interstate Banking and Branching Act of 1992 accelerated this trend and encouraged cross-regional consolidation. For instance, originated in San Francisco, Bank of America acquired Security Pacific Corporation in California and other western states in 1992. Two years later, it bought Continental Illinois National Bank of Chicago, marching toward the East Coast. After suffering a huge loss when Russia defaulted on its bond, the bank and its well-known trademark were acquired by NationsBank of Charlotte in 1998. Chase Manhattan Bank, for its part, was acquired by Chemical Bank in 1996 and then merged with JPMorgan & Company in 2000. Seeking to expand out of the East Coast, the new conglomerate acquired the Midwest compact Bank One Corporation in 2004.

The number of independent banks dropped from more than 12,000 in the 1970s to around 6,500 in the 2000s. Banking assets were concentrated into a handful of institutions (Figure 3.2), such that the three largest bank-holding companies managed between 10 and 15 percent of the total banking assets before 1990, but over 35 percent in the late 2000s. More recently, a full half of commercial banking assets in the United States have come under the control of just 10 banks.

More significant than this horizontal consolidation is the vertical integration of various financial activities. The Financial Services Modernization Act of 1999 legitimatized the "one-stop shop" model and led large national banks to expand further into asset and wealth management, trading, investment banking, venture capital, insurance, and real estate. In this process, the high-risk, high-reward culture once unique to Wall Street came to dominate the whole financial sector. Retail banking became a secondary business that provided capital for "high finance" ventures. The primary customers of these banks are no longer individual depositors or borrowers but other financial institutions. Figure 3.3 illustrates the sources of revenue for the four

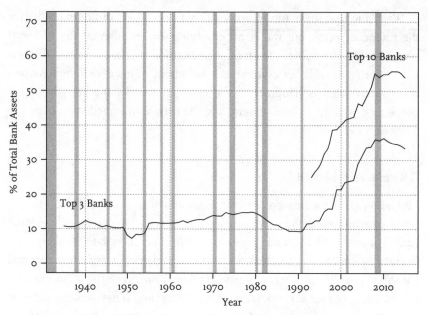

FIGURE 3.2 The Concentration of Assets in the Banking Industry

NOTE: The sample includes all FDIC-insured commercial banks. The total assets of the three largest banks between 1935 and 2006 were acquired through a Freedom of Information Act request to the Federal Deposit Insurance Corporation. Other data sources include FDIC Historical Statistics on Banking, Table CB09, and Statistics on Deposit Institutions.

largest banks between 2000 and 2017. It shows that, before the financial crisis, interests made up only between 36 and 59 percent of their revenue, while a significant portion of income was generated through deposit fees, trading, investment banking, credit card servicing, securitization, and insurance. The importance of interest income has increased for JPMorgan and CitiGroup since the financial crisis; however, it still constitutes only about 50 and 70 percent of their revenues, respectively.

The tremendous consolidation of the financial sector grants large firms enormous power to *condition* the markets. They are the hubs of capital market, able to bend the supply and demand of capital for their own interest. Financial economists David Humphrey and Lawrence Pulley (1997) noticed that the 1990s recovery of bank profits was mainly driven by large banks' ability to impose more deposit fees, set higher minimum balance requirements, and charge higher interest rates on consumer, small business, and middle-market corporate loans. Similar price hikes were not observed among smaller banks. An oligopolistic structure also facilitates fraud (Lattman 2013) and antitrust violations (Eisinger 2012; Silver-Greenberg 2012; Taibbi 2012) and generates frequent conflicts of interest (Bowley 2010;

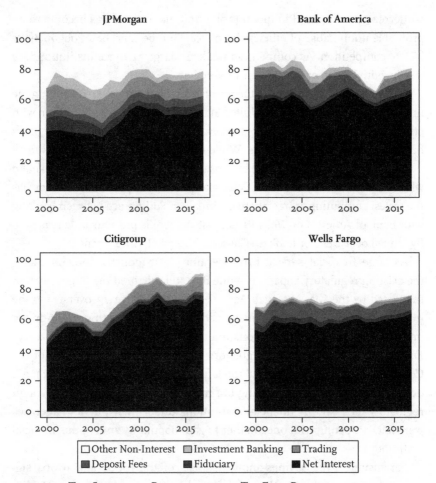

FIGURE 3.3 THE SOURCES OF REVENUE FOR THE TOP FOUR BANKS

NOTE: **Fiduciary revenue** includes revenue generated through investment management, investment advisory, personal and corporate trusts, transfer agent services, and certain employee benefit account services, as well as securities custody, securities lending, securities clearing and settlement, and functionally regulated securities broker-dealer and registered investment advisor activities. **Deposit fees** include revenue generated from the maintenance, minimum balance, immature account closing, ATM, overdraft, stop payment, and other related services. **Trading** denotes net gains and losses from trading cash instruments and off-balance sheet derivative contracts. **Investment banking** includes fees and commissions from underwriting securities, private placements of securities, investment advisory and management services, and merger and acquisition services. **Other noninterest income** includes venture capital, mortgage and credit card servicing, gains from securitization transactions, insurance underwriting, and sales. SOURCE: FDIC Statistics on Deposit Institutions.

Nocera 2013). The absence of threats from challenger firms leaves little incentive for incumbent firms to maintain their reputation.

Indeed, the consolidation has not brought greater efficiency but lower competition in the financial industry. Financial economists Germán

Gutiérrez and Thomas Philippon (2017) find that finance has become more profitable not because of efficiencies of scale but because of an oligopolistic lack of competition. As competition weakens, large financial institutions are less incentivized to enhance their productivity.

It should be no surprise that the four largest banks are regulars among the most "hated" companies in the United States.[1] What they have in common with other notorious companies is not simply that they are big, but that they profit from disempowering consumers. While monopoly is largely prohibited in all these markets, competition is all but absent. Unlike the electronics market, in which fans constantly debate which smartphone takes the best selfie or has the fastest computing scores, there is virtually no difference between banking with Bank of America or Wells Fargo, just as there is precious little reason to fly United over Delta or hook up Comcast instead of Time Warner.

As large financial service firms became cross-industry conglomerates, the existing regulatory apparatus—one that still mirrored the fragmentation mandated by the Glass-Steagall Act—became ineffective for overseeing the interconnection of various financial activities and preventing profit-driven practices that negatively affect consumers (Tomaskovic-Devey and Lin 2013). Furthermore, because many regulatory agencies, such as the Office of the Comptroller of the Currency and the Office of Thrift Supervision (OTS), did not receive governmental funding but maintained their operations through regulatory fees paid by financial institutions under their purview, agencies were left competing with one another to gain popularity among the financial institutions.

For instance, the savings-and-loan crisis of the 1980s and 1990s significantly reduced the number of financial institutions under the OTS. To maintain its revenue and staff, the OTS pitched itself as a regulator-against-regulation at industry meetings. In 2003, OTS chief James Gilleran even brought a chainsaw to a news meeting, hoping to demonstrate how determined he was to shred federal regulations (Kiel 2008). This grandstanding attracted various financial institutions, including American International Group and Countrywide, to set up a savings-and-loan function so as to switch their regulation to the OTS.

Deepening Political Involvement

In addition to market concentration, the financial sector's political involvement has been deepening. Figure 3.4 presents its total campaign donations from the 1990 to the 2016 election cycles. The figure shows not only that these firms have consistently outweighed labor unions (a main

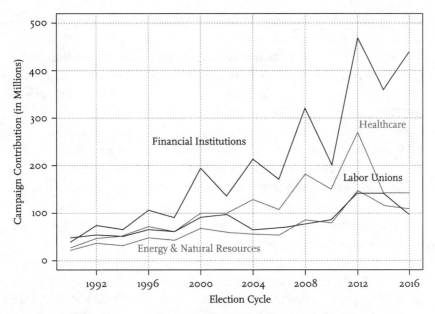

FIGURE 3.4 TOTAL CAMPAIGN CONTRIBUTION OF THE FINANCIAL SECTOR
NOTE: Financial institutions include commercial banks, savings and loans, credit unions,
student loan companies, payday lenders, venture capital, hedge funds, private equity, and
accountants but exclude insurance and real estate companies. The aggregate campaign
contribution and lobbying expense are estimated by the Center for Responsive Politics.
Campaign contribution is calculated based on itemized contributions reported to the Federal
Election Commission and state agencies. The total amount includes contributions from the
employees of the organizations, their family members, and their political action committees.
Contributions under $200 are not included in the statistics.

advocate for financial reform and policies that reduce inequality) in campaign contributions, but also that the gap has been widening over time. In
the late 1980s, financial firms spent twice as much as unions in campaign
contributions; now they spend almost six times as much. The financial
sector's expansion in political involvement has, in fact, far outpaced all other
major industries. In 2012, the securities and investment industry channeled
more resources into federal elections, spending almost twice as much on
political contributions as the healthcare sector in the midst of healthcare reform and almost three times as much as the energy and natural resources
sector while fighting against climate-change regulations.

Frequently, the financial sector is aided by other industries when proposing
or blocking regulatory policies. Comparing the energy, health, agriculture,
telecommunications, and financial sectors, political scientists Kevin Young
and Stefano Pagliari (2017) find that the financial sector enjoys the strongest
cross-sectoral business unity. Its efforts to loosen restrictions and deter new
regulations are often supported by other sectors, which might view finance

as a crucial driver of the economy or believe that it provides a key infrastructure, credit, for other businesses.

These political machinations have real consequences. An analysis of the 105th Congress finds that business contributions from related individuals and PACs led to more favorable votes on regulatory and tax policies (Fellowes and Wolf 2004). Another study shows that, after the telecommunication industry was deregulated in 1996, the cost of entry to a new market was positively associated with the political contribution of the incumbent firms (De Figueiredo and Edwards 2007). Examining the connection between campaign contributions and stock performance among public corporations between 1979 and 2004, finance professor Michael Cooper and his colleagues (2010) report that a public firm's future stock price is positively associated with the number and type of candidates it supports.

Economists Deniz Igan, Prachi Mishra, and Thierry Tressel (2012) at the International Monetary Fund suggest that lobbying efforts targeting mortgage lending and securitization regulation may have been a direct cause of the 2008 financial crisis. They found that mortgage lenders lobbying on these specific issues were more likely to drop their lending standards, originate lower-quality loans, and take higher risks. After the bubble burst, they were also more likely to receive funds under the Troubled Asset Relief Program (TARP). The size of the bailout was positively associated with cumulated lobbying expenditures.

Besides favorable policies and regulatory practices, failures to update policies and to enforce regulations are responsible for excessive earnings in the financial sector (Hacker and Pierson 2011). A well-known example in this regard is "carried interest" provisions in tax laws, which treat a part of venture capital, private equity, and hedge fund managers' income as capital gains instead of ordinary earning. This subjects their income to much lower tax rates. Economist Richard Freeman (2010) points out, too, that the FBI had detected an abnormal trend in mortgage fraud long before the subprime mortgage crisis, yet the Federal Reserve, blinded by macroeconomic and financial data, paid little attention to this and other clear warnings (Fligstein, Stuart Brundage, and Schultz 2017).

Private Intermediation of Public Policies

While the financial sector clearly has much to gain from fostering a close relationship with its regulators, federal and state governments depend on financial institutions to execute their economic, social, and foreign policies. To secure a financial system that draws international capital and promotes economic growth, the federal government guarantees the obligations of financial institutions not only through the well-known deposit insurance but also through emergency interventions like those during the S & L and the 2008 financial crises. To promote activities such as agriculture, homeownership, and education, the government also relies on private financial institutions to provide credit intermediation. Instead of directing more funds to make housing and college affordable, policymakers encourage private investors to lend by purchasing the loans or guaranteeing the return. This is particularly the case since the political reorientation in the last quarter of the 20th century, during which market-based instruments began to replace direct services as the default method for economic leveling. Mounting national debt also encourages the government to leverage the financial sector, instead of direct spending, to achieve policy goals.

Figure 3.5 contrasts government-guaranteed financial obligations with publicly held federal debt (e.g., Treasury and agency bonds), TARP, and three waves of quantitative easing following the 2008 financial crisis. It shows that the emergency bank bailout was but a drop in the ocean compared to the routine interventions taking place in financial markets, which amounted to more than $15 trillion in 2012 (Hamilton 2013). That is almost 50 percent higher than the widely debated national debt and 2.5 times larger than the total amount of quantitative easing, which added to $4.5 trillion. To be clear, these debt guarantees were in no way equivalent to national debt, but obligations explicitly or implicitly cosigned by the federal government. The risk of default for these loans was low in the absence of a catastrophic event, but of course, that is always unlikely until it happens. A visible government hand is present in much of today's financial activities.

More profound are a series of loose monetary policies enacted since 2001 and aimed at stimulating the economy. The low interest rates used to boost spending were among the most effective performance-enhancing drugs for the financial sector, which could borrow for free and earn handsome fees from asset appreciation. The low yields also made passive savings a much less attractive option than active investing, pushing pension funds and other investors to embrace private equity, venture capital, and high-fee hedge funds.

The private intermediation of public services, especially by a handful of financial institutions, is a classic example of a principal-agent problem, in which financial institutions' primary interest is to maximize their own profits, not achieving policy goals. With the understanding that government

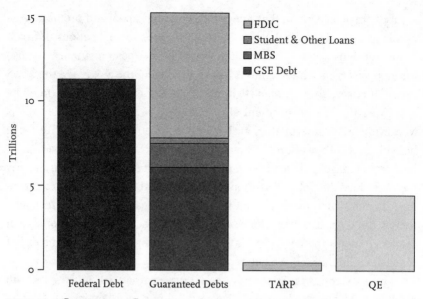

FIGURE 3.5 GOVERNMENT-GUARANTEED OBLIGATIONS, 2012

NOTE: **Federal debt** includes public debt and agency securities held by the public. **GSE debt** includes short- and long-term debt issued by government-sponsored enterprises such as Freddie Mac, Fannie Mae, Federal Home Loan Bank, Farm Credit System, Federal Agricultural Mortgage Corporation, Financing Corporation, and Resolution Funding Corporation, and the MBS guarantees of Fannie Mae and Freddie Mac. **MBS** includes mortgages held in pools from Government National Mortgage Association and Federal Farmers Home Administration plus mortgages held by Federal Financing Bank. **Student & other loans** includes Federal Family Education Loans and programs other than FHA, Rural Housing Services, and Veterans Housing Benefit Programs. **FDIC** refers to total insured deposits. **TARP** refers to the Troubled Asset Relief Program enacted in 2008. **QE** refers to the total amount of assets held by the Federal Reserve by the end of 2014, including around $900 billion in assets held prior to the first QE. SOURCE: Hamilton 2013.

intervention will meet any sign of instability, large financial institutions are virtually free to swing for the fences, embracing excessive risks on the possibility of extraordinary returns.

The agency problem was particularly evident in the ineffectiveness of quantitative easing during and in the aftermath of the recession. Aiming to provide liquidity and stimulate economic growth, the Federal Reserve increased the supply of money to banks through purchasing Treasury- and mortgage-backed securities. Banks, however, were hesitant to lend the money out to homebuyers and small businesses, since their funds would then be locked into long-term loans paying historically low interest. Instead, they deposited most of the funds and waited for interest rates to rise. It might have been more effective to channel the funds to state and municipal governments for fiscal spending, but that was deemed politically infeasible under the market-oriented governing model dominating in the late 2000s.

In the following section, we examine the bankruptcy reform of 2005 and student loan boom to illustrate how the concentration of market power, deepening political involvement, and private intermediation of public services jointly generate the extraordinary profits for the financial sector. Both cases show that the unusually high income of the financial sector is not from an increase in productivity but rather the ability to change the rules.

The Bankruptcy Reform of 2005

Prior to the 1980s, the bankruptcy rate in the United States was largely stable (Figure 3.6). Each year, about 1.2 in 1,000 adults filed for debt relief. Then came a dramatic surge, from 1.5 cases per 1,000 adults in 1980 to 7.7 in 2003. Contrary to the popular myth that bankruptcy filers are clever individuals trying to "game the system," the vast majority were families having trouble securing stable employment (Sullivan, Warren, and Westbrook 1997; Warren 2003). This upward trend drew some attention from the public but a much deeper concern in the financial sector. A significant rise in bankruptcy would severely undermine their profits.

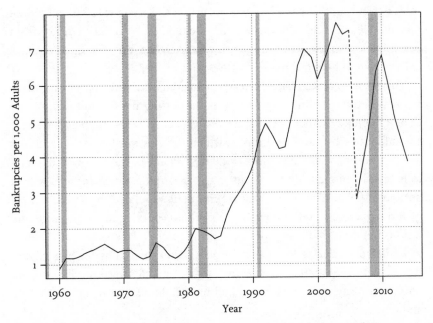

FIGURE 3.6 Number of Personal Bankruptcies per 1,000 American Adults

NOTE: The estimates from 1960 to 2005 are derived from determined bankruptcies, while the estimates from 2006 to 2014 are from bankruptcy filings, which are slightly larger. Adults include population aged 20+. SOURCE: Garrett 2007, the Administrative Office of the US Courts, and OECD Stat.

The proliferation of credit cards, aggressively advertised to middle- and working-class consumers and earning handsome revenue for banks and credit card companies, precipitated the bankruptcy boom. These credit cards were rarely the sole cause of bankruptcy, but high and revolving interest rates tend to quickly escalate economic hardship to a point of no return (Tabb 2006). And where one might logically expect banks and credit card companies to become more selective in card issuance or more decisive in card termination to reduce their losses from bankruptcy or even reduce bankruptcy all together, banks went a different way.

Curtailing credit would only be "smart" for banks if interest rates were low and late payment fees nonexistent. Instead, a controversial—but framed as bipartisan—initiative emerged in 1997 to deter households from seeking debt relief. Its proponents claimed that consumers were either financially illiterate or intentionally abusing lax bankruptcy laws for irresponsible consumption. The remedy, therefore, was to "catch" these abusers by raising the bar for bankruptcy filings. Unsurprisingly, most of these advocates worked on behalf of credit card issuers, an industry that experienced rapid consolidation in the decade prior to bankruptcy reform (Cappiello 2013). The market share of the top 10 credit issuers grew from 57 percent in 1995 to 87 percent in 2005. During this period, pretax profits for the credit card industry more than doubled. Concertedly, these companies sought to reduce their loss from bankruptcies while continuing to grow their profits from selling to families in dire need of financial relief.

The intent to protect bank instead of consumer interests was blatant when the new bankruptcy bill was first proposed during the Clinton administration. It mandated a means test and a counseling requirement before debtors could file for Chapter 7 bankruptcy, which forgives most debts. The means test determined whether debtors could repay some of their debts and, therefore, should instead file for Chapter 13 bankruptcy, which forgives only a portion of debts. The counseling requirement stipulated that debtors must go through credit counseling within six months of filing for bankruptcy protection. Yet many of these counseling firms received kickbacks from lenders when debtors enrolled in a payment plan rather than filing for bankruptcy; that is, there were abundant incentives for this mandated counseling to steer borrowers away from bankruptcy and toward decades of repayment (Dash and Bayot 2005).

Chapter 13 bankruptcy was reformed to add stricter borrower scrutiny during the repayment period. For example, it prohibited spending on luxury items and duplicate financed assets (e.g., cars and electronics). Lobbyists backing this bill framed these stipulations as necessary to deter financial recklessness, ignoring entirely the negligence of banks in providing excessive credit and how banks' business models count on borrowers struggling with debt. By casting Americans facing bankruptcy as ignorant, unscrupulous, or both, lobbyists and legislators passed the social cost of the credit card business to Main Street. This "reform" disproportionately harms black debtors, who tend to be steered to file Chapter 13 instead of Chapter 7 bankruptcy (Braucher, Cohen, and Lawless 2012).

To be sure, the clear bias in these stipulations brought immediate opposition. Rep. Jerrold Nadler (D-NY) labeled the bill "Mom versus Chemical Bank" to highlight the corporate interests involved (Seelye 1998). He testified that the bill was authored "by and for" credit card companies, saying on record: "This bill deals with a phony crisis, concocted with a $40 million lobbying and propaganda campaign of the big banks and credit card companies" (Nadler 1998: H10229). Sen. Ted Kennedy (D-MA) echoed this statement in his testimony: "All year long Congress has been teaming [sic] with credit card lobbyists pushing for legislation making it harder for consumers, for working Americans, to get relief from crushing debt woes" (Kennedy 1998: H9145).

One key actor driving this legislative mobilization was John Collinwood, the head of Bank of America's in-house lobbyist team. Before going into finance, Collinwood had served as an FBI congressional liaison and therefore had extensive knowledge of the inner workings of Congress. Other banks supplemented their lobbying efforts by funding research activities aimed at substantiating their claims. In 2002, Elizabeth Warren, then a professor at Harvard Law School, detailed how the consumer credit industry funded economic research conducted by Wharton Econometric Forecasting Associates, Ernst & Young, and the Credit Research Center (CRC) at Georgetown University (Warren 2002). The CRC, in particular, afforded credibility to the lobbying efforts, even though the research published by the Center aligned with the positions of the credit industry on every topic it investigated. The CRC's studies were widely disseminated by lobbyists, journalists, senators, and representatives, even appearing in the *Congressional Record*.

The growing size and might of the credit card industry enabled it to successfully lobby members of Congress and control the evidence informing their votes. Although Bill Clinton first vetoed the bill, it gained new momentum after the 2004 elections, in which the Republicans won additional congressional seats. George W. Bush eventually signed the law in 2004. The Bankruptcy Abuse Prevention and Consumer Protection Act of 2005 led to a large drop in bankruptcy filings in the following year (Figure 3.6). Yet the number surged again during the recession and returned to 1990s levels, despite the new restrictions. Clearly, the reform did nothing to alleviate the economic hardship experienced by many Americans.

Student Loans

The increasing debt load carried by college students is another example of private lenders incurring historic profits through regulatory manipulation. In 2015–2016, the federal government provided $87.9 billion in loans to students pursuing higher education (Hillman 2016). Students graduating in 2016 borrowed an average of $37,173 in total debt (Picchi 2016). Today, seven out of 10 college graduates have student loans, and one-fifth have loans from private lenders, which entail few protections and high costs (Cochrane and Cheng 2016). The overall outstanding balance for student loans amounted to $1.3 trillion and counting in 2016 (Kamenetz 2016).

Policy reform to alleviate student debt burden has been a central focus of public debate. Some have even dubbed student debt the "next bubble" likely to generate a financial crisis (Holland 2015). Investors on Wall Street have already begun betting that a large portion of the outstanding debt will be defaulted (Kelly 2017), while policymakers are brainstorming solutions to a potentially catastrophic economic and social problem.

The idea that finance could and should promote education was proposed by economist Milton Friedman ([1962] 2002), a renowned champion of free markets, more than 50 years ago. He forcefully argued that investments in education would increase human capital, to the benefit of workers, future employers, and the economy as a whole. Uncharacteristic of his preference for market solutions, Friedman believed that government was the best provider of the necessary capital for disadvantaged individuals to advance their economic prospects via education, because the return to education is difficult to predict and likely varies greatly across individuals. The high risk and administrative costs of managing loans of this type would deter private capital from investing in education or make it an unaffordable option for students altogether.

Friedman proposed that educational finance take the form of a government equity investment, instead of a subsidized loan, to prevent overinvestment in human capital. Specifically, he called for a repayment plan based on a proportion of the borrower's income for each $1,000 lent by the government. According to Friedman, "The individuals who received the training would in effect bear the whole cost" ([1962] 2002: 106). By providing disadvantaged individuals the opportunity to pursue higher education, he believed, this investment would allow for greater equality in opportunity and mobility.

What the Higher Education Act of 1965 introduced, however, was federal grants and a guaranteed loan program that incentivized private lenders to carry out education policy. Since the loans were guaranteed, private lenders were encouraged to provide as many loans as legally allowed without considering the consequences. When tuition began to rise in the 1980s, the demand for student loans increased; the built-in moral hazard had become a serious issue. A series of scandals, dubious lending practices, and lobbying efforts from private lenders emerged in the 2000s.

At the center of this storm was Sallie Mae, the largest student loan provider in the country. Established in 1972 as the Student Loan Marketing Association, Sallie Mae was a government-sponsored enterprise (GSE) that aimed to expand access to federal student loan funds. With the backing of the federal government, Sallie Mae could borrow at lower costs, then purchase student loans from private lenders and stimulate more lending. By 1990, it held nearly half of the outstanding federal loans in the market.

Sallie Mae began to cut ties with the federal government in 1997 and became a fully privatized public company in 2004, as the government came to prefer direct lending. In this process, the company expanded its portfolio of uninsured, private student loans from 165 in 2000 to 43,000 in 2006. Although they charged much higher interest than guaranteed loans, the private loans did not bring profits to Sallie Mae: between 50 and 92 percent of the borrowers with such loans defaulted from 2000 to 2007 (Cowley and Silver-Greenberg 2017).

Still, Sallie Mae pushed subprime loans to greater numbers of students each year. This was because the Department of Education stipulates that no more than 90 percent of a school's tuition payments can come from federal sources. Sallie Mae used private loans to meet the 10 percent requirement and boost the number of federally guaranteed loans it could sell to schools nearing the cap. To Sallie Mae, borrowers' financial ruin when they defaulted on private loans was a necessary evil for greater sales of guaranteed loans. No matter that many of the borrowers were, of course, low income.

Schools, particularly for-profit schools, benefited from this arrangement since almost all their students depended on loans for tuition. Some even subsidized Sallie Mae's lose-some-to-win-more model, agreeing to rebate 20 to 25 percent of the tuition paid by private loans to Sallie Mae. In other deals, lenders simply bribed financial aid officers. A 2007 investigation by the New York State attorney general discovered that JPMorgan Chase provided student aid officers perks to receive the "preferred lender" status (Abramson

2007; Vielkind 2010). More than 2,000 student aid officers were even invited to a $70,000 party cruise in New York harbor to celebrate their extraordinary salesmanship.

Student loan providers worked to influence Congress, too. Between 1999 and 2005, Sallie Mae spent $9 million on lobbying efforts and made over $130,000 in campaign contributions to those legislators in charge of revising bankruptcy regulations (Siegel 2007). As a result, the Bankruptcy Reform Act of 2005 made it more difficult to discharge educational loans, even when private lenders had originated them. Student debt was rendered an artificially "safe" investment for lenders, because the threat of default losses was de jure nil.

Meanwhile, former New York congressman Rick Lazio headed the lobbying efforts for JPMorgan Chase from 2004 to 2008 (Vielkind 2010). The bank paid him and others millions to lobby against restrictions on private student lending. In 2007 alone, JPMorgan Chase spent a total of $5.44 million on lobbying. This effectively stymied a legislative effort to redirect $20 billion from subsidies for private lenders to direct federal loans. George Miller, the California representative who sponsored the bill, remarked after an investigation into JPMorgan Chase's activities: "The 2007 student loan scandals finally exposed the millions of dollars lenders were spending to violate the law. It was very clear that the taxpayer subsidies these lenders were receiving were not only excessive but were essentially financing bad lender behavior." As a result of these bad behaviors, the share of nonfederal loans grew to 25 percent, a notable increase from its 2000 level of 12 percent (Baum et al. 2017).

There had been several attempts to eliminate the moral hazard. In the 1990s, the George H. W. Bush and Clinton administrations shifted funding to direct lending driven by a concern for minimizing the costs to students and the government. The mounting malpractices of private lenders and increasing rates of student loan default during the economic recession finally led to the Student Aid and Fiscal Responsibility Act of 2010, which eliminated guaranteed loans altogether. Since then, Sallie Mae and JPMorgan Chase have significantly changed their lending practices. In 2008, Sallie Mae's chief executive, Thomas Fitzpatrick, resigned, and the lender ceased subprime lending because of growing defaults. Sallie Mae spun off into two separate companies in 2014, transferring its troubled assets to the newly formed Navient. Meanwhile, JPMorgan Chase announced that it would stop issuing student loans in 2013 (Henry 2013). These pivots show how dependent these lenders had been on governmental subsidies in making their profits.

Despite the policy change, much damage has been done. By 2018, the total amount of student loans had climbed to a total of $1.5 trillion. A recent Brookings report indicates that the cumulative default rate could be as high as 40 percent for some cohorts of borrowers (Scott-Clayton 2018). The pattern of mass default is particularly serious among black college graduates, who are five times more likely to default than both white college graduates and dropouts.

Earnings in Finance

The bankruptcy reform and student loan crisis illustrate how the combination of market consolidation, political involvement, and private intermediation of public services came together to create opportunities for financial institutions to reap excessive rewards from potentially harmful activities. As profits grew (Figure 1.1), financial sector workers' compensation spiked. Figure 3.7 compares the annual earnings in finance with that of other industries. They moved largely in tandem in the 1970s, but a significant gap opened in the 1980s and expanded dramatically in the next three decades. Recently, workers in finance have come to earn, on average, 35 to 40 percent more than other workers. Adjusting for demographic, educational, geographical, and other differences does not eliminate this gap. At its peak, similar individuals could earn a quarter more in finance than other industries.

Importantly, Figure 3.7 shows that rising compensation in finance, at least initially, was not driven by the sector employing more skilled workers. A more plausible explanation is that the abnormal compensation lured highly credentialed workers into the industry, which in turn justified extraordinary charges for their services. Indeed, recent studies on the "Ivy League–Wall Street Pipeline" indicate that around 30 percent of the Harvard, Yale, and Princeton graduates take their first job in the financial sector (Rampell 2011). In contrast, only 10 percent of these schools' graduates start their postcollege careers in public or nonprofit services. One study shows that 70 percent of Harvard's senior class submits résumés to Wall Street and consulting firms (Rivera 2015).

In addition to the six-figure paychecks that already appear astronomical to many college seniors, sociologist Amy Binder (2016) finds that financial firms' aggressive recruitment aggrandizes life on Wall Street. To attract fresh talents with elite pedigrees, these firms deploy a wide range of tactics, from signing up to be "platinum" members of the schools' career

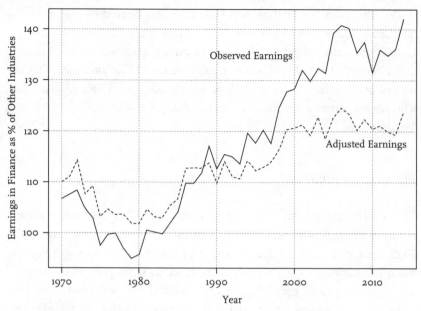

FIGURE 3.7 Earnings in Finance as Percentage of Other Industries

NOTE: The sample includes full-time, full-year workers aged 25–65. The financial sector is defined as the combination of the banking and securities industries. The adjusted earnings take into account age and its squared term; the interaction between region and metropolitan area status; race; level of education; and the three-way interaction between gender, marital, and parental status. SOURCE: Current Population Survey.

services programs to hosting concerted recruitment events and bombarding students' inboxes with advertisements. These firms imprint a narrow definition of success on the minds of students at elite institutions. This manufactured prestige convinces a large portion of seniors to consider finance *the* place to go, especially when they lack a clear vocation or face immediate pressure to repay their student loans.

Besides the enormous transfer of income from the economy to the financial sector in terms of profit and compensation, there are also great within-sector profit disparities. The largest national banks command the lion's share of profits compared to their smaller, community-oriented counterparts. In 2015, the top 10 financial conglomerates took away 60 percent of all the profits in this industry, far above their asset share of 51 percent (Figure 3.2). The four largest banks together captured 45 percent.

This "winners take all" pattern also manifests in the distribution of compensation among financial workers. Figure 3.8 examines how compensation varies across the earnings distribution from 1970 onward, revealing that the "financial premium" was sizable at the bottom of the earnings distribution (e.g., the 10th percentile) in the 1970s. Low-paid financial workers such as

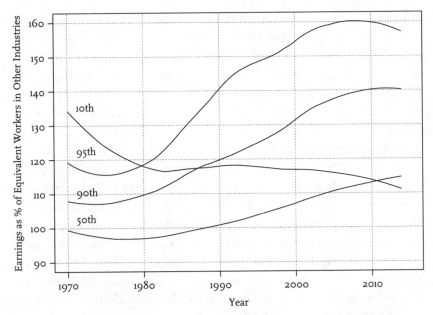

FIGURE 3.8 ADJUSTED EARNINGS IN FINANCE AS PERCENTAGE OF OTHER INDUSTRIES ACROSS EARNINGS DISTRIBUTION

NOTE: The sample includes full-time, full-year workers aged 25–65. The financial sector is defined as the combination of the banking and securities industries. The adjusted earnings take into account age and its squared term; the interaction between region and metropolitan area status; race; level of education; and the three-way interaction between gender, marital, and parental status. The yearly estimates are smoothed with local polynomial regression. SOURCE: Current Population Survey.

tellers and bookkeepers tended to earn between 20 and 30 percent more than their nonfinancial counterparts. This seems surprising, considering that low-wage workers in the financial sector, or service sector in general, were rarely unionized. But it is likely that the financial sector, compared to other industries, is much more vulnerable to internal theft and fraud, so paying low-level workers higher wages could attract more honest individuals, create positive social norms, and increase the cost of losing jobs (Chen and Sandino 2012). Supporting this idea, we see that, as electronic technology became widely adopted for data processing and ATMs proliferated throughout the 1970s, the premium for low-paid financial workers dropped from more than 30 to around 10 percent.

Where did all the money go? Only a fraction went to median financial workers. A steady increase began to emerge in the 1990s, as their compensation rose to around 15 percent more than similar workers in other industries. Yet most of the surge in the financial premium went to elite financial workers, including securities brokers, traders, analysts, and portfolio managers (Lin 2015). In the 1970s, these workers received only about a 10 percent premium for working in finance. The difference in earnings grew fourfold between 1990 and 2010 to 40 percent. The rise of the financial premium is even more dramatic further up the chain of command. At the 95th percentile, the dividend for working in finance increased from 18 to 60 percent in the late 2000s, amounting to an annual difference of $90,000.

How do elite financial workers appropriate their enormous compensation packages? In his detailed ethnography of financial institutions, sociologist Olivier Godechot (2016b) finds that compartmentalized operations in finance and exclusive control over certain domains or assets allow elite workers to make credible claims that *they* are the ultimate source of profits. In other words, any revenue generated from the "seats" is personalized, believed to belong to the people who are sitting on them. Few question whether similar profits would be generated should a different person hold that seat, how the outcome is a result of collaborative efforts, or to what degree the gains reflect market dynamics. These factors are only brought up when there are losses.

In sum, Figure 3.8 provides a similar yet different picture from looking at the average premium (Figure 3.7). The compensation for financial workers has increased over time, but only workers in the middle and upper half of the earnings distribution received the pay bump. Those at the bottom faced a decline in compensation relative to the 1970s level. Furthermore, even though the average premium began to plateau in the first decade of the 21st century, the premium for the elite workers rose. Compensation in the financial sector has greatly exacerbated overall inequality in the United States.

Several ethnographic studies of financial firms also identify stark disparities in terms of compensation and upward mobility between men and women, even when comparing those with similar performance and qualifications (Blair-Loy and Wharton 2004; Madden 2012; Roth 2006; Turco 2010). These are consistent with industrial surveys, which indicate that, being a high-paying industry, financial services has one of largest gender wage gaps (Catalyst 2015).

Sociologist Louise Roth (2006) argues that performance-based compensation systems, preferences for social similarities, and the failure to fully implement family-friendly, sexual harassment, and diversity policies all contribute to gender disparities in high finance. She documents how supposedly meritocratic performance-based reward systems leave ample space for arbitrariness, misinformation, and discrimination. Roth outlines how a perception of similarity preferences leads managers to assign men the client-facing positions that build social capital and client relationships. Even though many Wall Street firms adopted family-friendly policies in the 1990s, she shows how the industry's informal expectation for working around the clock remains a significant barrier for women who carry a greater burden of balancing family needs and career advancement.

Of course, the old-boy network that dominates high finance remains an obstacle, too. In a business that demands trust and connection, men tend to monopolize the most valuable connections, while women struggle to access informal networks (Ho 2009; Neely 2018; Roth 2006). Even women who do successfully establish professional relations accrue fewer benefits than their male counterparts, because women's networks (and, in turn, resources) are limited by job segregation (McGuire 2000, 2002).

Gender gaps in finance amplify for men and women who become fathers and mothers. Studies have clearly identified that employers tend to perceive mothers as less competent and worthy, but rate fathers as more appealing employees (Benard and Correll 2010; Correll, Benard, and Paik 2007). Compared to childless men, fathers are likely to be seen as more responsible and in need of additional compensation as breadwinners. In contrast, mothers are viewed as less dedicated than women without children and therefore should be moved to secondary functions. Patrimonialism, a system of leadership based on trust and loyalty, further ensures the reproduction of gender segregation and male domination on Wall Street (Neely 2018). Through hiring, grooming, and seed investing practices, a select group of elite white men reproduce a new generation of financiers who share both their demographic and social backgrounds. And their resulting success is used to justify their fitness for this business.

Race also plays a significant role in determining who profits from the dominance of finance. Some studies (e.g., Castilla 2008; Heywood and Parent 2012; Wilson and Roscigno 2010) indicate that minority men, like women, do not benefit from performance-based pay. Building on expert reports submitted in racial discrimination litigations, sociologist William Bielby (2012) finds that limited access to white wealth, pigeonholing minority workers, and mal-aligned diversity policies prevent black financial professionals from receiving equal pay even in a performance-based pay compensation system. As a result, black financial advisors earn one-third to 40 percent less than their white colleagues, and the disadvantage accumulated throughout their careers (Madden and Vekker 2008).

Figure 3.9 compares annual earnings by demographic characteristics of elite workers, demonstrating that the payoff for working in finance varies significantly by race, gender, and parental status. White men, particularly

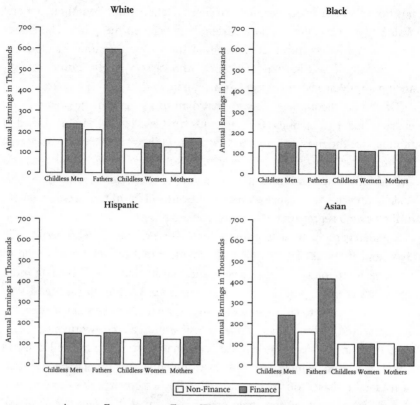

FIGURE 3.9 Annual Earnings of Elite Workers (95th percentile) in Finance and Other Industries

NOTE: The sample includes full-time, full-year workers aged 25–65 in 2010–2015. The estimates are generated at the 95th percentile of the earnings distribution with Re-centered Influence Function regression. The financial sector is defined as the combination of the banking and securities industries. The adjusted earnings take into account age and its squared term; the interaction between region and metropolitan area status; level of education; and marital status. SOURCE: Current Population Survey.

fathers, are the clear winners on Wall Street, taking home about $600,000 every year. Asian fathers also enjoy a significant level of privilege, making 1.5 times more on Wall Street than Main Street. In contrast, women in general do not gain substantial advantages for working in finance (Lin and Neely 2017). Consistent with the large racial disparities in pay, black men recount obstacles from racially segregated networks in industries such as financial services, yet identify themselves as more easily accessing these white male-dominated networks than women of all racial and ethnic backgrounds (Wingfield 2014).

This apparent contradiction between perception and reality may owe to the sector's convention of not sharing compensation information with colleagues and how that silence leads to greater actual than perceived disparities (Rosenfeld and Denice 2015). Although this norm appears to be regularly broken (Indiviglio 2010), colleagues may only share this information with their closest confidants, isolating African Americans and curtailing their knowledge about their peers' earnings. As such, they may perceive their firms as largely meritocratic even though they, in fact, earn much less than their white peers. Further, while black men report having access to the men's inner circles at their firms, they may encounter racial barriers when they attempt to extend their networks beyond the workplace into the wider industry, which is still dominated by white men. For example, African American men in sociologist Catherine Turco's (2010) study expressed frustration with their interactions with white executives at different firms during business negotiations. Since the earnings in high finance are largely tied to locating sales and investment opportunities, disadvantages of this kind could generate significant disparities in pay.

Summary

The common emphasis on the stability of our financial system overlooks the fact that the financial sector has harmed the US economy and undermined the livelihood of middle- and working-class Americans. Finance has transformed from a sector of feudalistic enterprises to one dominated by a handful of conglomerates. Stability and constraining financial power were once the primary principles behind the sector's governance, but deregulation emerged as a plausible solution to the banking crisis of the 1970s. The ascending belief in free markets further weakened the enforcement of the remaining regulatory apparatus and allowed financial firms to seek profits in legislative gray areas. During this transformation, personal relationships became less and less crucial to the success of banking.

The deregulation of the financial sector and technological advancement did not result in higher efficiency and therefore lower prices for customers, such as large corporations, small businesses, or households. Instead, the financial sector began to absorb a growing share of resources from the rest of the economy. Its expanding profits and compensations were driven by three developments: the concentration of market power, the deepening involvement of finance in politics, and the private intermediation of public services.

Financial deregulation did heighten competition and undermine the traditional business model in the 1980s, but shortly thereafter came a rapid consolidation of the financial sector in both geographical and operational terms. The new mega-institutions have branches across the United States and simultaneously operate in deposit-taking, loan-making, asset and wealth management, trading, investment banking, venture capital, insurance, and real estate. Their gargantuan size enables them to set the prices of their services and utilize the information gained from one division to benefit another. The resulting oligopoly facilitates collusion among large banks to profit from fraud, antitrust violations, and other malpractices.

These bank-centered financial conglomerates make political investments to support politicians who advocate for their interests, regardless of their party affiliation. In the last 20 years, the financial sector spent more money in campaign contributions and lobbying than any other industry, including healthcare and energy. And the returns on their political investments have allowed firms to gain from high-risk, at times predatory, activities with scant regulatory oversight, consequences be damned. Political investments even grant financial firms opportunities to bend the rules in their favor and suppress potential reform.

This considerable political influence is exacerbated by the government's dependency on the financial sector to execute its economic, social, and foreign policies. From maintaining a stable financial system to promoting agriculture, homeownership, education, and retirement savings as well as sanctioning foreign governments, the state relies on private financial institutions to achieve its policy goals. As a result, various subsidies, in the forms of emergency funds, insurance, guarantees, and tax exemptions, are set in place to encourage financial institutions to provide public functions. The private intermediation of public policies creates a principal-agent problem, by which financial institutions prioritize their interests over the government's.

As the financial sector claimed ever more of the nation's wealth, compensations for its workers grew quickly (though in ways that reflect race and gender hierarchies). Before the 1980s, the average salary in finance was no different from the rest of the economy but has since increased dramatically. At its peak, the average salary in finance was 40 percent higher than that of nonfinancial workers. Importantly, we show that the excessive earnings preceded the educational upgrade in the financial sector, which indicates that rising compensation was not driven by an influx of increasingly skilled workers. Instead, highly skilled workers were attracted to the sector by its outsized financial rewards.

Finance is supposed to serve the economy by allocating capital to its most productive uses. Instead, it has morphed into a snake ruthlessly devouring its own tail. Financialization escalated American inequality by transferring income into the financial sector and distributing most of the rewards to a small group of elite workers. Where did this money come from? Who are the casualties? In the following chapters, we examine developments in the corporate world and households where most Americans work and live.

CHAPTER 4 | The Financial Turn
of Corporate America

AS THE FINANCIALIZATION OF the US economy transferred tremendous profits and compensation into the financial sector, it too broadly affected the distribution of income and employment growth in nonfinancial sectors. Wall Street's logic—its metrics that determine who wins and loses—became the dominant "rules of the game" throughout the economy. For many corporations, the most important customers are no longer consumers of their products but investors of their stocks.

In this chapter, we turn our focus to financialization in the supposedly "nonfinancial" sector and how it results in greater inequality. As mentioned earlier in this book, the last 40 years have seen a turn in which many nonfinancial firms have increased their participation in financial markets. That is, rather than invest in buildings, machinery, stores, research, and workers, more and more companies have invested in financial assets (Figure 2.6). Consequently, a substantial portion of even nonfinancial firms' profits comes from interest and dividends rather than sales (Figure 1.3), and the bulk of the profits are then channeled right back to financial markets through dividends and stock buybacks (Figure 1.2). To maximize shareholder profits, corporations have been taking up an unprecedented level of debt, which erodes their financial standing and slows long-term growth.

All these developments drain valuable resources into the financial sector (and its investors' pockets) from other economic activities. Those who benefit are often in the upper or upper-middle class and have significant wealth (Chapter 6), a fact that reveals how fundamentally financialization has undermined the capital-labor accord established after World War II, elevating the bargaining power of shareholders and managers while weakening the demand for labor. Stockowners and corporate executives saw their rewards soar, as most workers' compensation and employment security diminished.

How did all these developments unfold? In the following sections, we describe why nonfinancial firms took a financial turn in the late 1960s and early 1970s. We focus on two aspects of financialization: the advent of nonfinancial firms actively lending and trading in financial markets and the rise of the shareholder-value model in corporate governance. We conclude by identifying the "winners and losers" created by these developments and how financialization has devastated working Americans.

When Car Makers Became Money Dealers

Nonfinancial firms have provided some level of financial services since the early 20th century. The first automaker to provide lending was General Motors, which established General Motors Acceptance Corporation (GMAC) to finance customers' and dealers' automobile purchases in 1919. At that time, cars were viewed as luxury goods and most bankers viewed automobile loans as a risky business. The fact that almost all customers had to purchase cars with cash severely limited the market base for GM and other automakers. The need to pay cash on the delivery also limited the number of potential dealerships and the size of their GM inventories. The new financial service, GMAC, was a quick and unambiguous success. For its first 40 years, GMAC financed a total of 40 million vehicle sales. Its "Time Payment Plan" was widely advertised in newspapers and magazines, promising Americans families could buy a new car "on time." Its services included additional assistance with car insurance and borrower's life insurance. Prudently, these advertisements also warned customers, "Just don't overdo it" and that "you should pay down as much as you comfortably can, then pay the balance as soon as you can" (Figure 4.1). Thus, we see that GMAC's main purpose was to promote automobile sales, not to earn interest or late fees from making loans—GM's financial arm was meant to supplement its sales rather than generate income in and of itself.

Noting GMAC's success in promoting sales through finance, Ford established Ford Motor Credit in 1959 and Chrysler debuted Chrysler Credit Corp in 1964. Providing credit became a standard practice among car manufacturers. And though these subsidiaries violated the separation of finance and commerce outlined in the Glass-Steagall and Bank Holding

Just don't overdo it

Go easy on "easy terms" when you buy a car, because the *longer* you pay, the *more* you pay. It's wiser to pay down as much as you comfortably can, then pay the balance as soon as you can. On the GMAC Plan you get terms arranged to suit your needs—at reasonable cost. It's the way over 2,000,000 families bought their cars last year. Ask your General Motors Dealer who uses the GMAC Plan to explain all the benefits of financing where you buy.

GMAC
GENERAL MOTORS ACCEPTANCE CORPORATION
TIME PAYMENT
PLAN

ASK YOUR DEALER in CHEVROLET • PONTIAC •
OLDSMOBILE • BUICK • CADILLAC new cars, and used cars
of all makes; also FRIGIDAIRE • DELCO APPLIANCES

THE PLAN THAT HAS HELPED MILLIONS BUY CARS "ON TIME"

FIGURE 4.1 GMAC Print Advertisement, 1957

Company Acts, they were tolerated by regulators because they did not accept demand deposits and their activities were auxiliary. That is, they did exactly what finance *should* do: stabilize and promote the production and consumption of, in this case, automobiles. Other industries soon took note: GE Capital was established in 1943 to provide loans for the purchase of General Electric radios, refrigerators, and televisions and, for business customers, generators, engines, and other industrial machinery.

In the corporate reconfiguration of the 1960s, the rapid economic growth of the post–World War II era slowed. Manufacturers from Europe and Asia had regained their footing, and, in the United States, the Warren-led Supreme Court expanded the purview of antitrust legislation to prohibit within-industry consolidation (the Court viewed the overconcentration of economic power as a barrier to a just society). To maintain growth and profitability, large US corporations began to transform into conglomerates, simultaneously operating in a large set of unrelated industries.

In the process of diversification, finance gradually elevated from a technology for accounting and budgeting to a "science" of decision-making (Fligstein 2001; Crotty 2003). Financial professionals began to replace industrial specialists in corporate headquarters. In contrast to their predecessors and to the workers who engaged in the actual production of goods and services, these financial professionals often had less firm- or industry-specific knowledge. What they had was a deep conviction that a firm's performance could be optimized with sophisticated cost-benefit analysis. In their view, all parts of the firm were tradable financial assets that should be evaluated, eliminated, or expanded according to their profitability.

This transition into finance became evident in the growing disintermediation in the 1960s, when large firms began to issue and trade a large amount of commercial paper among themselves. They cut out banks as the middlemen. Financialization accelerated during the monetary turmoil of the 1970s and in the 1980s, when the shareholder-value model, including short-term performance and stock price gains, began to dominate corporate strategy, displacing long-term market share as the measure of success. In the meantime, the financial deregulation under the Reagan administration not only loosened the control over the financial sector but also weakened the long-standing separation of finance and commerce. In 1982, the Office of the Comptroller of the Currency, the main regulators of national banks, issued an official approval for nonfinancial corporations to operate "nonbank banks." As long as these subsidiaries did not simultaneously make commercial loans and receive demand deposits, they were not technically "banks" and therefore free to operate outside the regulations for bank-holding companies and the supervision of the Federal Reserve.

As corporate management became dominated by financiers and the demand for profits intensified through the shareholder-value movement, the permission of lending pointed toward a new direction for nonfinancial corporations to "grow fast in a slow-growth economy." Consequently, many firms' financial arms broadened their portfolios in the 1980s. In 1985, GMAC entered mortgage lending, launching a financial service entirely unrelated to automotive products, and Ford purchased First Nationwide Financial Corporation to enter the savings and residential loan markets. In the following decade, GMAC and Ford Motor Credit both expanded their services to insurance, banking, and commercial lending.

General Electric undertook the most aggressive border-crossing when, under the leadership of Jack Welch, GE Capital expanded from customer lending to small business loans, real estate, mortgage lending, credit cards, and insurance (more on this shortly). Sears, one of the nation's retail titans, entered the real estate brokerage and securities businesses in 1981 and issued the Discover Card, a one-stop financial services credit card that also offered savings accounts, in 1985. AT&T started its financial arm the same year, entered the small business loan market in 1992, and soon became one of the largest nonbank lenders in the country.

Banking became a lucrative business for these blue-chip corporations because their large assets and triple-A credit ratings allowed them to borrow at rates lower than households, small businesses, and sometimes even banks. By lending out these borrowed funds at higher rates, firms' financial arms could bring steady profits with little risks. Through their already established relations with consumers and other businesses, they had more direct access to potential borrowers than banks did, and, because these financial institutions were not banks, they were not subject to interstate branching restrictions. Some even argued that these firms' insider knowledge about the industry and consumption patterns provided them an edge over banks in terms of accurately assessing the potential return of various ventures.

As you might expect, the proliferation of "nonbank" banks troubled the Federal Reserve and threatened traditional banks. The former worried that a mounting volume of financial activities were taking place outside its jurisdiction, while the latter was concerned with their shrinking market share and the new, uneven playing field. In an attempt to restrict any further expansion of nonbank lenders, the Federal Reserve took regulatory action to broaden the definitions of "demand deposit" and "commercial loan" in 1984. However, the move was struck down by the Supreme Court two years later. Community banks vehemently urged members of Congress to stop the further creation of nonbank institutions, yet there was little consensus regarding the proper scope of a potential banking amendment. Obviously, this was not the type of financial deregulation banks hoped to see.

The resulting Competitive Equality Banking Act of 1987 (CEBA) was, in many ways, a product of multiple compromises. It expanded the definition of "bank" to include all financial institutions that were FDIC insured or accepted demand deposits and made commercial loans, but explicitly exempted industrial loan corporations (ILCs), credit card banks, limited-purpose trust companies, credit unions, and savings associations. Some nonbanks that already had a strong foothold in financial markets were "grandfathered" in, and their financial activities, which would otherwise be prohibited under the new law, were left untouched.

The ILC exemption under CEBA is particularly notable because it actually opened a *new* window for nonfinancial firms to enter banking. Industrial loan companies had existed in the United States since the early 20th century. Their original purpose was to extend credit to industrial workers who had steady incomes but no collateral for securing bank loans. As banks gradually entered this market, ILCs expanded into other banking activities, yet their presence was mostly negligible in finance by the time CEBA was drafted (in 1987, the whole industry controlled only $4.2 billion worth of assets, while the commercial banks held $3.5 trillion). Shortly after CEBA's enactment, however, General Motors acquired an ILC charter. Many other nonfinancial firms followed, trying to tap into financial markets (Baradaran 2015; Johnson and Kaufman 2007). Total ILC assets ballooned to $270.3 billion by 2007. In the early 2000s, Target earned 15 percent of its total profits from its in-house credit card operation—it's little wonder then that all the cashiers at Target are trained to promote the REDcard. BMW, Volkswagen, Harley-Davidson, UPS, and Nordstrom all came to offer banking products, including business loans, home equity loans, credit cards, and checking accounts (Saranow 2004). Retail giant Walmart planned to obtain an ILC in 1999 and 2005, but was stopped by tremendous opposition from community bankers, labor unions, and other retail stores.

Among these developments, the most visible financial operation for household consumers is the retail credit card. Unlike earlier installment plans, which would allow consumers to make payments toward large purchases such as cars and pianos, store credit cards promise discounts, bonus points, and loyalty programs to their consumers in order to persuade them to buy clothing, furniture, appliances, and electronics with credit. These perks are far outweighed by the cards' high interest rates—some double the rates charged by the average credit card. In 2016, discount retailer Kohl's credit card revenue accounted for 35 percent of profits, and Macy's credit revenue was almost 40 percent.[1] The importance of this credit card business is so high that Macy's is perhaps more appropriately described, not as a retailer, but as a credit card and real estate company; the combination of those revenues constitutes more than half of Macy's annual operating income.

Cashiers constantly push customers to open cards—it's a "no-brainer," they insist—because their livings are as dependent on their ability to sell credit cards as products and services.

Airlines benefit from their branded cards, too, though less directly. Whenever cardholders make purchases, the managing banks take a cut (via the fees they charge to the sellers for processing the transactions). A portion of those fees is then used to purchase miles from airlines, distributed back to cardholders as "awards." This operation can account for as much as 12 percent of airlines' overall sales. Essentially, consumers pay out of pocket to purchase these miles through their everyday spending but believe that these miles are rewards for their brand loyalty.

The separation of banking and commerce was temporarily strengthened in the Gramm-Leach-Bliley Act of 1999, which closed the S & L (but not ILC) loophole some companies had used to build their financial subsidiaries. Yet these restrictions did not curb nonfinancial firms' interest in profiting from finance. Some began to emulate hedge funds, investing their assets in financial markets. Edward Lampert's attempt to reinvent the retail industry provides a case in point. After the Sears-Kmart merger in 2005, Lampert turned the company's retail stores into a business generating cash flow for speculative trading. A year before the 2008 financial collapse, a third of Sears's pretax income was generated through trading. Lampert's financial savvy saw him widely heralded as the next Warren Buffett.

Similarly, before its bankruptcy in 2001, Enron was more of a commodities and derivatives trading company than an energy company (we will explore this more in a bit). It created the market for electricity trading and had trading floors that processed $2.5–$3 billion of commodities transactions a day. One Wall Street analyst estimated in 2000 that almost 40 percent of S&P 500 companies' earnings stemmed from lending, trading, venture investments, and other financial activities. A third of that had been earned by nonfinancial companies.[2]

The financialization of US corporations shifted their focus away from production and sales, undermining the stability and potential growth of their core businesses. At Sears, because a significant proportion of the cash flow generated by retail outlets was channeled into financial activities, less was available for store improvement and advertisement. Under Lampert's management, Sears spent only $1.5–$2 per square foot to maintain its retail stores, against the industry standard of $6–$8. These and other cost-cutting programs drove up employee turnover and led to low-quality service. Unsurprisingly, customers came to see shopping at Sears and Kmart as a dreadful experience and gradually took their business elsewhere.

A more pernicious erosion in quality was happening inside these companies. Financialization provides a means to profit without production, and so it weakens the interdependence between capital and labor. Where industry-specific knowledge, experienced workers, productive investments, and product innovation were once the pathways to prosperity, they are now secondary to talents in financial engineering and money dealing. This upside-down world of financialization was particularly salient in 2004, when GM reported that 66 percent of its $1.3 billion quarterly profits came from GMAC. Just a day earlier, Ford had reported a loss in its automotive operation, but $1.17 billion in net income (mostly via its financial subsidiaries). The most "valuable" workers are no longer those who make and sell cars but those who move money around.

A Revolution in the Name of the Shareholder

The financial turn of US corporations was concurrent with a rapid transformation of corporate governance. As the global market share and profits of US firms dropped to a record low in the 1970s, corporate America and academics alike began to question why large, hierarchical conglomerates were performing so poorly compared to their foreign competitors. Managers and scholars were eager to find an alternative, more efficient model to stop the empire from falling apart.

Agency theory emerged as the dominant diagnosis for the illness afflicting US corporations. In their pathbreaking 1976 paper, financial economists Michael Jensen and William Meckling argued that the sole purpose of a firm is to serve its shareholders and that the fundamental inefficiency in the 1970s had come out of a misalignment between ownership and control. Because managers at the time were "mistakenly" rewarded by the size and stability of the company, they often grew and diversified their firms even when the expansion led to lower rates of return. Moreover, since these managers were spending "other people's money," they were willing to pay excessive wages and benefits, make charitable contributions, build extravagant headquarters, and fly on corporate jets to gain the admiration of their peers, workers, and communities, all of which led to a significant waste of corporate resources.

Jensen and Meckling's proposed solution was to reassert the centrality of the shareholder in corporate governance and align manager interests with those of shareholders. Specifically, they suggested that executive compensation needed to include more equity-based components, so that managers would act more like shareholders. Conglomerates should contract in scope and devote their resources to only the most profitable ventures, and firms' spending should be financed with debt to ensure that any investment would yield above-market (measured by the interest obligation) returns. Managers should be monitored closely by an independent board of directors and replaced if the firm's stock underperforms. All these prescriptions encouraged companies to shift their focus from growth and stability to profit and risk-taking.

If agency theory identified the public enemies and outlined the strategy for revolution, retirement reforms provided the ammunition. The Employee Retirement Income Security Act of 1974 (ERISA), attempting to diversify risk, adopted a market-centered approach and demanded that no pension fund hold more than 10 percent of its portfolio in the employer's securities. This triggered a massive outflow of funds into financial markets. ERISA's mandates on employee protection also significantly increased operating costs, which pushed many firms to outsource their pension funds to the financial services industry.

In an effort to settle the uncertainty surrounding cash or deferred arrangement (CODA), the Revenue Act of 1978 added a new subsection (k) to Section 401 of the Internal Revenue Code, allowing the use of salary reductions for retirement plan contributions. Unexpectedly, some of the largest US firms quickly embraced the new legislation. In 1982, firms such as Johnson & Johnson, PepsiCo, JC Penney, and Hughes Aircraft Company began to operate 401(k) plans. In 1986, Congress acted to replace the federal pension plan with a less generous defined-benefit plan and a more generous defined-contribution plan similar to the 401(k). This boosted the public's confidence—and investments—in defined-contribution plans. In 1985, the ratio between defined-benefit and 401(k) participants was three to one, but by the early 2010s, it had reversed to one to three.

The massive influx of retirement funds spawned a new class of mega-investors in the equity markets: mutual funds. These are professionally managed financial firms that pool money from large numbers of individuals to invest in securities, and they quickly became the most common vehicle for defined-contribution plans like 401(k) and individual retirement accounts (IRAs). Figure 4.2 traces the total mutual fund assets as a percentage of GDP in the United States. It shows that mutual funds' assets under management have increased steadily in the past 35 years, from around 5 percent of GDP in 1980 to around 100 percent in the 2010s.

Besides mutual funds, state and municipal pension funds also increased their presence in the stock market (Figure 4.3). Before 1960, these public pension funds invested almost all their assets in low-risk, fixed-income

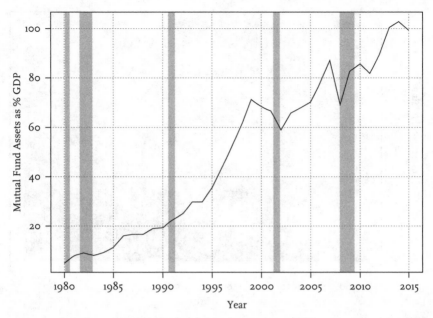

FIGURE 4.2 Mutual Fund Asset Size as Percentage of GDP

NOTE: A mutual fund is a type of managed collective investment scheme that pools money from many investors to purchase securities and is the most common vehicle for defined-contribution plans and individual retirement accounts (IRAs). SOURCE: World Bank, Federal Reserve Bank of St. Louis, Federal Reserve Economic Data (DDDI07USA156NWDB).

securities such as Treasury notes, governmental and corporate bonds, and mortgages. Their portfolios began to change dramatically in the 1960s, as these funds ventured into the stock market through both direct holding of corporate equity and investments in financial vehicles such as hedge funds and private equity. In total, these higher-risk investments increased from only 3 percent in 1957 to more than 75 percent of total public pension fund assets in recent years.

A direct consequence of these developments is that the seats of many publicly traded firms have gradually come to be occupied by representatives of institutional investors (Davis 2010). The tension between ownership and control has existed since the invention of the modern corporation, but the concentration of ownership has given institutional investors unprecedented power to negotiate with management. The significant presence of retirement funds in the stock market also changed the rhetoric about shareholders. Rather than representing wealthy individuals or "greedy capitalists," fund managers can now credibly claim to protect the retirement savings of hard-working, middle-class Americans. Who can be against middle-class Americans?

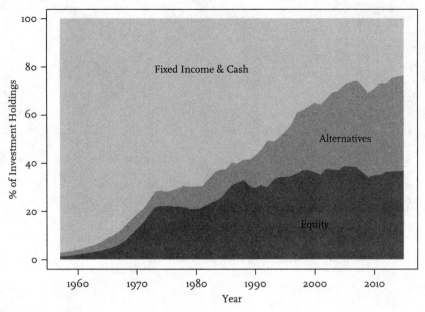

FIGURE 4.3 INVESTMENT HOLDINGS OF STATE AND LOCAL PENSION FUNDS

NOTE: Fixed income includes governmental securities such as Treasury and municipal bonds, corporate bonds, and mortgages. Equity refers to the direct ownership of corporate stocks. Alternatives include the investment in private equity and hedge funds, foreign securities, real estates, and other investments. SOURCE: 1957–1992 Historical Data Base on Public Employee-Retirement Systems; 1993–2015 Annual Survey of Public Pensions.

So we have the cause (agency theory) and the ammunition (large institutional investors) of the shareholder revolution; what about the battleground? These skirmishes have, by and large, occurred in corporate boardrooms. The combination of high inflation, a bear stock market, and low interest rates in the 1970s made it a lucrative practice to purchase the control of firms with weak stock performance through debt financing. A new wave of mergers and acquisitions in the late 1970s and 1980s, some of which came without the consent of the targeted firm, were frequently facilitated, if not encouraged, by bankers, charging advisory fees and issuing "bridge loans" for takeovers. These banks knew before the public what tender offer would be made to purchase a target firm's stocks, and so they could take positions in the stock market so as to cash out when the merger was announced.

To maintain control, executives began to adopt defensive tactics such as the "poison pill" and "golden parachute" (Useem 1993). The former allows existing shareholders to purchase more shares at a discount rate, thereby increasing the cost of outsider takeover. The latter guarantees a handsome severance package for top executives who lose control of their firms. In several high-profile cases, ransoms or "greenmails" were even arranged between management and corporate raiders to buy back raiders' shares at a premium. Under the threat of takeover, defending executives learned to load firms with debt to decrease the net value of their assets. Managers closely monitored and manipulated their firms' equity price, further encouraging borrowing and stock buybacks.

Of course, takeovers represent only an extreme form of shareholder activism. More frequently, fund managers express their discontent and demands for greater returns directly to management or through the media, so much so that large corporations have begun to devote sizable resources just to manage their investors. Just as politicians spend most of their energy courting donors, today's corporate executives devote intense efforts into building relationships with institutional investors. Managers who could not adapt to this new environment were gradually replaced with more investor-minded types.

To be clear, the ascendance of shareholders does not imply the extinction of commanding CEOs who prioritize long-term growth. Founders and family-owned enterprises often retain significant control by either limiting the shares of their corporations sold to the public or creating dual-class shares with unequal voting rights. The issuance of dual-class shares is particularly prevalent in the tech industry. For example, when Google went public in 2004, it created two classes of stocks, A and B. The A shares were sold to the public and each share entitled its owner to one vote (in elections for directors and on major corporate decisions), while the B shares were held by the three founders and a few other executives and entitled owners to 10 votes. In 2014, Google created a C share with the same economic rights as A and B shares (i.e., receiving the same amount of dividend), but no voting rights. A tiered stock design like this concentrates control in the hands of executives and prevents outside investors from intervening in executive decisions. Facebook, similarly, sought to maintain its founder-centered leadership by issuing two classes of stocks in 2012, then a class of nonvoting shares in 2016. These negative cases suggest that even the most successful CEOs need ways to curtail the power of institutional investors.

The success of the shareholder-value revolution becomes even more inarguable when we look at how much corporate America has been spending to reward shareholders. In most of the post-World War II period, the corporate sector distributed between 20 and 40 percent of profits as annual dividends to shareholders. The payout increased dramatically in the 1980s, after John Shad, the first Wall Street executive to serve as the chairman of the Securities and Exchange Commission, decided to narrow the definition of stock manipulation in 1982. This interpretation of the law opened the floodgate for stock buybacks, since fewer outstanding shares would create the illusion of better financial performance. In 1984, the sum of dividends and stock repurchases jumped to around 80 percent of all corporate profits and more than 100 percent in 1986 (Figure 1.2). Today, US corporations frequently give away most of their earnings or even borrow to reward their shareholders.

The triumph of shareholder activism is evident in the stock market, too (Figure 4.4). After a decade of sagging performance (from the early 1970s to the early 1980s), stock prices began to soar. Up until the late 1980s, the S&P 500 index tracked the GDP fairly well. The decoupling began in the go-go 1990s, when equity market growth outpaced national economic growth (except during the 2008 financial crisis). The low-interest regime maintained by the Federal Reserve under chair Alan Greenspan (1987–2006) and the quantitative easing enacted between 2009 and 2014 (to help the economy recover from recession) also pushed savings from the bond to the stock market, further encouraging the deviation of stock prices from economic fundamentals.

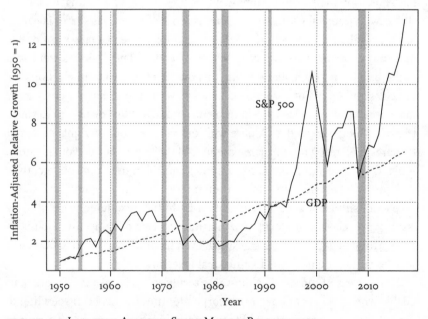

FIGURE 4.4 INFLATION-ADJUSTED STOCK MARKET PERFORMANCE

NOTE: S&P 500 refers to the closing price of the Standard & Poor's 500 stock market index on the first trading day in December of each year. Unlike the Dow Jones Industrial Average, S&P 500 is capitalization-weighted and includes a diverse set of companies, which make it more representative to the US stock market. Both trends are adjusted for inflation using the consumer price index and standardized with the values of 1950. SOURCE: Standard & Poor's; Bureau of Economic Analysis, National Economic Account, Table 1.1.5.

To illustrate how the financial turn transformed corporate America, we take a closer look at two companies. Each was once considered a pioneer demonstrating exemplary success in the era of financialization. One ended in a complete disaster in the early 2000s, and the other barely survived the 2008 financial crisis with public and private bailouts. Both have fundamentally reshaped corporate America's ideas about success.

GE: The Shining City upon a Hill

Founded in 1892, General Electric Company was a consolidation of Thomas Edison's various ventures, including the Edison Lamp Company, Edison Machine Works, and Edison Electric Light Company. General Electric went public seven years later and became one of the original 12 corporations listed in the Dow Jones Industrial Average. GE expanded swiftly: it was the fourth largest US corporation when the Fortune 500 was established in 1955. When the legendary Jack Welch became chief executive in 1981, GE was a model corporation of the postwar economy. It offered all the distinguishing characteristics of the standard employment contract: lifelong employment, high wages, health benefits, and retirement plans. A GE employee could count on stable employment, incremental raises, and steady promotion over the course of his career. These practices were a boon to the US economy and the welfare of workers, because, by 1980, GE was the fourth largest corporate employer of US workers.

As the youngest chairman and CEO in GE's history, Welch pioneered a new corporate paradigm that favored the bottom line over loyalty to workers. Frustrated by GE's bureaucracy in his early years, Welch was a natural ally for shareholder value. He believed that building a lean and agile organization, free from superfluous layers and corporate red tape, was the key to efficiency and profit.[3] Welch's slogan was "Fix it, close it, or sell it." Within his first five years of leadership, Welch would begin selling off units and downsizing employees, eliminating 71 business units and over 100,000 workers. This earned him the nickname "Neutron Jack," after the strategic nuclear weapon that massacres its victims but leaves assets intact.

During his chairmanship, Welch expanded GE's earnings by $7.8 billion, yet $5–$7 billion of those earnings stemmed from downsizing (Kennedy 2001). Despite being feared by his employees, Welch was widely praised in financial circles. His 1981 speech, "Growing Fast in a Slow-Growth Economy," given to the investors in New York City, cemented the legitimacy of the shareholder-value model. He was later named "Manager of the Century" by

Fortune magazine in 1999. Welch is credited with growing GE's market value from $12 billion in 1981 to almost $300 billion in 2001. Between 1989 and 2001, GE met or beat analysts' forecasts in 46 out of 48 quarters, an unprecedented record later revealed to be a result of financial engineering.

GE's extraordinary growth sprang from Welch's extraordinary measures. Under his leadership, Welch implemented an annual review program called the "vitality curve" or "rank and yank," in which managers were forced to recommend the top 20 percent of performers for mentoring and the bottom 10 percent for dismissal. Welch referred to the mentees as "products," and managers were responsible for developing the product (Tichy and Charan 1989; Welch and Byrne 2003). Instead of lifetime employment, Welch vowed to provide GE employees with training that would ensure *future* employment—at other firms. GE's competitors quickly adopted his "survival of the fittest" system.

As he revolutionized the terms of employment, Welch transformed the company's financial arm into a "money machine," relying on the help of Harvard Business School graduate Gary Wendt. Like other major manufacturers, GE had a financial arm—the aforementioned General Electric Contracts Corporation—as early as 1932 to provide small loans to customers of the corporation's many products in the midst of the Great Depression.[4] As finance became an increasingly profitable venture in the 1970s, its successor, GE Capital, extended credit beyond financing for General Electric's products. Under Welch and Wendt, GE Capital's growth outpaced GE's manufacturing businesses. And after running a close second for decades, GE Capital topped GMAC as the nation's largest nonbank lender in 1992.

By the late 1990s, GE Capital was bringing in a majority of the company's revenue. The Fortune 500 began labeling GE as a "diversified financial" firm to capture the scale of its activities in financing commercial real estate, residential mortgages, insurance, aircraft, railcars, and credit cards. Contracting to over 300 retailers, GE Capital serviced more credit cards than American Express. On the eve of the 2008 financial crisis, the company managed $696 billion in assets. Only four US banks were larger, and GE Capital was the largest financial company outside the banking sector (O'Boyle 1999; Colvin, Benner, and Burk 2008; Lohr 2008).

While GE Capital's financial dealings increased the overall profits of General Electric, the operation also drained resources away from GE's industrial roots. During Welch's tenure, GE's research-and-development spending plummeted, as a percentage of revenue, by half. Its new exposure in financial markets made the company more vulnerable to market turmoil, and after decades of steady growth, GE faced its first significant setback. During the collapse of the dot-com bubble, its share price dropped more than 60 percent in less than three years (from almost $60 in 2000 to $22 in 2003).

GE recouped some of these losses by 2007. Before the financial crisis, its share price was $41. Yet when credit quickly tightened in 2008, GE Capital's expected earnings plunged; its share price began another free fall, dropping 83 percent to a low of $7 in early 2009. This century-old American company would have gone under if not for a lifeline from public and private sources. As the magnitude of the crisis escalated, GE requested the Obama administration guarantee GE Capital's $139 billion debt in exchange for the company coming under FDIC regulation. Besides raising $12 billion through a public stock offering, GE's then CEO Jeffrey Immelt reached out to Warren Buffett for a personal $3 billion investment.

After the financial crisis, GE Capital was identified as "too big to fail" by the Financial Stability Oversight Council. It was labeled a Systemically Important Financial Institution (SIFI), mandated by the Dodd-Frank Wall Street Reform and Consumer Protection Act of 2010 to receive stricter oversight from the Federal Reserve, including taking annual stress tests, preparing bankruptcy plans (known as living wills), and meeting higher capital requirements. These requirements were expected to strengthen the robustness of these financial institutions, but also meant that SIFIs would be less profitable than their competitors without such designation.

Because of the "too big to fail" status and the risks exposed during the crisis, GE has since taken steps to wind down its lending activities. In 2014, GE spun off Synchrony Capital, the unit that financed credit cards, in a $2.9 billion initial public offering. GE then sold assets managed by GE Capital, including $26.5 billion in real estate assets to Wells Fargo and $16 billion in customer deposits to Goldman Sachs. Overall, GE Capital has decreased as a share of GE revenue since 2008, dropping from 42 to 28 percent of total revenue. These efforts were successful, and GE shed its SIFI status in 2016 (Merced and Sorkin 2015; Merced 2016).

By returning to its industrial base, GE has come full circle. After 30 years as the locomotive of the conglomerate, GE Capital had begun to be viewed as a liability preventing the company from moving forward. With energy costs declining and foreign labor costs rising, manufacturing in the United States has, again, become a profitable venture. GE opened more than 20 new plants and added 16,000 new workers in the last decade, and Immelt doubled GE's R & D spending and directed funding to upgrade and connect its industrial equipment to specialized analytical software.

Financialization, at least in this one company, seems to be coming to an end. Yet its ghost continued to haunt the enterprise. The board of directors ousted Immelt in June 2017 for not following the shareholder-value model as aggressively as Welch. New CEO John Flannery, hoping to distance himself from his predecessor, quickly announced a plan to cut $2 billion in expenses, lift profits, and raise dividend payments to the shareholders. In addition, even though GE sold out most of its financial operation under Immelt's watch, certain assets and liabilities were retained due to a lack of interested buyers. In January 2018, GE acknowledged that it had been overly optimistic about the profitability of its past reinsurance operation and now had to write down $7.5 billion in losses and massively expand its insurance reserve. In February 2018, GE announced that the company might be investigated by the Department of Justice for violating federal lending laws in 2006 and 2007. These disclosures pulled GE stock down to financial crisis levels and kicked off speculation that the company might never fully recover. After a century of dominance, GE was booted from the Dow Jones in June 2018.

The Perfect Storm That Was Enron

Unlike GE, Enron did not survive its financial ventures. With $66 billion in prefiling assets, Enron's 2001 bankruptcy was, at the time, the largest in US history. Still, just before the bankruptcy and resulting investigation, industry leaders had applauded Enron's innovations in natural gas and electricity. As a long-standing energy company, it had grown rapidly during the late 1980s and early 1990s, drawing acclaim from investors and industry leaders alike. A string of bad business deals fell through in the late 1990s, and Enron's profits waned; however, its stock price remained high, inflated by financial engineering. When these activities were exposed during the bankruptcy proceedings, Enron's practices began to look more like fraud than innovation. Policymakers cast Enron as a "bad apple" driven by greed and corruption (Langley 2008), yet behind the headlines that decried corporate excess is a less conspicuous account of financialization.

From its inception, Enron was a self-identified "new type of corporation" that fully embraced shareholder value. Founder Kenneth Lay was the son of a Baptist preacher and an economist by training. Lay subscribed to two ideologies: free markets and Christian values (McLean and Elkind 2004). After completing his PhD in 1970, Lay worked as an energy deputy undersecretary for the US Department of Interior in the Nixon administration, where he led the push to free corporations from regulatory constraints. His tenure in public service was brief. Lay returned to the energy sector, where he used his insider knowledge and networks to profit from the deregulation of the energy market. Lay was soon an executive at Houston Natural Gas, then negotiated a merger with Omaha-based InterNorth. Enron, the resulting company, was formed in 1985.

In just one decade, 1991 to 2001, Enron's revenues ballooned from $13.5 billion to $101 billion (Salter 2008). Much of that growth was fueled by financialization. In 1989, Enron created Gas Bank, a division that guaranteed producers and wholesale buyers the ability to sell or purchase future gas supplies at a fixed price. Headed by Jeffrey Skilling, a Harvard Business School graduate and former McKinsey consultant, this financial arm brought tremendous profits to the firm. Gas Bank soon expanded into Enron Capital & Trade, the largest market maker for energy commodities and derivatives, which included swaps, options, or futures contracts on electric power, coal, steel, and water (Henriques 2001).[5] At the height of the dot-com bubble, Enron even entered the market of broadband telecommunication, planning to trade internet bandwidth as it did other commodities.

Enron's financial turn transformed its identity from an energy producer to a trader in the 1990s, and it divested more than 5,000 miles of pipelines in North America. Former banker Skilling's prowess was not limited to trading and deal making, but also "managing" Enron's bottom line. So, following the dominant practice in the securities industry, Skilling implemented mark-to-market accounting, which would pad the value of Enron's assets. Instead of measuring the value of an asset based on its historical costs, mark-to-market accounting prices the asset based on its market value. Skilling claimed that this practice more accurately reflected the true value of Enron's assets, and "there's no way around it" (McLean and Elkind 2004). However, since there was no market for many of the assets Enron held, the mark-to-market accounting was more often mark-to-model, a practice assessing value based on projected earnings. This allowed Enron to claim profits from assets that had yet to generate any revenue—and to do it based on the highest *possible* earnings. The accounting practice gave the appearance of rapid growth, even though few of the investments panned out.

To conceal these toxic assets from Enron's balance sheet and maintain its high stock price, Skilling enlisted Andrew Fastow, a Kellogg School MBA and former financier, to help create thousands of special purpose entities (SPEs). Many of these SPEs went under the name "Project Raptor," after birds of prey whose keen vision enables them to feed on nearsighted rodents.[6] These off-balance sheet "partners"—with names like Raptor I, II, and III and Jedi I and II—allowed Enron to secretly profit from transactions that might not serve the interests of its clients. Project Raptor also served as a firewall separating Enron from its bad dealings—at least temporarily—by preventing more than $500 million in losses from appearing on Enron's balance sheet in 2000 (McLean and Elkind 2004). By the time the scheme was uncovered, Raptors had collectively shielded $1 billion in losses. The intervening years had provided Enron executives, who were compensated by equity, time to silently cash out their stock options before the company collapsed.

Central to Skilling's financial maneuvers was the oversight—or lack thereof—of Enron's accounting firm, Arthur Andersen, which approved the firm's financial statements, giving it the appearance of sound financial health. Skilling's and Fastow's fraudulent disclosure practices began to draw skepticism in the spring of 2001 when a series of risky investments started to deteriorate Enron's cash flow. Losing confidence in Enron's future, investors sold off their shares in droves, driving the stock price from around $80 in February to below $40 in August.

Since most of the SPEs were backed by Enron shares, the enormous drop in the company's stock price meant Enron would have to issue an additional 58 million shares just to keep the SPEs solvent. That would drag the stock price down further. Enron finally decided to end the Raptor operation in October and put all the underperforming assets back on its balance sheet. This decision also revealed that Enron's trading operation had actually taken on a much higher level of risk than it had appeared to investors, and the shrinking stock price exacerbated its financial distress (Partnoy 2006). Overall, this financial restatement added $591 million in losses and $628 million in debts, pushing Enron's stock price down to about $10 and dropping its credit rating to just above "junk" status (Thomas 2002).

By the time Enron filed bankruptcy, it had defrauded investors of over $70 billion (Frontain 2010). More than half of the employees who participated in the company's pension plan saw their savings vaporized (Oppel 2001). In the year following Enron's demise, the AFL-CIO estimated that 28,500 employees lost their jobs at Enron, WorldCom (a subsequent accounting scandal), and Arthur Andersen, and American workers lost $1.5 trillion in retirement savings (Valenti 2006). Former CEOs Kenneth Lay and Jeffrey Skilling were convicted of securities and wire fraud, and 22 Enron employees were found guilty of criminal offenses associated with financial malfeasance (Frontain 2010). Enron's accounting firm, Arthur Andersen, was convicted of fraud for destroying evidence (shredding Enron-related documents) and forced to close. In 2002, Congress passed the Sarbanes-Oxley Act, which established the Public Company Accounting Oversight Board to hold external auditors accountable (Norris 2002). While these responses did penalize a handful of criminals and improve oversight, they failed to address the unprecedented level of risk from derivative financial products that had come to characterize the US economy.

Just as the name Enron is now shorthand for corporate excess, it should also be shorthand for the cascade of problems that can ensue when a nonfinancial firm becomes financialized. Enron's usage of derivatives and SPEs was initially viewed as innovative and commendable, but these practices ultimately led to its bankruptcy. With hindsight, they were deemed symptoms of pervasive corruption. In this respect, Enron captures the potential pitfalls of a rapidly changing corporate model that incentivizes taking financial risks. It also demonstrates what is at stake when finance takes precedence over the productive economy.

Inequality Consequences

Who benefits from the financialization of corporate America? The obvious winners are financial professionals: there is a lucrative, growing demand for their expertise outside of the traditional financial sector. Thus, as finance became the guiding principle and a primary source of profits for US corporations, Wall Street became a springboard for corporate executives and other key personnel. In recent years, about 30 percent of Fortune 500 CEOs spent their formative years in finance; market acumen is now a key qualification for corporate executives (Sanders 2011).

The marketization of US retirement system and the exponential growth of stock prices also made fund managers the chosen people in the shareholder revolution, compensated based on the volume of assets under their management and the amount of returns they can provide. Investment bankers cheered and profited handsomely from the spin-offs, mergers, and acquisitions driven by the shareholder-value movement. Among the 400 richest Americans listed by *Forbes* magazine, the number of people working in the securities and investment industry increased from 24 in 1982 to almost 100 in 2015.

Perhaps the most unexpected outcome of this financial turn is the skyrocketing compensation for corporation executives, supposedly the "villains" behind excessive corporate spending. Figure 4.5 illustrates the inflation-adjusted average compensation for the CEOs of the top 350 firms (ranked by sales) between 1965 and 2015. Before 1980, these CEOs made about $1 million a year. In the 1990s, stock options became a popular form of compensation (Murphy 2002). By the end of the century, the average top

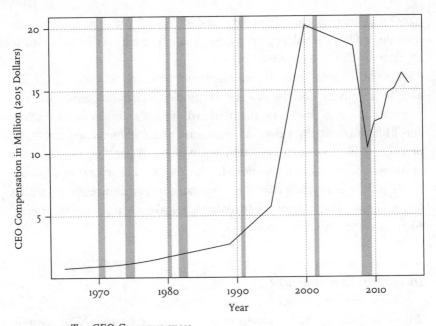

FIGURE 4.5 TOP CEO COMPENSATION

NOTE: CEO annual compensation is computed using the "options realized" compensation se-ries, which includes salary, bonus, restricted stock grants, options exercised, and long-term incentive payouts for CEOs at the top 350 US firms ranked by sales. SOURCE: Table 1 in Mishel and Schieder 2016 using Compustat's ExecuComp.

CEO compensation reached the $20 million mark, almost 400 times the pay received by their companies' typical workers (Mishel and Schieder 2016).

Since stock options now tie much of that pay to the equity market, CEOs took a substantial hit during the Great Recession. But their recovery was equally dramatic. While the CEO-to-worker compensation ratio went under 200 in 2009, in just three years, it had surged to more than 300. In 2015, the average among these CEOs took home about $15 million per year. Not only have today's CEOs out-earned their predecessors by more than 1,400 per-cent, they also out-earn their peers in every other advanced economy. A 2016 Bloomberg study shows that the CEO-to-worker pay ratio in the United States overshadows those in the United Kingdom, Canada, Switzerland, Germany, Spain, and the Netherlands. In countries such as Sweden, France, Singapore, and Finland, the ratios hover between 60 and 80.[7]

Political economist David Gordon (1996) argues that the shareholder-value movement expanded rather than curtailed managerial power, since more managerial supervision is needed to extract additional effort from already squeezed workforces. Instead of making corporations "lean and mean," the shareholder-value movement made them "fat and mean" by augmenting managerial power. Analyzing CEO compensation of public firms, sociologist Taekjin Shin (2012) finds that the more CEOs are willing to conform to the shareholder-value ideology—either by adopting performance-based strategies or by signaling their beliefs in public, the more monetary rewards they receive from their boards of directors (Shin and You 2017). Furthermore, when comparing CEOs with and without financial backgrounds, the former tend to earn much higher salaries than the latter (Shin 2014).

The ascendance of managerial pay and power is not limited to those at the very top. Examining industrial dynamics between 1984 and 2001, sociologist Adam Goldstein (2012) shows that shareholder-value strategies such as mergers and acquisitions are linked to growth in compensation for managers at all levels. The proportion of business income that goes to managerial workers increased from under 17 percent in 1989 to almost 23 percent in 2001, while the proportion allocated to nonsupervisory workers dropped from more than 35 percent to 27 percent.

Meanwhile, average Americans have not benefited from the financial turn. While the boom should have rewarded household savers, the reality is that many Americans are nowhere near the stock market (continued in Chapter 6). The proportion of workers who receive any employment-based retirement benefits declined from 55 percent in 1980 to about 40 percent in 2014 (Figure 4.6). The vast majority of workers at the bottom half of the earnings distribution receive no retirement benefits. The drop was most significant at the top quintile, whose participation declined from 80 percent in the early 1980s to around 60 percent. A recent Gallup study indicates that, even when counting all types of investment, from direct purchase to mutual funds and IRAs, half of Americans have no stake in the stock market (McCarthy 2015).

Even for the half of Americans who are fortunate enough to participate in the Great 401(k) Experiment, retirement accounts cannot promise a bright future. Vanguard, one of the largest mutual funds in the United States, reported that the median savings for its customers aged 55 to 64 in 2013 was only $76,381. A portion of their savings has been eaten away by fees, and the extreme swings in the stock market mean that money may not be there when retirees need it. It is no surprise that, when asked by the National Institute on Retirement Security, 86 percent of Americans believed that the nation was facing a retirement crisis and three in four were highly anxious about their retirement outlook (Oakley and Kenneally 2015).

Why did the shareholder-value movement lead to these unintended consequences? In part, in the process of addressing the agency problem, the shareholder-value revolution created a *new* agency problem—between

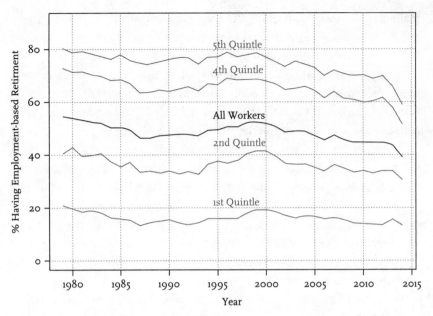

FIGURE 4.6 THE PERCENTAGE OF WORKERS RECEIVING RETIREMENT BENEFITS
NOTE: Estimates include all private sector employees aged 25–65. The CPS redesigned the questionnaire in 2014, which is believed to contribute to lower estimates for 2013 and 2014.
SOURCE: Bureau of Labor Statistics, Current Population Survey Annual Social and Economic Supplement.

fund managers and household investors. Sociologists Frank Dobbin and Jiwook Jung (2010) argue that the shareholder-value model actually created "fund-manager value." Since fund managers are paid based on the annual return of their portfolios but do not have to cover the losses, they are incentivized to push for short-term gains. They also profit much more from a stock market with ups and downs, which encourages them to fuel rather than burst bubbles. Similarly, executives with stock options will gain tremendously when the share price rises but lose nothing when it falls below the option price. Combined with their shorter tenures, this incentive structure encourages CEOs to pursue risky strategies rather than promoting the long-term, sustainable growth of their companies.

In addition to jeopardizing the future of millions of retiring Americans, financialization devastated the "basic bargain" of American society—that if you are willing to work hard, you can make a decent living for your family. As firms begin to emulate banks and investment firms, corporate resources are directed away from the production and sales of goods and services into financial subsidiaries and markets. More money is invested in mortgages, credit card debt, business loans, and derivatives trading, while far less is spent developing human resources and innovation. Prior to the Great Recession, the industries that most depended on financial revenue (e.g., interest, dividends, and capital gains) tended to have a lower share of income going to labor, higher compensation for executives, and elevated earnings inequality. The reliance on financial income decouples the generation of surplus from production and sales, strengthening shareholders' and elite workers' claims on profit over other workers' (Lin and Tomaskovic-Devey 2013; see Alvarez 2015 for similar findings in France).

As financial professionals started to dictate how large corporations should be run, cost-cutting became a path to glory. In addition to stagnant wages (see Figure 2.3), most workers now face more precarious employment conditions. Mass layoffs, once perceived as managerial failures, are now a fashionable business practice that promotes shareholder value (Jung 2015, 2016). The casualties spread from the blue-collar workers in the Midwest to office workers on the coasts. To maintain profit-oriented flexibility, many firms replace permanent positions with part-time or temporary workers who can be dismissed at will.

Besides mass layoffs, the revenue and employment size of the largest nonfinancial companies in the United States began to diverge in the 1980s. That is, as industrial giants play a greater role in shaping the US economy, their share of employment actually declines. This disjuncture is in part driven by financialization. The rising profitability of financial over manufacturing activities and the dominance of Wall Street culture have both prompted executives to venture into finance to seek higher returns. In the meantime, executives who believe that any investment activities should be disciplined by debt and the purpose of a firm is to maximize shareholder value have stopped focusing on promoting growth. Now, rather than engineering new products, they are engineering equity prices through debt financing and stock buybacks. Firms increasingly divert resources away from creating jobs and toward dealing money and paying their creditors and shareholders (Lin 2016).

Similar dynamics were observed by economists Eileen Appelbaum and Rosemary Batt (2014) in the extreme case of private equity. To maximize their returns on investments, private equity firms often borrow heavily with acquired assets and implement draconian cost-cutting strategies, both of which sacrifice the financial stability of the targeted firm and the employment security of its workers. A recent example is the bankruptcy of Toys "R" Us, which was loaded with more than $5 billion of debt when it was acquired by private equity firms Bain Capital, KKR & Co., and Vornado Realty Trust. After the acquisition, the toy store's revenue remained stable even when facing competition from online stores. The debt payment, however, ate away a significant portion of its revenue. Eventually, all 735 stores closed for business in 2018. Without severance, 33,000 workers lost their jobs. By then, CEO Dave Brandon had already fled the sinking ship with millions in the form of a "golden parachute" paid out before the company concluded its bankruptcy filing.

Besides weakening employment, financialization encouraged other developments that undermined the capital-labor accord. Sociologists Neil Fligstein and Taekjin Shin (2007) report that, across industries, the prevalence of shareholder-value strategies such as mergers and acquisitions is associated with increased investments in computer technology and reductions in the share of unionized workforce. Milberg (2008) argues that financialization also motivates the global disintegration of production: to create profits for shareholders in a slow-growth economy, US firms offshore production to developing countries, further diminishing ordinary Americans' economic prospects.

Importantly, political economist Thibault Darcillon (2015) proposes that the rise of finance has adverse effects on labor market institutions meant to protect workers. Across Organization for Economic Cooperation and Development countries, he finds that financialization undercuts workers' bargaining power by reducing union density, dismantling collective wage-setting, and reducing the coverage of collective bargaining agreements (i.e., the extent to which nonunion workers receive the same employment terms as union workers). It also erodes the protection of regular workers against individual dismissal, eases the regulation of temporary employment, and lessens requirements for mass layoffs. Other scholars link financialization to the deterioration of coordinated wage bargaining and greater firm-level deviation from collective agreements (Meyer 2017). Together, these studies suggest that in addition to siphoning resources from the nonfinancial to the financial sector, financialization has fundamentally restructured the economy. The capital-labor accord that drove postwar prosperity has taken hits on multiple fronts: firms became fragile, labor-replacing technology became popular, outsourcing prevailed, and union and labor protections were dismantled. Consequently, worker's share of national income declined, stable employment dwindled, and economic resources were concentrated in the hands (and wallets) of a small number of individuals.

Summary

Besides transferring income to Wall Street, financialization has had widespread impacts on the income and employment dynamics of Main Street.

Focusing on the financial turn of large US corporations since the 1970s, we saw that nonfinancial firms have increased their involvement in financial markets, taking both active and passive positions. These companies expanded their involvement in financial markets, profiting from lending money to households and small businesses, and trading stocks and other securities. At the same time, the emerging dominance of the shareholder-value governance model imported the logics and practices of Wall Street to Main Street, making stock price the sole measure of a firm's performance.

While large manufacturers such as General Motors and General Electric began to provide financial services to their consumers in the first half of the 20th century, the main purpose of these services had been to promote the sales of their products such as automobiles and home appliances. As finance became a profitable venture in the 1970s, these services took on a life of their own. Customers were no longer limited to those who wished to purchase cars, pianos, and refrigerators, but expanded to any small businesses and households in need of credit. The number of nonfinancial firms providing financial services mushroomed, blurring the long-standing separation of banking and commerce.

In addition to traditional banking activities, some corporations found their way into high finance. Between 2005 and 2008, Sears used the cash generated from its big-box stores to invest in risky derivatives, operating more like a hedge fund than a retailer. Before its ultimate collapse in 2001, Enron shifted from an energy producer to a trader of various commodities, including natural gas and broadband fiber optic capacity. The rise of finance from a secondary, supportive function to the principal driver of these firms' profitability diverted resources away from investments in productive assets and employment and often brought tremendous risk to their financial health.

While so many of these nonfinancial firms expanded their financial operations, a concurrent shift was occurring in corporate America. The managerialism that had dominated the corporate world since the early 20th century was questioned in the crisis of 1970s and eventually overthrown by the shareholder-value model. Advocated by fund managers and corporate consultants, this new governance model holds that a firm's sole purpose is the delivery of financial rewards to its owners.

To bolster the centrality of shareholders in corporate governance, financial economists prescribed a variety of sticks and carrots. Among these, equity-based compensation incentivized executives to pursue strategies such as downsizing and stock buybacks that would immediately boost stock price. The expansive use of debt, as a source of capital and a deterrence for takeover, pushed firms to operate under high financial pressure. And this emphasis on shareholder value *did* boost the stock market to unprecedented levels.

Yet what is good for the stock market is not necessarily good for most Americans. The clear winners in the financial turn are fund managers and corporate executives. The former are compensated based on the size of their assets under management and returns to their investors. Booming financial markets, even when they do not reflect the economic realities, enrich these financial professionals. And as stock options become the main component in their compensation packages, executives benefit from the resulting inflated share prices. Meanwhile, less than half of ordinary Americans even have a 401(K) or IRA account,[8] and even those who do reap no benefits when market volatility is high. Sure, we can get creative and theorize how *some* part-time and on-call retail workers could benefit *indirectly* from a bull market. But financialization helped to create these unstable jobs in the first place.

Financialization not only failed average American workers, it fundamentally undermined the capital-labor accord—the agreement that authorizes managers full control in return for providing workers living wages and job security—in the United States. The imperative to maximize shareholder value has meant the redirection of corporate resources from the production and development of goods and services into financial ventures, expediting trends like the decline in labor's share of income, widened gaps in earnings, and stagnant growth in employment.

Importantly, the rise of finance also weakened the livelihood of American workers by facilitating antilabor developments. In the pursuit of shareholder value, new technologies have been adopted to replace unionized workforces (thus undercutting American labor's main champion). The outsourced tasks mainly went to nonunionized firms and temporary staffing agencies, creating an abundance of nonstandard and potentially exploitive employment. The cost-cutting mandate also motivated the global disintegration of production, not only shipping jobs to low-wage countries but also creating hazardous working conditions for those foreign workers. It is no surprise that many American families now borrow to get by.

CHAPTER 5 | American Life in Debt

You wanna know what's more important than throwin' away money at a
strip club?
Credit.

—JAY-Z ("THE STORY OF O.J." 2017)

IN THE PREVIOUS TWO chapters, we discussed how the rise of finance widened
economic inequality in the United States. An essential component of this
process was a massive expansion of household debt (Figure 1.4). Before
1980, the average American family's debt hovered around 65 percent of its
disposable income. The amount of debt climbed steadily in the following
two decades, increasing to more than 100 percent in 2002. The trend continued during the 2000s and hit an all-time high of 132 percent at the onset
of the Great Recession. Irresponsible lending is, of course, one driver: subprime mortgage issuers, for instance, lured low-income families into their
products with low introductory payments. As actual rates kicked in after the
first few months, many families could no longer afford the payments on
their homes.

While such reckless and predatory lending practices undoubtedly cause
harm, the ever-expanding debt held by American families has less straight-
forward ramifications for inequality. On the one hand, rising household
debt may indicate deepening economic divisions: an increasing number
of American families cannot make ends meet and need to borrow to get
by (Leicht and Fitzgerald 2006). A heightened debt burden, in turn,
may trap these families in a downward financial spiral, making their
lives ever harder to manage. The beneficiaries of credit expansion are
modern usurers, preying on the economically vulnerable and financially
precarious.

On the other hand, this trend may suggest that financialization has alleviated consumption inequality by allowing more families to live middle-class lifestyles. American families have had much greater access to credit in the era of financialization, and this has allowed them to buy homes and cars, obtain college degrees, and purchase consumer goods. These newfound opportunities may improve families' quality of life, strengthen their long-term economic prospects, and equalize access to goods and services between the haves and have-nots. One may even argue that the debt-to-disposable-income ratio[1] exaggerates the actual increase of debt burden carried by American families, who are borrowing at much lower interest rates than before, all thanks to financialization.

Indeed, the picture looks quite different when we shift the focus from how much American families owe to how much they pay for their debt. Figure 5.1 presents the *debt burden* of American households, measured as debt service payments over disposable personal income. Compared to the dramatic growth of debt seen in Figure 1.4, the debt burden has been largely stable, suggesting that rising amount of debt is largely driven by its declining

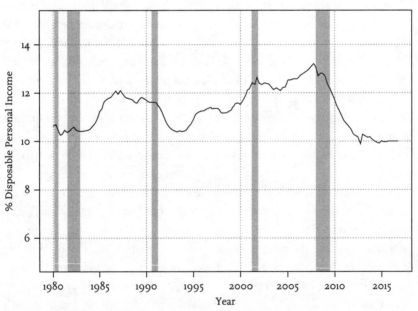

FIGURE 5.1 HOUSEHOLD DEBT SERVICE PAYMENTS AS PERCENTAGE OF DISPOSABLE PERSONAL INCOME

NOTE: Calculated as the ratios of the Federal Reserve household debt service payments and financial obligations over the percentage of disposable personal income. SOURCE: Federal Reserve Bank of St. Louis, Federal Reserve Economic Data.

cost. American families, *on average*, use between 10 and 13 percent of their income to repay their debts.

This chapter argues that neither the optimistic nor pessimistic view of the growing household debt provides an adequate understanding of the issue. This is because national accounts obscure the fact that both debt and debt burden are unequally distributed among American families. Importantly, *those with high debt are rarely those with high debt burden.* Among affluent households, having a large sum of outstanding debt is not a sign of financial ruin, but a reflection of their advantageous access to credit and wealth-building potential. Residential and student loans provide alternatives to dipping into these families' savings or investments, which tend to yield higher returns or tax benefits than the interest payments consume. That is, for upper-class families, debt can be profitable.

Middle-class families, with less wealth than the affluent but greater access to credit than the poor, have become more leveraged—they have taken on more debt relative to their net worth—in the era of financialization (Wolff 2015). As such, these families tend to have higher debt loads when compared to their net worth. The availability of credit enables these families to advance educational attainment, improve lifestyles, and "keep up with the Joneses," but these debts also expose them to greater financial risks (Fligstein and Goldstein 2015). Without much savings, many families are one paycheck or medical bill away from losing their home.

Low-income households have not benefited much from the expansion of credit. Most of these families have little access to credit from mainstream lenders. For those who are able to borrow, credit tends to come with an expensive price tag, which puts a destructive burden on their financial health. Consequently, the expansion of credit has made the majority of American families economically vulnerable, except for those already with abundant resources. This development is particularly ironic, considering credit has been promoted as a market-based *solution* to inequality.

In this chapter, we examine how financialization exacerbates inequality through the expansion of household debt. We identify three primary avenues through which household debt has become a primary driver of inequality among families. First, families have unequal access to credit. Those who need it the most are the least likely to have access to credit; when they do, these families face the heaviest financial burden for taking out credit. Second, those who are well off have abundant access to cheap credit and use that credit as a part of a household investment strategy that bolsters their wealth. Thus, the wealthy use credit as a resource, while the poor pay usurious rates. Third, though policymakers have long championed credit as a solution to inequalities in wages and in labor markets, the expansion of credit is inadequate for addressing economic hardship. Credit can provide relief to a family in the short term, but it deepens economic divisions over time. Credit provides a distraction rather than a solution to the problem of inequality.

We first provide a historical account of how consumer finance emerged as a remedy for inequality and catalyst for growth in the 20th century and how decades of policies have reinforced its role in American society. We then examine how credit is distributed across households and the unequal consequences of borrowing.

A History of Household Debt

> A bank is a place that will lend you money if you can prove that you don't need it.
>
> —BOB HOPE

Consumer finance has a long history in the United States. What used to be a stigmatized practice associated with dire poverty and frivolity has come, over time, to be considered an elixir for these very ills. That transformation stemmed from an unlikely alliance between two separate and often competing interests in the Progressive Era (Anderson, Carruthers, and Guinnane 2015; Trumbull 2014). While manufacturers and retailers saw credit as a stimulus for the consumption of their goods and services, progressive reformists viewed consumer credit as a tool for smoothing the economic instability afflicting working-class Americans. Both advocated for policies that would grant more public access to credit. This alliance continued throughout the 20th century, as consumer credit and home loans became a popular means to meet unfulfilled needs. In this section, we trace how consumer lending evolved from an illicit activity to a reputable financial service—and then the focus of public wrath in the wake of the 2008 crisis.

Origins of Credit as a Solution to Inequality

At the turn of the 20th century, moral boundaries were drawn between "good" and "bad" debts. "Society," as it were, viewed applying for loans to buy a farm or start a business as a productive use of finance that would promote economy and build communities, while borrowing for consumption was denounced as frivolous. Strict usury laws before 1916 limited interest rates to under 6 to 8 percent (Calder 2001). These ceilings deterred community banks from establishing personal lending departments, because it was impossible to make a profit with low interest rates and no collateral. Families in need of financial relief had few options, and many sought small, informal loans from friends or family or used charge accounts to buy from neighborhood stores. In desperate situations, people would turn to pawnshops or other shady lenders willing to lend small sums at high interests with valuable collateral, such as a watch or a necklace.

After World War I, the types of credit available to the common American expanded. Economic historian Louis Hyman (2012) identifies two financial innovations that would define modern consumer credit: installment credit and legalized personal loans. Installment credit allowed consumers to purchase big-ticket items—such as cars, pianos, washing machines, televisions, and refrigerators—through a payment plan. Sears, the largest national retailer at the time, introduced credit options to its customers in 1911, and JC Penny followed suit shortly thereafter. In 1919, General Motors, led by Alfred P. Sloan, became the first automobile company to establish a financing subsidiary, the General Motors Acceptance Corporation, which financed installment payments to expand its customer base (Farber 2002).

In the meantime, reformists viewed borrowing as a necessity for working-class and poor Americans coping with unexpected medical expenses or unemployment. To curtail predatory lending,[2] nonprofit banks were established. In 1910, Arthur Morris founded the first Morris Plan bank in Virginia, which made small loans to workers with good references and scheduled a repayment plan that went toward a certificate of deposit. Morris believed that he could instill in his borrowers a "habit of thrift through systematic investing" (quoted in Trumbull 2014: 26). The Morris Plan banks expanded to more than 100 locations in the following years and became an icon of charitable lending.

To further encourage the entry of for-profit financial institutions into consumer markets, progressive organizations such as the Russell Sage Foundation began to create a blueprint for usury law reform by states. Believing that higher interest rates were necessary if banks were to engage in this riskier venture, they advocated for less restrictive interest ceilings for personal finance coupled with the proper regulation of the lending practices. New Jersey became the first state to adopt such laws in 1916; 25 other states passed similar small-loan laws by the 1930s. Eager to access these new markets, commercial banks began to establish personal lending departments in the 1920s and 1930s. By 1934, 13,000 consumer lenders were registered with the Federal Reserve.

Credit provided an appealing alternative to the public welfare programs and redistribution policies that had begun to gain popularity across the Atlantic. Instead of creating a formal, public safety net, politicians and industrialists believed that private financial institutions could be the main providers of economic relief in a fast-changing economy. However, since most financial institutions would not lend without expecting profits, the beneficiaries of these reforms were mostly middle-class white men with stable employment. The most disadvantaged households' economic hardship was left unaddressed by usury reform.

This piecemeal, finance-based safety net was tolerable in the roaring Twenties, when reliable incomes allowed households to repay their debts, yet its shortcomings became apparent as the Great Depression unfolded. Mass unemployment not only reduced the income of many American families but also blocked their access to credit. In response, Franklin D. Roosevelt's administration introduced a series of social programs to ensure that the welfare of the middle- and working-class Americans did not suffer during the period of economic turmoil. Among these, the Homeowner Refinancing Act of 1933 and the National Housing Act of 1934 provided much-needed relief to construction workers, homeowners, and mortgage lenders (Prasad 2012).

In a formal statement upon signing the acts, Roosevelt said, "I feel that we have taken another important step toward the ending of deflation which was rapidly depriving many millions of farm and home owners from the title and equity to their property."[3] He then appealed to lenders to avoid pursuing foreclosures and dispossessing homeowners until the refinancing provided through the law was fully implemented. Since almost all mortgages were held on banks' balance sheets at the time, the banks indeed had discretion over foreclosures. The act also established the Federal Housing Authority to insure home loans made by lenders, which led to lower interest rates, lower down payments, and extended repayment periods.

Expansion of Household Credit after World War II

A popular myth holds that the "Greatest Generation," those who fought in World War II and returned home to create a baby boom, earned its way through hard work and thrift. Less is known about how consumer credit played a critical role in promoting widespread prosperity after the war. As soldiers returned and embarked on family life in the suburbs, access to low-interest credit for home purchase or entrepreneurship stimulated the postwar economy. Manufacturers, too, provided attractive payment plans to stimulate demand for their products. After two decades of turmoil, consumer credit seemed again a catalyst for rapid economic growth and an equalizer for standards of living.

Organized labor, like the reformers of the earlier era, supported credit expansion because it provided a much-needed safety net for the working class. Political economist Gunnar Trumbull (2014: 13) recounts, "Credit seemed to create a virtuous cycle, with new credit purchases driving scale in manufacturing, the resulting productivity increases enabling increases in wages." Credit was applauded for allowing the middle and working classes to improve their quality of life.

The introduction of consumer credit cards also contributed to the debt of American households. Western Union introduced the first charge card in 1914, followed by hotel chains, department stores, and oil companies in the 1920s. Multiple-purpose cards, like the ones we know today, did not enter the mainstream until after World War II. The Diners Club card, introduced in 1950, led the trend by extending credit to restaurant-goers. The card charged a 7 percent interest rate and an annual fee but was extremely popular among affluent households who frequented high-end restaurants. In one year, it attracted 20,000 new members. Other lenders quickly started similar services, such as National Credit Card Inc., which provided a card targeted to traveling businessmen. American Express joined the credit business in 1958, sending 8 million potential customers application forms for credit cards modeled after the Diners Club. The number of banks offering credit cards grew from 27 in 1958 to 1,500 in 1967, servicing an estimated 11–13 million active accounts.

Despite taking on significantly more debt than their parents had, most American families were able to pay back their debts and build savings, owing to rapid wage growth and employment security grounded in the New Deal legislation. Every year after World War II, household borrowing grew, and so did repayment. Rates of outstanding debts remained constant over time. This ready access to credit provided the semblance of equality at least among working- and middle-class suburban households (the wealthy did not need to borrow for consumption, and the poor were still excluded from the credit market). Although half of clerical and factory workers lived in the suburbs— consistent with overall trends during the era—they were 1.5 times more likely to be in debt than their neighbors who worked as managers and professionals (Cherlin 2014). To some extent, these trends fulfilled the goals of progressive advocates for personal lending: debt helped to level inequality in consumption among households at the middle of the distribution, creating the enduring perception that most Americans were middle class.

The triumph of the postwar credit system was on display during the six-week American National Exhibition in Moscow in 1959. Richard Nixon, then vice president and chief ambassador of American capitalism, showcased a suburban model home, fully furnished with modern appliances including a television, washing machine, refrigerator, range, and dishwasher. Knowing that the United States was lagging behind the Soviet Union in space technology at the time, Nixon proudly proclaimed that this model house was not some unrealistic propaganda but a home that a "typical" American could afford. What he did not mention was that the home and all the appliances were only affordable though a mortgage and payment plans.

Nixon also failed to mention that the financing available to black households made middle-class lifestyles come at a much higher price. Discriminatory lending and employment practices meant that black Americans had to pay higher interest, and they already earned roughly half the income of their white counterparts. As a result, these households were far less able to accumulate wealth. Lower savings and lower income compounded their financial distress by making them more reliant on borrowing in times of need. Among all indebted households, the percentage with no savings amounted to only 24 percent of white households compared to 69 percent of black households. Racial disparities were most salient in the suburbs, where black households carried a debt burden twice as large as their white neighbors (Hyman 2012).

Other forms of institutional racism compounded this debt burden. In the 1930s, the Federal Housing Administration (FHA) explicitly refused to insure mortgages to people of color and other borrowers in neighborhoods dominated by minorities. After World War II, even black veterans were denied access to government-guaranteed mortgages, as financial institutions identified nonwhite borrowers as lacking sufficient capital and credit history. In New York and New Jersey, for example, racial and ethnic minorities held fewer than 100 of the 67,000 GI Bill-insured mortgages (Katznelson 2005).

In the late 1940s, under pressure from the NAACP, the FHA launched an initiative to improve its lending neutrality—and its image among racial and ethnic minorities. However, discriminatory lending and insuring practices continued under the presumption that black neighborhoods presented more risk for investors (a claim readily undermined by the increasing value of these homes and black wealth overall during this period). Later, the Fair Housing Act, Title VIII of the Civil Rights Act of 1968, prohibited discrimination in the sale, financing, or leasing of any residence. Yet the legacy of earlier discriminatory programs continues to shape racial disparities in wealth today, and the movement to extend credit to African Americans and other groups would reaffirm the faith in credit as a solution to inequality in the United States (Massey and Denton 1993).

We refer to a movement that began in the late 1960s and 1970s and aimed to promote access to credit for groups previously deemed "uncreditworthy" by the banks, specifically women and minority men. Whereas labor rights groups took the lead in the first half of the twentieth century, the cause was taken up by advocacy groups such as the National Organization for Women and the National Welfare Rights Organization in the latter half. This movement resulted in a series of new laws. The Equal Credit Opportunity Act of 1974 prohibited discrimination based on sex or marital status and was amended in 1977 to include race, religion, and national origin. To curb "redlining," the Home Mortgage Disclosure Act of 1975 required lenders in metropolitan areas to disclose their mortgage loans by classification and geographic location. The Community Reinvestment Act (CRA) of 1977 required banks to service lower-income minorities in their community; in a Clinton-era revision, paperwork requirements were replaced by performance tests to stimulate lending in low-income communities. While these policies attempted to equalize access to credit, they also allowed policymakers to further transfer the responsibility of tackling inequality to financial institutions (Krippner 2011). And that meant inequality went substantively unaddressed.

The Financial Turn of the 1980s

As early developments in household lending made credit more accessible to some Americans, household debt remained low—a fraction of what it is today. Up until about 1980, consumer credit was considered as a secondary means of funding a suburban lifestyle. Starting in the 1980s, however, credit transitioned. The deregulation of finance allowed consumer debt to proliferate, rivaling income as a driver of American households' prosperity. As the state gradually relaxed the restrictions set in place to promote stability and prevent excessive financial power in the aftermath of the Great Depression, new and "convenient" financial products enticed household borrowers. The removal of interest rate ceilings allowed banks to charge household lenders high interest rates and fees that would have been deemed predatory in the Progressive Era. Meanwhile, stagnant wages of middle- and working-class families (see Figure 2.3) created a need for more access to credit.

The proliferation of securitization accelerated an upward trend in lending. By bundling household debts into tradable securities, lenders could sell their loans to foreign and domestic investors and acquire funds for another round of lending. As demand for these debts grew in capital markets, financial vehicles such as collateralized debt obligations, mortgage-backed securities, and credit default swaps flourished. Two decades of strong demand for consumer debt (in terms of both end-consumers and financial markets ready to buy up the loans) encouraged banks and other financial institutions to lend as much and as fast as possible. Furthermore, because lenders no longer held the loans on their balance sheets, loan *quality* was secondary to *quantity*. Politicians and regulators cheered on this development, still apparently believing that ready access to credit was the most efficient remedy for poverty and inequality.

While residential loans drove much of the increase in household debt, other types of consumer debt also expanded rapidly. Figure 5.2 illustrates the inflation-adjusted consumer debt per capita over the last five decades, excluding the amount borrowed for home purchase. Before the 1980s, household debt fluctuated, but mostly followed the business cycle: American families borrowed more for spending during economic booms and less during recessions. While the same pattern persisted in later years, the upsurge in consumer debt began to outpace repayment rates in the 1980s.

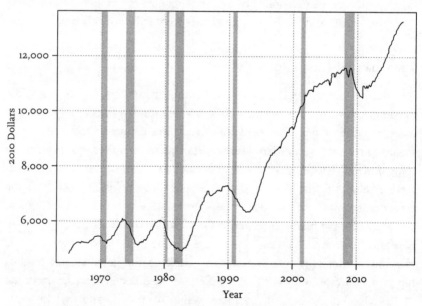

FIGURE 5.2 CONSUMER CREDIT OUTSTANDING PER CAPITA

NOTE: Calculated as the total outstanding consumer credit owned and securitized (TOTALSL) over the civilian, noninstitutional population (CNP16OV) with the adjustment of the consumer price index: Total All Items for the United States (CPALTT01USM661S). Consumer credit includes credit card debt, student loan, automobile loan, and other plans used to purchase goods and services but does not include mortgage and other investment loans. SOURCE: Federal Reserve Bank of St. Louis, Federal Reserve Economic Data.

Between 1982 and 2016, the debt of an average American increased from around $5,000 to $13,000 (adjusted for inflation), driven by the expansion of credit cards, auto loans, and, in recent years, student loans.

Overall, the 1980s marked a new era in consumer credit, driven by selling financial rather than manufacturing products. Consumer credit that had once primarily served to stabilize and promote the consumption of goods and services had become an end in itself: financial institutions made credit available as a consumer good and profited from loan origination through escalating interest rates, hidden service fees, and late payment fees as well as the repackaging of those loans in financial markets.

The expansion of household credit would eventually lead to the 2008 financial crisis. Once in office, the Obama administration implemented several reforms to curb the crash: first, the Credit Card Accountability, Responsibility, and Disclosure Act, passed in 2009, provided greater protections for consumers by making credit terms more transparent and requiring more accountability for lenders. Then, in 2010, the Dodd-Frank Wall Street Reform and Consumer Protection Act was passed to revive the Volcker Rule prohibiting deposit-taking financial institutions from investing in proprietary trading of securities, derivatives, commodity futures, and options. It also established the Consumer Financial Protection Bureau (CFPB) to provide more oversight of mortgage lenders and brokers so as to protect homeowners and their families. The CFPB, which has been significantly disarmed recently, aimed to increase transparency on the terms of home loans, credit cards, and student loans. In theory, these policies should reduce the potential negative consequences attending consumer and mortgage debt by regulating lending practices and containing the consequences of risky investment. The real impact of these interventions remains unknown, especially as the Trump administration makes strides to scale them back.

These postrecession reforms may improve conditions for borrowers, but they leave intact the century-old policy model by which *the problem of inequality is misconstrued as a problem of illiquidity*. Rather than ask why poor and working-class families do not have the means or upward mobility to secure a middle-class lifestyle, policymakers, reformists, and bankers alike ask how they can help poor households gain access to credit. Rather than provide a real safety net, the government seeks to safeguard Americans with financial spider webs. That is, the federal government frequently provides financial sector subsidies and mandates to lend, without proposing sound educational, housing, retirement, and welfare policies to narrow the class divide (Kus 2013). And since private lenders are profit-driven, the most disadvantaged households remain unlikely to receive credit without paying the high fees and interest so detrimental to their long-term financial standing.

The misconception that credit will solve the problem of inequality was most evident in the policies of the Clinton administration. To ensure that banks lent to low- and moderate-income communities, President Clinton pushed for both regulatory and legislative changes to strengthen the Community Reinvestment Act. In the meantime, the Personal Responsibility and Work Opportunity Act broke the New Deal by imposing a work requirement on welfare recipients and setting a five-year limit for governmental assistance. The requirements funneled single mothers and other disadvantaged families into low-wage, low-security employment with employers who knew that these Americans needed jobs to qualify for welfare (but also that welfare was there, so the pay need not be so high as to provide a living wage). Taken together, these policies solidified the central idea that the United States is a nation of credit, not welfare.

The Distribution of Credit

But where does all the credit actually go? Did the decades-long effort to channel credit to low-income and marginalized communities prove effective? Has financial deregulation "democratized" credit? In this section, we begin to answer these questions using data from the Survey of Consumer Finance, a triennial representative survey that collects information about the financial and demographic characteristics of American families. For our analysis, we exclude families with household heads either younger than 25 years old or older than 65 years; this avoids the interferences of education, retirement, and other changes associated with the life course.[4] We then divide families into six groups based on their total household income. The first group consists of families in the top 10 percent of the income distribution. The second group includes families in the next 10 percent of the distribution. The remaining American families are then evenly divided into four groups based on their level of income.

Figure 5.3 examines how household credit is distributed across these six groups of American families. Perhaps unsurprisingly, the distribution of credit is highly skewed. A large sum of household credit flows to families in the top 10 percent. For every year between 1989 and 2016, only a tenth of the households obtained about 30 percent of household credit. If we add the next 10 percent of families, the top-fifth households captured almost 50 percent of all household credit in the past three decades. The bottom fifth of

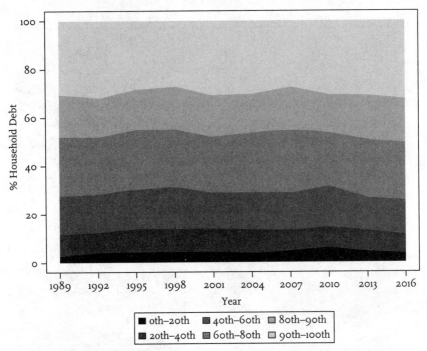

FIGURE 5.3 DISTRIBUTION OF HOUSEHOLD CREDIT ACROSS INCOME
PERCENTILE GROUPS
NOTE: The share of household debt for each income group is calculated by summing the total
value of debt held by the households in a given year. Sample weights are used to correct for the
oversampling of affluent households. Income includes all sources of household income in the
previous year. Families with household heads aged <25 or >65 are excluded from the sample.
SOURCE: Survey of Consumer Finance 1989–2016, Federal Reserve.

families, in contrast, received only a smidgen. Their share of credit increased
from 2.7 percent in 1989 to about 6.4 percent in 2010 but fell to 3.9 percent
in 2016.

Figure 5.4 dissects the distribution of credit by four main types of debt: residential, credit card, education, and vehicle.[5] In all four markets, affluent
households dominate access to credit, but the degree varies. Credit is most
unevenly distributed in the residential loan market, in which borrowing normally requires a prime credit score and a substantial amount of savings,
but leads to a direct accumulation of wealth. The level of concentration of
borrowing among the well-off changed only slightly during this period. The
share of debt owed by the bottom fifth of families increased from 1.6 percent
in 1989 to 3.1 percent in 2016, while the share owed by the top fifth increased
from 49 to 52 percent.

Credit card debt (i.e., carrying a balance), which entails high interest rates
and does not build wealth, has become less concentrated in the hands of the

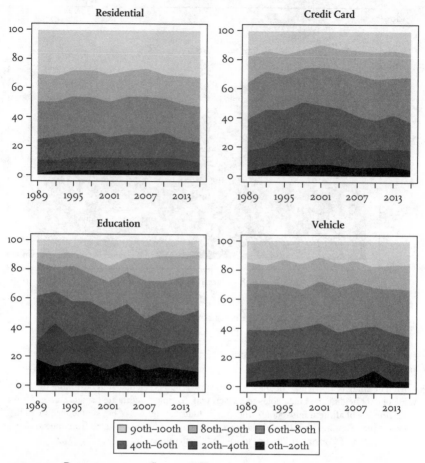

FIGURE 5.4 DISTRIBUTION OF CREDIT BY TYPE

NOTE: The share of household debt for each income group is calculated by summing the total value of debt held by the households. Sample weights are used to correct for the oversampling of affluent households. Income includes all sources of household income in the previous year. Families with household heads aged <25 or >65 are excluded from the sample. SOURCE: Survey of Consumer Finance 1989–2016, Federal Reserve.

affluent over time. The top 20 percent of families used to carry more than 35 percent of credit card debt. This number shrank to 31 percent in 2016 as "plastics" were made more available to middle- and working-class families. The main expansion took place among the families between the 60th and the 80th percentile, whose debt surged from 25 to 31 percent. The bottom 60 percent families experienced an increase in their credit card debt in the 1990s and then a decline in the 2000s.

Educational debt is the most evenly distributed of the four types of credit. The subsidy and guarantee provided by the federal government enabled the bottom 40 percent of families to obtain around 35 percent of the student loans. In recent years, upper-middle-class families have begun to take on more student loans as interest rates have dropped (essentially, education debt became much "cheaper"). The share of debt owed by families in the 80th to 90th percentiles increased from 6.6 percent in 1989 to 14 percent in 2016.

The distribution of vehicle loans (including cars, trucks, SUVs, motorcycles, boats, airplanes, etc.) largely follows business cycles. Affluent households took on higher proportions of debt, often for luxury vehicles, during economic booms, while low-income households assumed higher proportions of auto lending during recessions. The top 10 percent of families capture between 10 and 16 percent of this market, while the bottom fifth of families take around 5 percent.

Together, Figures 5.3 and 5.4 show that the actual distribution of credit deviates significantly from the public perception. Although debt is commonly associated with poverty, upper-class families use the majority of credit. The working class and the poor receive only a small fraction. The uneven distribution of debt is not merely because low-income families borrow less than the affluent, but also because they are less *able* to borrow. In recent years, only about 60 percent of the families in the bottom fifth of the income distribution reported having any debt, compared to more than 90 percent among those well-off.

Thus, the expansion of household credit has mostly benefited the haves, who borrow to take advantage of low interest rates and tax incentives—even when they could afford to make the purchase upfront. For example, the deductions for home mortgage and equity loan interest allow homeowners to subtract interest payments for their primary residence from their taxable income. Similarly, financial advisors frequently recommend wealthy families take out federal student loans to gain from the low cost of borrowing, make higher returns on other investments, and take advantage of the opportunities to receive merit-based aid.[6] Middle- and lower-class families have only seen substantial gains in their share of credit card balances (a costly debt that does little to accumulate wealth).

Figure 5.5 shows the proportion of families who were denied credit or feared being denied in the past five years by income and racial status. Unsurprisingly, high-income families have less trouble borrowing than their low-income counterparts. What is unexpected is that the expansion of credit did little to narrow this gap. The difficulty of low- and middle-income families remained high in the past three decades: between 30 and 40 percent of white families had problems obtaining credit in the five years before the interview. In contrast, white families in the top tenth of the distribution seemed to gain

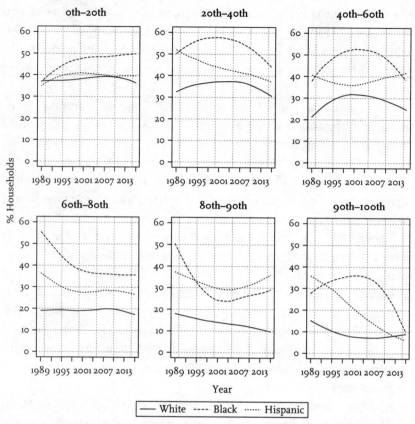

FIGURE 5.5 TURNED DOWN FOR OR FEARING DENIED CREDIT IN THE PAST FIVE YEARS
NOTE: White refers to non-Hispanic white. Families with household heads aged <25 or >65 are excluded from the sample. The trends are smoothed with local polynomial regression.
SOURCE: Survey of Consumer Finance 1989–2016, Federal Reserve.

greater access to credit over time. Their chances of being rejected dropped from around 15 percent in 1989 to under 10 percent in 2016.

Racial status plays a significant role in determining access to credit. Across the income spectrum, black and Hispanic families are much more likely than their white peers to find it difficult to borrow (Killewald 2013). The differences are particularly stark at the middle of the income distribution, where it is consistently more difficult for minority families to borrow. The gaps seem to converge at the very top of the income distribution, with high-income black and Hispanic families having access to credit similar to that of their white counterparts in recent years.

These racial disparities are likely due to a combination of lending discrimination and wealth disparities—an outcome of systemic racism. While numerous policies have been implemented to curtail discriminatory lending, various forms of "redlining" persist. For example, recent studies have shown that black and Hispanic applicants are less likely to receive mortgages than their white counterparts even when sharing similar characteristics (Cherian 2014; Munnell et al. 1996; Ross and Yinger 2002). Among the successful cases, researchers found that minority families are more likely to receive subprime loans, which feature higher interest rates and fees (Williams, Nesiba, and McConnell 2005).

Race-based discriminatory lending is not limited to the mortgage market. Black-owned small businesses are twice as likely to be denied credit as white-owned businesses, even when creditworthiness and other factors are taken into account (Blanchflower, Levine, and Zimmerman 2003). Similarly, observational and experimental studies show that black borrowers are less likely to receive funding than whites with similar credit profiles on peer-to-peer lending websites (Harkness 2016; Pope and Sydnor 2011).

Besides discrimination, wealth disparities also prohibit minority lenders from gaining equal access to credit. Since wealth is accumulated over multiple generations, the black-white wealth gap is considerably wider than other indicators of economic inequality (Oliver and Shapiro 2006). One recent estimate indicates that the median net worth of white families is 12 times higher than that of black families and 10 times higher than that of Hispanics.[7] The enormous difference in wealth implies that minority borrowers are less able to afford a down payment or offer collateral. Thus, even when they have sufficient means to repay debt, they may be denied credit.

Overall, the rapid expansion of household debt has looked nothing like the promised "democratization" of credit. The distribution of credit has remained highly uneven in the past three decades, with borrowing concentrated in the balance sheets of the most affluent households. Families in the top tenth of the income distribution incur more than half of household debt in the United States. Low-income and minority families still face great difficulty in obtaining credit. The bottom 20 percent of American families receive, at most, 5 percent of all household loans. Black and Hispanic families are most likely to be excluded from the credit market.

For American families unable to access traditional lines of credit, high-interest loans are a last resort. The "fringe lending industry" fulfills the needs of 20 percent of US households that are underbanked or denied access to credit by commercial banks and credit card companies. Common forms of fringe lending include high-fee money orders, check cashing, rent-to-own services, remittances, payday loans, pawnshop loans, (tax) refund anticipation loans, and auto title loans. Many lenders providing such credit promise "fast cash," "no credit check," or "no payment for six months." To lure cash-strapped families to take on high-interest debt, Mariner Finance, along with other consumer installment lenders, even mails low-income households checks, hoping they will cash the checks and incur high-interest debt when they are in need (Whoriskey 2018). These seemingly lenient business models are only profitable when the lenders can count on the majority of borrowers *not* being able to repay their debt on time. In other words, fringe lenders *aim* to extend credit to those who prove that they cannot repay it.

Payday loans, which allow workers with a low credit score to borrow against their paycheck, are the most common form of short-term lending. These service some 12 million Americans annually. For many borrowers, a payday loan is not a one-time but revolving event. These small loans, often under $500, incur large interest rates and fees. The average payday borrower takes out eight loans of $375 each and pays $520 in interest on those loans per year. Most payday borrowers are actually white women between the ages of 25 and 44, but overall the people who are most likely to use these loans are less educated, home renters, lower income, and divorced or separated. Black Americans are disproportionately likely to borrow relative to other racial and ethnic groups (Baradaran 2017; Burhouse et al. 2013; Kiel and Waldman 2015; 2012).

The Consequences of Debt

> The frequently troubled lives of the creative impress me less than
> those of the poor. It takes as much genius—in the way of courage,
> dreams, patience and impatience, innocence and ruse—to find
> the rent money and clothe the children as to put together a
> masterpiece.
>
> —CHRISTIAN BOBIN

Consumer finance has transformed from a shameful resource to a common or even advantageous practice, but its implications remain unclear. Some view credit expansion as a worrisome development. As the amount of household debt grows (Figures 1.4 and 5.2), American families have come under greater financial stress. Others think the expansion of household debt is a generally healthy trend. It is rational, they argue, for American families to borrow more in response to declining interest rates and other incentives. Financial innovation also allows lenders to more accurately assess the risks and extend credit to populations that were previously deemed too risky. Above all, the debt burden among American households appears largely stable

(Figure 5.1), suggesting that household debt has not become the crushing burden that one might imagine.

But we do not live our daily lives as a nation. We live in individual families with diverse economic resources and constraints. Those who earn high incomes are rarely paying high interest. Those who have high debt are not necessarily carrying a heavy debt burden. In this section, we examine the consequences of debt for families across the income spectrum. We show that the effects of debt vary dramatically across the income distribution and cannot be adequately understood without familial context. High-income families capture most of the credit, and low- and middle-income families carry the heaviest debt burdens.

From the outset, borrowing costs more for low-income and minority families. Figure 5.6 illustrates the average monthly payment for $100 of debt by income and racial status. To repay the same amount of debt, families in the bottom 20 percent of the distribution have to pay between two and three times more each month than the families in the top 10 percent. These disparities are driven by high-earners' ability to borrow by pledging collateral, at lower interest rates, and pay back over longer maturities (smaller

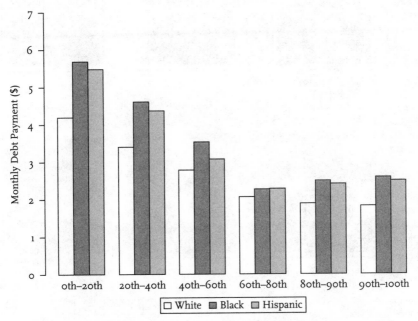

FIGURE 5.6 Average Monthly Payment for Every $100 of Debt

NOTE: Sample excludes households with no debt. White refers to non-Hispanic white. Families with household heads aged <25 or >65 are excluded from the sample. SOURCE: Survey of Consumer Finance 1989–2016, Federal Reserve.

payments for longer periods of time). Black and Hispanic families also pay more than white families with similar income. For instance, middle-class black families, on average, pay $3.56 per month for $100 of debt, while white families in the same income bracket pay just $2.78. The disparity is greatest at the lower end of the income distribution, where black families pay $5.68 to whites' $4.18.

Not only do low-income families pay more for the same amount of debt, debt payment also consumes a larger portion of their paychecks. Figure 5.7 presents the monthly debt payments to monthly income ratio across the six income groups. For each income group, we assign all households to one of the five categories according to their levels of debt burden. The first captures families without debt payments, often because they lack access to credit. The second is those who carry a light debt burden, using under 10 percent of

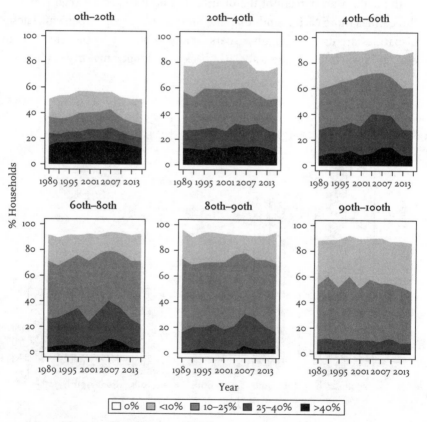

FIGURE 5.7 MONTHLY DEBT PAYMENT TO MONTHLY INCOME RATIO
NOTE: Income includes all sources of household income in the previous year. Families with household heads aged <25 or >65 are excluded from the sample. SOURCE: Survey of Consumer Finance 1989–2016, Federal Reserve.

their income to pay debt. Households with a moderate debt burden, paying between 10 and a quarter of their monthly income in debt obligations, fall in the third category. The fourth is comprised of families who face a heavy debt burden, which drains between 25 and 40 percent of their income. The final category includes families in extreme debt, surrendering more than 40 percent of their income to creditors.

The level of debt burden is most bifurcated at the bottom quintile of the income distribution. About half of low-income households do not make any debt payment, while more than 15 percent face heavy or extreme debt burden. In fact, despite their limited access to credit, these families are more likely to be in extreme debt than families in any other income group. Given these families have little income to begin with, facing a high debt-payment-to-income ratio often means severe difficulty paying for necessities such as food, utilities, and housing.

Moving toward the middle of income distribution, fewer families have extreme levels of debt and more have access to credit. Nevertheless, we also see a larger proportion of families spending a substantial portion of their monthly income on debt services. For example, around 30 percent of middle-income families use more than a quarter of their income to fulfill debt obligations. The proportion increased to almost 40 percent during the credit boom of the 2000s and has since declined to just below 30 percent.

Families in the top quintile are the clear winners in the era of financialization. Like their middle-income counterparts, most of these families borrow. Very few, however, carry unsustainable amounts of debt. For example, only about 2 percent of the families in the top decile pay more than 40 percent of their income for their debt, compared to around 10 percent of the middle-quintile families and about 17 percent of the bottom-quintile families. Most high-income families hit the "sweet spot" by taking on some debt without having to commit a significant portion of their income to debt servicing.

The unequal consequences of debt also manifest in the likelihood of falling behind on payments. Figure 5.8 presents the proportion of debtors who had any payment 60 or more days past due in the last year. Compared to the debt-payment-to-income ratio, late payment is a more extreme but less ambiguous indicator that a family is in financial distress; delinquency is associated with additional interests and fees and is harmful to one's ability to borrow in the future. The figure shows that not only are lower-income families more likely to fall behind on payments when they borrow, this disparity has increased over time. At the bottom of the income distribution, the proportion of late payers increased from 15 percent in 1995 to

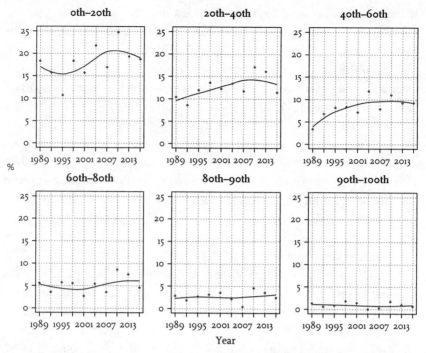

FIGURE 5.8 ANY DEBT PAYMENTS 60+ DAYS PAST DUE IN LAST YEAR AMONG HOUSEHOLDS WITH DEBT

NOTE: Sample excludes households with no debt. The trends are smoothed with local polynomial regression. Income includes all sources of household income in the previous year. Families with household heads aged <25 or >65 are excluded from the sample. SOURCE: Survey of Consumer Finance 1989–2016, Federal Reserve.

more than 20 percent in 2013. The upward trend is not unique: even those with middle-class incomes find it increasingly difficult to pay their debt on time.

As the debt burden snowballs among low- and middle-income families, their wealth begins to melt away. Figure 5.9 presents the proportion of families with negative net worth—meaning they owe more than they own—across the income distribution. It shows that financialization has led to a broad-based erosion of wealth. More families have become insolvent—"underwater"—meaning that the joint value of their home, vehicles, saving, business, and retirement account is less than the total amount of debt they carry. This is most salient among families with middle and lower-middle incomes; the proportion of families with a negative net worth in the former increased from 7 to 15 percent, while that in the latter increased from 10 to almost 20 percent. The bankruptcy reform of 2005 (see Chapter 3) made the financial lives of these families even *less* manageable.

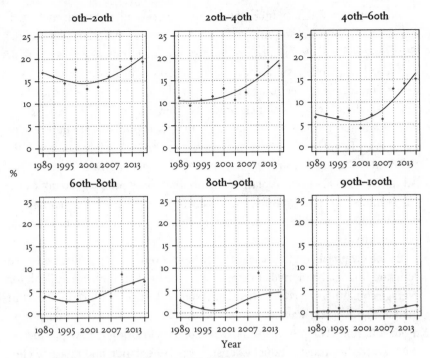

FIGURE 5.9 FAMILIES WITH NEGATIVE NET WORTH

NOTE: Families are classified as with negative worth when their total value of debts exceeds their total value of assets. The trends are smoothed with local polynomial regression. Income includes all sources of household income in the previous year. Families with household heads aged <25 or >65 are excluded from the sample. SOURCE: Survey of Consumer Finance 1989–2016, Federal Reserve.

But They Are Adults

Some argue that the excessive debt burden carried by American families is not a supply- but a demand-side problem—too few borrowers are equipped with adequate financial skills. Indeed, a recent national survey shows that a quarter of Americans have difficulty calculating interest payments and 40 percent of them do not understand the concept of inflation (Lin et al. 2016). In this conception, financial illiteracy is the cause of families living beyond their means, and the clear remedy is consumer education rather than government regulation. Governmental agencies, such as the Office of Financial Education and the Financial Literacy and Education Commission, were established to advance these financial skills, and April was designated "National Financial Literacy Month." Even corporations such as Home Depot and Delta Air Lines provide financial wellness programs to their employees so as to improve their "financial fitness."

Advocates for financial literacy have been successful, not in promoting financial knowledge among Americans, but in setting a different standard for financial products. When it comes to most products consumers use in their everyday lives, from toys, food, appliances, cars, and furniture to an ever-expanding variety of electronic devices, manufacturers and retailers are held responsible for the safety of their products. They are expected to issue voluntary recalls and refunds when they learn that their products are defective or hazardous. Regulators such as the Consumer Product Safety Commission, the Food and Drug Administration, and the National Highway Traffic Safety Administration are even in place to ensure that these products do not cause harm under normal circumstances. Nowhere are consumers harmed by such products castigated for their lack of chemistry, mechanics, electronics, or carpentry literacy.

So the emphasis on financial literacy looks even more peculiar when we compare financial and medicinal products side by side. Both are difficult for average consumers to comprehend and should be used with caution and in moderation, yet the ways these two products are distributed could not be more different. For pharmaceutical companies to bring a new product to the market, they must conduct extensive experimentation and repeated clinical trials to establish its effectiveness. The Food and Drug Administration then assesses whether the product's benefit outweighs its harm and gives approval only to those products that meet their high standard. To purchase potentially harmful medicine, consumers are required to visit a physician, who conducts medical exams, selects the appropriate product, and provides a prescription. A pharmacist then independently evaluates the suitability of that medicine and supplies the consumers with instructions and information about potential adverse reactions. Should harm arise, medical practitioners, pharmacists, and drug companies are required to report those harms to the FDA; in extreme cases, drugs are pulled from the market.

The consumer financial market operates in an almost opposite fashion. While there are also laws and governmental agencies to prevent discriminatory, predatory, or deceptive practices, interventions rarely take place. When regulations are enforced, it is generally on an ad hoc basis and only after the product has caused widespread harm. Financial services firms are allowed to create and sell "innovative" products without considering their consequences or ensuring that they provide more good than harm. Compounding the issue, financial companies are *incentivized* to promote harmful or even addictive products, since these bring the highest profits and the forced arbitration clauses hidden in many contracts prevent victims from pursuing justice collectively. The conventional wisdom, at least before the 2008 financial crisis, was that inferior products would not survive the test of market. Thus, most regulations focus on increasing the transparency of financial products and encouraging comparison shopping. However, only resourceful consumers have access to independent professionals. Most are expected to be their own "doctor," deciding which financial medicine to take when they are under great distress; and generally the patient is blamed should things go wrong.

Moreover, promoting financial literacy above financial regulation avoids the reality that many families' incomes are now highly volatile (Western, Bloome, and Percheski 2008). Compounded with unexpected expenses when their cars break down or water pipes burst, it is often trying for poor or near-poor families to budget and save for long-term goals. Ingenious coping strategies are developed by these families to make extra income, cut expenses, and preserve savings. Where these measures are insufficient to make ends meet, these families get by through emergency borrowing, either from friends of families or high-interest lenders (Morduch and Schneider 2017).

Summary

The financialization of the US economy not only manifests on Wall Street and in the boardrooms of large corporations, but also among American families. This chapter examined the origins, distribution, and consequences of household debt since the 1980s. We contrasted two dominant perspectives: one in which booming household debt is seen as an unsustainable, if not destructive, solution for wage stagnation and rising inequality, and another in which it is seen as a positive development, indicating that more American families are taking advantage of declining interest rates and a growing variety of financial services to advance their standard of living.

These broad-stroke accounts mask the unequal distribution of debt and debt burden by which the meaning and consequence of debt vary significantly across American families. Affluent households still capture the lion's share of credit in the era of financialization. The expansion of credit provides them with the opportunity to invest or meet short-term financial need with low cost. Meanwhile, middle- and low-income households carry the heaviest debt burdens. Accordingly, a policy of expanding household debt has become a regressive system that benefits the rich and devastates the poor.

We traced the evolution of consumer finance back to the turn of the 20th century, during which progressive reformists, industrialists, and politicians began to view consumer credit as necessary to mitigate the financial hardship and political turmoil of a fast-changing economy. This belief was solidified in the postwar era, as the state, manufacturers, and labor activists came to see credit as a means of promoting mobility into middle-class lifestyles and spurring economic growth. Even though finance played an increasingly significant role in American life, the level of household debt remained largely stable during this period.

The 1980s marked a watershed in the growth of consumer finance. The deregulation of interest rates and the securitization of debt created favorable conditions for banks and other lenders to expand their credit offerings. The influx of foreign capital and the stagnation of wage growth only fueled this upward trend. American families began to increase their usage of debt in both quantity and variety, with the eager, bipartisan support of politicians holding to the century-old belief that offering liquidity will solve the problem of inequality.

Indeed, financialization increased the share of debt held by low-income households, but it did not lead to the "democratization" of credit. The majority of household credit in the United States is still captured by a tenth of American families. The distribution is most skewed in the residential loan market, where the top fifth of American families receives about half of the credit. Even in the education loan market, where low-income borrowing is subsidized, the bottom 40 percent of families only obtain around 35 percent of available student loans. We see no evidence that borrowing has become easier for low-income and minority families over time.

Credit is a game for the rich: they borrow the most and it costs them the least. Low-income families pay more than the high-income families for the same amount of debt, and being a minority comes with additional penalty. As a result, low-income families are most likely to be in extreme debt even when they are least able to borrow. Beyond the bottom of the income distribution, we observe a steady increase in debt burden among middle-class families. More Americans are unable to meet their obligations on time, except those with abundant resources in the first place. As a result, increasing numbers of families have become insolvent, owning less than what they owe. Taken together, in all its iterations, the expansion of household debt has been a cause of, rather than a solution to, inequality.

CHAPTER 6

A People's Portfolio of the
United States

FINANCIALIZATION MOVES EXPONENTIALLY, TRANSFERRING an escalating amount of resources from workers to Wall Street. But Wall Street's "winners" are not abstract. They are concrete organizations and individuals that represent and act in the economic interests of affluent American families. As resources are redistributed from financial outsiders to insiders, however, tangible assets and business profits are actually less significant in generating wealth for the rich than the cultivation of a diverse portfolio of financial assets. The simple fact of having a seat at the high rollers' table amasses money in their coffers. To a much lesser extent, middle-class families also have a stake in the stock market, tying their economic securities to the action on the floor of a virtual stock exchange. And for everyone else, the ante is much too high—they are left out of the big money game. Access to the stock market is now central to American households' wealth accumulation, and differential access is largely responsible for the extreme wealth gap across households.

The previous chapter examined the origin of and recent trends in household debt. We showed that the rapid expansion of credit since the 1980s has been a cause of rather than a solution to inequality. The influx of credit has allowed affluent households to gain financial flexibility, while middle-class and low-income families face heavier debt burdens and struggle to make ends meet, let alone improve their financial well-being and build wealth.

In this chapter, we look at the other side of the coin, focusing on how finance has transformed household wealth—a trend with long-term implications for how social class inequality becomes entrenched. We first review the uneven distribution of wealth in the United States. Wealth inequality has risen since the last quarter of the 20th century. Today, fewer American families have sufficient means to accumulate wealth over time, and the concentration of capital in the hands of a select few has widened the fault line between the richest and the rest. And it isn't just about money: wealth is strongly associated with a wide range of improved life outcomes from education to marriage, health, and longevity. Its transferability ensures that such advantages are passed down from one generation to the next, refocusing our attention on the fact that Americans do not start their lives from a place of equality.

Certainly, financial assets drive much of the wealth divide. Not only do stocks and bonds constitute a higher proportion of affluent families' portfolios, the importance of other financial assets has grown over time. A parallel increase is observed for the remaining upper half of the wealth distribution, but to a much less extent. For those in the bottom half, however, wealth has not become financialized; if these families have any wealth to speak of, it is stored in tangible assets such as homes and motor vehicles, rather than in financial portfolios.

Thus, like access to credit, the democratization of the stock market—the shift to what has been called the "ownership society"—is more slogan than practice. Households in the top 10 percent of the wealth distribution own about 80 percent of the equity market (if we count only those stocks owned by Americans). The racial gap has expanded in the past 30 years, with white households allocating a higher proportion of their assets to the stock market than black households. Financial firms managing these assets profit from the high concentration of wealth and the wealth divides among families. The emerging global network of financial-legal services, in the meantime, enables affluent families to retain a greater amount of wealth through both legitimate and criminal tax avoidance.

This chapter also examines how the distribution of wealth has changed across generations—more precisely, what social scientists call "cohorts." That is, wealth for the baby boomer generation differs greatly from wealth among the millennials. Since wealth accumulation develops over the course of a person's life (Killewald, Pfeffer, and Schachner 2017), we pay particular attention to families in young adulthood and near retirement. Most young adults today possess less wealth than their predecessors. The significant growth in wealth is seen among families entering retirement (except those at the bottom). We find that across these generations wealth inequality has consistently widened for both sets of families. These developments show that the tension between capital and labor has been reinscribed as tensions between privileged and marginalized workers and between older and younger generations.

The Wealth of Families

Like income inequality, the trajectory of wealth inequality has followed a clear U-curve over the past century. The early 1900s was marked by acute inequality: the top 0.1 percent of American families owned about a fourth of total national wealth (Saez and Zucman 2016). The aftermath of the Great Crash of 1929 and the massive destruction of two world wars served as leveling factors, narrowing the divide between the haves and have-nots. Inequality remained at a lower level from the 1950s to the 1970s, during which the bottom 90 percent were able to increase their share of national wealth from 20 to 35 percent. The trend reversed in the 1980s. While the total national wealth continued to increase, nearly all the profits from the boom were captured by the wealthiest 20 percent. Other households experienced declines—both absolute and relative—in wealth (Keister 2000b).

The increasing concentration of wealth among the rich did not simply mean that some people could afford fancier cars, sail on luxurious boats, or live in grandiose mansions. These "lifestyles of the rich and famous" visions dominate portrayals in television and film, but the majority of the top 10 percent do not, in fact, spend much of their money on extravagances. Wealth inequality is less a matter of *luxury* than it is of *opportunity*. As the very richest accumulate more wealth, rather than spending it on frivolities, they hoard their wealth, transferring it to subsequent generations along with all the improved life chances wealth signals. By "life chances," we refer to the resources and opportunities provided to a person, shaping her quality of life and ability to change it.

So the significance of wealth begins at birth. Early exposure to wealth substantially improves your financial standing for your *entire* life.[1] Affluent parents make greater investments in child care, educational goods, and enrichment activities for their young children. In fact, the rich have tripled these kinds of parental investments since the 1970s. Their monthly spending per child increased from around $700 in 1972 to more than $2,500 in 2012, adjusted for inflation (Kornrich 2016; Kornrich and Furstenberg 2013). Families with fewer economic resources cannot keep up, and so a considerable developmental gap emerges between those young children whose families are well off and those who are less privileged. Income inequality exacerbates this dynamic. In contexts with higher income inequality, high-earning parents are able to continually increase their investment in child-rearing, perhaps spurred by the perception that rising inequality raises the stakes and the likelihood of residential segregation by income (Schneider,

Hastings, and LaBriola 2018). For the affluent, keeping up with the Joneses has become keeping ahead of the Joneses.

The disparity continues to expand as children attend school. Children from wealthy families attend public or private schools with more resources (often fueled by higher tax bases), populated by similarly high-achieving peers. School-age children's cognitive development, particularly math scores (Friedline, Masa, and Chowa 2015; Yeung and Conley 2008), is more advanced when they come from wealth, and so these children are more likely to apply, be admitted to, and complete their bachelor's degrees at selective colleges (Jez 2014; Lovenheim and Reynolds 2013). While part of the association between wealth and these educational outcomes could be attributed to the intergenerational transmission of parental traits that promote both wealth accumulation and educational advancement, the wealth effects remain robust even when researchers adjust their studies to take such traits into consideration (Doren and Grodsky 2016).

The disparity in parental investments is especially pronounced when adult children begin to establish their own households, careers, and families. In this later phase, sociologist Thomas Shapiro (2004) finds that the transfer of family wealth through assistance with a down payment on a house or tuition to attend college is rarely recognized as "inheritance" or having an unfair advantage; it is downplayed by its recipients as getting "a little help" from their parents. Shapiro calls these forms of inherited wealth "transformative assets" because such wealth is so central to class status, affecting whether you form a family, own or rent a home, where you live, the schools your children attend, and so much more (Addo 2014; Benton and Keister 2017; Nau, Dwyer, and Hodson 2015).

The transferability of wealth also explains part of the persistent economic inequality and residential segregation between black and white households (Conley 2010). Inherited wealth, along with its associated educational and housing advantages, allows whites to outperform black households when it comes to homeownership and labor market outcomes (Charles and Hurst 2002). Since white adults tend to receive wealth early in life, they are more able and likely to invest in financial assets that generate additional wealth throughout the life course (Keister 2004). Black young adults, in contrast, take on substantially more debt than their white counterparts, which severely limits their ability to own a home or start a family (Addo, Houle, and Simon 2016).

What drives up wealth inequality in the United States? Obviously, the increasing concentration of earnings plays a significant role in funneling economic resources into the hands of few. Despite being able to afford a comfortable lifestyle, high-wage households are able to save and invest between 30 and 50 percent of their earnings. They can transform income into profitable assets while so many other American families make barely enough to stay out of the red (Dynan, Skinner, and Zeldes 2004; Saez and Zucman 2016). Financialization has tremendously increased the rate of return on these investments (Piketty 2014), allowing the wealthy to *further* improve their children's life chances. As a result, income inequality increases and polarizes wealth disparities from one generation to the next.

A series of tax cuts enacted since the 1970s have figured into this self-reinforcing cycle. The effective tax rate for the top 1 percent was around 42 percent in the mid-20th century but has more recently declined to around 36 percent (Piketty, Saez, and Zucman 2017). And when wealth changes hands, the tax burden has lessened dramatically: the estate tax exemption increased from $0.27 million per inheritor (adjusted for inflation) in 1976 to $11.18 million in 2018, while the top rate decreased from 77 to 40 percent. You may know this tax as "the death tax," and it affects direct inheritances; a higher exemption means those receiving inheritances keep a larger slice of the pie. Similarly, cash gifts were once taxed at 70 percent in excess of $5 million over the course of the donor's lifetime. Now the rate stands at only 40 percent. Such reductions allow high earners to retain more economic resources and enable wealthy parents or grandparents to pass down most, if not all, their assets to their children and grandchildren.

Multiply and Preserve Wealth through Finance

Thanks to these tax reductions, the top 1 percent can invest more of their money in financial markets, elevating wealth inequality. Sociologist Lisa Keister (2000b) argues that the greater concentration of wealth among the rich is driven, in part, by differences in how the upper and middle classes invest their money. Affluent families can afford volatility, and so they are more likely to invest their wealth in high-risk, high-yield financial assets. Since financialization began, stock market booms (Figure 4.4) have brought extraordinary returns to these households (Nau 2013). The middle class, on the other hand, preserves most of its wealth in real estate, which yields a lower return and is difficult to liquidate.

Wealth inequality has been attended by an intensifying difference in asset allocation. Figure 6.1 shows the portfolios of households in the top 1 percent, the next 9 percent, the next 40 percent, and the bottom 50 percent of the wealth distribution between 1989 and 2016. Among the top 1 percent

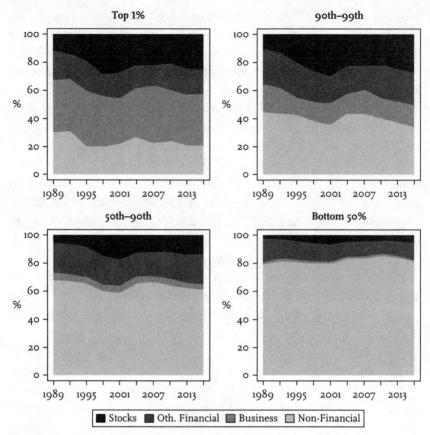

FIGURE 6.1 ASSET ALLOCATION BY WEALTH

NOTE: **Stocks** includes directly held stock, stock mutual funds, retirement accounts, annuities, and trusts. For combination assets and financial vehicles (e.g., stock + bond), the SCF divides the total value to compute the value of stock for each item. **Other Financial** assets include all other financial assets such as accounts and bonds. **Business** interests include both actively and non-actively managed businesses. **Nonfinancial** assets include vehicles, value of primary residence, value of other residential real estate, and net equity in nonresidential real estate. SOURCE: Survey of Consumer Finance 1989–2016, Federal Reserve.

of households, an average of about 37 percent of assets are devoted to business endeavors; that is, private business ownership remains the key source of wealth for the wealthiest families. Since the mid-1990s, however, financial assets have surpassed business interests, rising from around 32 percent of the wealthiest families' total assets in 1989 to 42 percent in 2016. Stock ownership doubled from 12 percent to a quarter of total assets in the same period, while nonfinancial assets, such as cars and homes, declined in significance, falling from 30 to only 20 percent of the top 1 percent's holdings.

We see similar trends among families in the rest of the top decile, though they invest much less in business endeavors than their peers at the very top.

Stocks constituted around 10 percent of their portfolios in 1989 but have since expanded to 28 percent, with total financial assets increasing from 36 to 51 percent. Again, tangible assets such as motor vehicles and real estate became less crucial, declining from 45 to 34 percent.

As we look down the line, similar trends are observed among the next 40 percent, whose stocks and total financial assets increased from 6 and 27 percent to 15 and 35 percent, respectively, from 1989 to 2016. But then we look to the bottom half.

In contrast to upper-half households, those in the bottom half did not see wealth become financialized. The importance of stocks increased slightly from 2.5 to 5.3 percent for these households in our focal period, yet the share of total financial assets actually declined from 20 to 18 percent. Nonfinancial assets still constitute the vast majority of these families' wealth—around 80 percent of their total assets. Put differently, the least wealthy 50 percent do not have surplus to invest in their families' futures; they must use what resources they have to acquire a house for stability and a car to get by. These assets are necessities that help stabilize families' lives, but they do very little toward accumulating wealth.

Despite an overall increase in American stock ownership, participation in the stock market has remained highly unequal. Studies have identified that, compared to whites, black families are less likely to invest in risky but high-yield assets (Keister 2000a; Stevenson and Plath 2002). Figure 6.2 estimates the amount of stock owned by black and white families in 1989 and 2016. Similar to Figure 6.1, it shows that stock ownership is positively associated with wealth and has expanded between 1989 and 2016. Nevertheless, compared to white families, affluent black families invest less in the stock market. The clear racial gap we see in 1989 has expanded over time, particularly at the upper end of the wealth distribution. These numbers suggest that progress toward a more equal and equitable distribution of financial resources among white and black families has not only stalled, it has potentially regressed in the era of big finance.

Racial disparities arise from many factors, including both discrimination in the financial sector and the financial decisions of peers (Gutter and Fontes 2006; Hong, Kubik, and Stein 2004). Enduring discriminatory practices, such as the high-interest loans and residential redlining explored in the last chapter, could, in fact, lead minority households to distrust financial institutions. Racism in marketing campaigns could also reduce the exposure and access of black households to financial services. Again, as we saw in the last chapter, excluding people from home loan advertisements based on race/ethnicity, religion, nationality, age, family status, and disability violates the

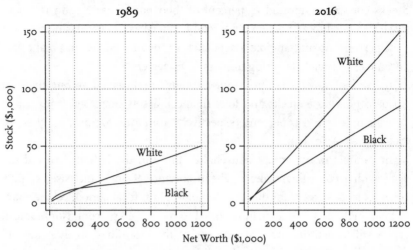

FIGURE 6.2 ESTIMATED STOCK OWNERSHIP BY RACE AND WEALTH

NOTE: Sample includes all households with positive net worth. Stocks include both directly and indirectly held equity. The estimates account for the sex of household head, family structure, logged family income, education, and age. These characteristics are held at their population means. Thus, the figures underestimate the stockholding of high-net-worth households and overestimate that of low-net-worth households. SOURCE: Survey of Consumer Finance 1989–2016, Federal Reserve.

federal Fair Housing Act of 1968 and the Fair Housing Act Amendments Act of 1988, yet lenders continue to racially target some and exclude other prospective borrowers. A 2016 public outcry erupted when it was revealed that Facebook offered housing advertisers the ability to filter users based on race and ethnicity (Noble 2018), but it certainly didn't mean advertisers hadn't been doing that before Facebook. Peer effects come into play when even distant painful memories of negative racial experiences are sustained and amplified through social interaction with friends, coworkers, and neighbors, or passed down from one generation to another.

Saving for retirement is another key avenue through which wealth disparities persist. Defined-contribution plans, which distribute financial risks to individual workers, have become the dominant retirement vehicle among American workers (replacing the pensions that provided stability to many postwar families). Few workers enroll in these voluntary plans, however, and so they lose both access to financial markets and retirement benefits (Morrissey 2016; see also Figure 4.6). Using administrative records, sociologists Christopher Tamborini and ChangHwan Kim (2017) find that many eligible workers do not participate because they simply cannot afford the monthly contribution. In contrast, high earners participate at high rates and set aside more money, taking advantage of tax deductions and matching contributions from their employers. Their ability to do so not only builds retirement accounts, it means their total compensation is actually higher than even differences in hourly pay or salary would indicate.

Indeed, the concentration of stock ownership in the hands of a select few is even greater than the concentration of wealth overall. Figure 6.3 charts the proportion of stocks owned by the families in the top 1 percent, the next 9 percent, and the bottom 90 percent of the wealth distribution (including directly held stocks as well as stocks held through mutual funds, hedge funds, retirement accounts, and other investment vehicles). One percent of U.S. families control around 40 percent of the equity market owned by Americans, and the next 9 percent take another 40 percent. The bottom 90 percent of families, together, own only about 20 percent of the total stock ownership. More importantly, stock ownership has become even more concentrated among the rich in recent years, countering the theory that retirement investment vehicles such as 401(k) and IRAs might democratize the stock market. Clearly, reality is again distant from rhetoric: what investment

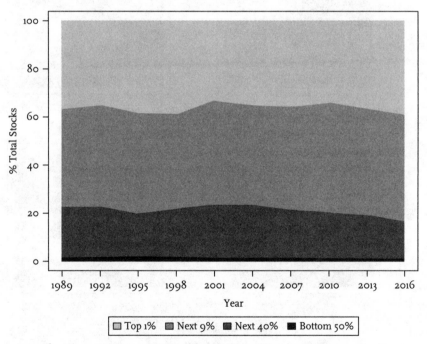

FIGURE 6.3 DISTRIBUTION OF STOCK OWNERSHIP BY WEALTH GROUPS

NOTE: The estimates include directly held stock, stock mutual funds, retirement accounts, annuities, and trusts. For combination assets and financial vehicles (e.g., stock + bond), the SCF divides the total value to compute the value of stock for each item. SOURCE: Survey of Consumer Finance 1989–2016, Federal Reserve.

firms promote is not the savings of hard-working, middle-class Americans but mostly the wealth of the wealthiest.

Notably, financial institutions increasingly mediate how households participate in the stock market. Figure 6.4 contrasts the proportion of stock directly held by American families with the proportion held via managing entities such as mutual and hedge funds. Across the wealth spectrum, American families have decreased the proportion of equity they directly own, and instead have their investments managed by professionals. Consistently, the most privileged families have delegated rising shares of their sizable investments in the stock market to fund managers. Managed equity, as a portion of wealth families' total equity, increased from 40 percent to 75 percent over the past 30 years, while direct stock ownership

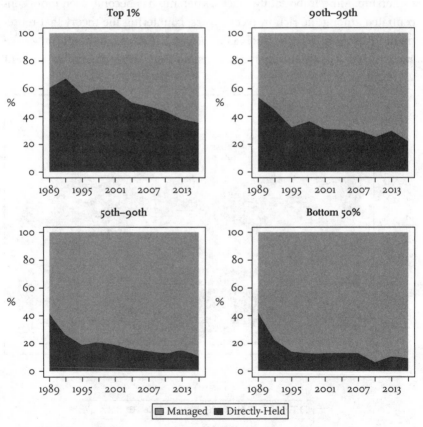

FIGURE 6.4 DIRECTLY HELD AND MANAGED EQUITY BY WEALTH GROUPS
NOTE: The estimates include directly held stock, stock mutual funds, retirement accounts, annuities, and trusts. For combination assets and financial vehicles (e.g., stock + bond), the SCF divides the total value to compute the value of stock for each item. SOURCE: Survey of Consumer Finance 1989–2016, Federal Reserve.

hovers around 10 percent of the portfolios of the bottom 90 percent of the wealth distribution (in 2016). These trends question whether "market populism," the idea that a growing number of Americans are actively picking stocks for investment (Harrington 2008), actually emerges beyond the small circle of amateur investors and, if so, how prevalent and successful they are.

In addition to generating greater return for economic elites, a growing wealth management industry developed to preserve elite's wealth and avoid holding them accountable. Sociologist Brook Harrington (2016) spent over eight years studying the global industry, finding that wealth managers work as financial architects. They design a complex set of financial-legal structures to prevent taxes, debts, fees, penalties, and alimony from reducing their clients' wealth. Offshore banks accounts, shell corporations, foundations, and trusts are used to separate the rights from the obligations of controlling wealth. Apart from helping the rich obscure ownership and evade responsibility for tax liabilities and culpability for wrongdoing, individual wealth managers and their trade associations help institutionalize wealth inequality by lobbying to adapt international tax and legal codes in support of their clients' interests.

How much wealth is hidden away from the public eye? Exploring the discrepancy between recorded liabilities and identifiable assets, economist Gabriel Zucman (2013) estimates that more than $4.5 trillion, or 6 percent of global financial wealth, has no traceable owner. The figure is two or three times larger if you include physical assets like precious metals, antiques, artwork, and real estate (Palan, Murphy, and Chavagneux 2013). Families in the United States alone store more than $1 trillion of their financial wealth offshore, almost half of it in Caribbean tax heavens (Alstadsæter, Johannesen, and Zucman 2018). Official accounts underestimate levels of wealth inequality, and the extent to which resources actually trickle *out* rather than *down*.

As wealth compounds for a select few, major banks like Bank of America, JPMorgan Chase, and Wells Fargo queue up to cater to the needs and demands of high-net-worth clients. Seeking the profits that come from the wealthiest clients, banks provide full service for select individuals: portfolio management, estate planning, and tax and legal advice can all be had for a fee calculated as a percentage of the assets under management. In recent years, wealth management has brought in around 21 percent of Bank of America's total revenue, for a pretax profit margin of 27 percent, and more than 12 percent of JPMorgan Chase's total revenue (with even higher returns). The social costs of these services remain uncountable.

Thus far, we have discussed overall trends in inequality and how financialization has helped to concentrate wealth among the richest. A key omission concerns how wealth is accumulated over the course of your life. That is, the *importance* of wealth varies depending on where you are in your life course. The "haves" could be families near the conclusion of their working lives. Rather than affording them luxury, wealth provides economic security when careers have ended and end-of-life care means mounting costs. So, too, could many of the "have-nots" be young families at the beginning of their careers, having foregone earnings in exchange for developing their human capital in school, knowing that this invisible asset will later return higher earnings and greater wealth. In other words, rising wealth inequality *could* simply reflect differing rates of accumulation throughout the life cycle, and the variation of wealth in each cohort might remain stable.

To see whether and how the wealth divide has changed between and within cohorts, this section focuses on disparities in wealth among households with heads aged 30–34 and among households with heads aged 60–64. The former are in the beginning of their adulthood, likely to have completed their formal education and just begun to build their wealth, perhaps by buying their first home or opening a retirement savings plan. The latter are in or approaching retirement, close to the peak of their wealth accumulation. We trace how wealth has changed among these families across a set of six-year birth cohorts. By contextualizing wealth in specific life stages, we gain better insight into how wealth inequality has impacted the lives of American families.

Millennial Wealth Slump

We start by focusing on the wealth distribution among households with heads aged 30–34, who capture the older end of the millennial generation. Figure 6.4 presents the net worth at the 95th, 90th, 75th, 50th, 25th, and 10th percentiles for four different cohorts of people born between 1965 and 1982. To compare wealth over time, we adjust all amounts to 2016 dollars. To account for the delay of marriage (Fitch and Ruggles 2000; Goldstein and Kenney 2001), we divide the net worth of married or cohabitated couples by two to obtain a measure of wealth per individual.[2]

Figure 6.5 shows that, while young wealth grew steadily across the cohorts born before the mid-1970s, it has dropped significantly for those who were born around 1980. The 95th percentile decreased from \$323,000 for the

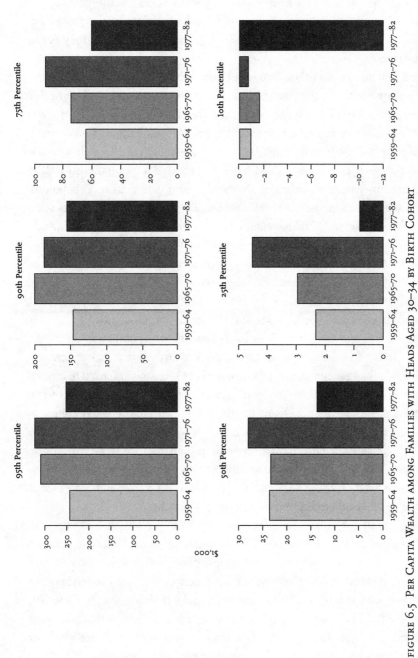

FIGURE 6.5 PER CAPITA WEALTH AMONG FAMILIES WITH HEADS AGED 30–34 BY BIRTH COHORT

NOTE: The sample is restricted to households with heads aged 30–34. All amounts are inflation-adjusted to the 2016 dollar. To account for the delay of marriage and the increase in divorce, the net worth of married couples is divided by two. SOURCE: Survey of Consumer Finance 1989–2016, Federal Reserve.

1971–1976 cohort to $252,000 for the 1977–1982 generation. The 90th percentile declined from $187,000 to $155,000. The contraction of wealth was even more apparent in the middle and lower halves of the distribution, with median wealth halving from $28,000 to $14,000 and the 25th percentile nearly evaporating with a drop from $4,500 to $800. At the bottom, the most recent cohort is more heavily indebted than their predecessors—at least 10 percent of this generation owed $12,000 or more when they began their careers.

The millennials' wealth slump is not inexplicable. Compared to the cohort of people who began their careers during the 1990s economic boom, this cohort entered the labor force during the worst recession since World War II. Many struggled to find employment opportunities that matched their education, and so they were trapped in lower-wage jobs. This wage downgrade could last as long as 10 years, and it can be expected to permanently reduce their lifetime earnings and their ability to accumulate wealth (Oreopoulos, von Wachter, and Heisz 2012). Millennials also carry the largest education debt of any cohort in US history. Lenders, educators, and policymakers all told them that an investment in education would yield higher future earnings—indeed, that was true for nearly all earlier generations. But millennials' massive student debt actually extended the lower tail of wealth distribution and shaped the options available to young adults as they planned their careers, formed families, and began to save for the future (Houle 2014).

Figure 6.6 shows that student loans have gained popularity across the four cohorts. The share of households carrying any student loans increased from around 20 percent among those born between 1959 and 1970 to around 30 percent for those born between 1971 and 1976. The prevalence of student loans exceeded 40 percent for the 1977–1983 cohort. Each cohort of borrowers took out more loans than the previous one. Adjusted to 2016 dollars, the median postgraduation student loan balance was only $3,000 for those born in 1954–1964 and around $5,500 for those who born in 1965–1970. The figure exceeded $9,000 for the following cohort and increased to more than $11,000 among those born in 1977–1982.

The payoff for education borrowing did not increase in lockstep with the increase in loan amounts. When comparing annual income between borrowers and nonborrowers, we see little difference for cohorts born in 1970 or earlier. This is expected: college-related expenses remained stable between 1960 and 1986 and were affordable to even many middle-class families.[3] The benefit of taking out student loans became significant for those born between 1971 and 1976—the first cohort to encounter rising tuitions. Those who took out student loans earned higher median annual incomes—almost $12,000

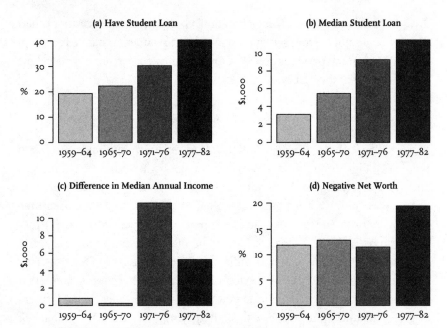

FIGURE 6.6 WEALTH CHARACTERISTICS, FAMILIES WITH HEADS AGED 30–34 BY
BIRTH COHORT

NOTE: The sample is restricted to households with heads aged 30–34. All amounts are
inflation-adjusted to the 2016 dollar. Median student loan sample includes only those who
were currently carrying student loans. To account for the delay of marriage and the increase
in divorce, the income of married couples is divided by two. SOURCE: Survey of Consumer
Finance 1989–2016, Federal Reserve.

higher—than their peers without student loans. The next cohort, nevertheless, did not share the same fortune. The median annual income among
these borrowers was only $5,000 higher than those who did not borrow. The
reduction is likely due to both the Great Recession and efforts to make loans
more accessible to students from less well-off families. There are also more
borrowers who dropped out before finishing their degrees. The combination
of larger volumes of student loans and lower returns to borrowing makes
the millennials the poorest generation in recent history. A fifth of this cohort
remained "underwater" (still owing student loans and having total negative
net worth) when they reached their early thirties. That had been true for only
about 12 percent of the previous three cohorts.

Overall, wealth accumulation is already more challenging for early
millennials, and we expect it to get even harder as later millennials, who
entered the labor force during the recession, carry even greater debt. Except
for those at the top, likely to receive wealth from their parents, this cohort
owns less and owes more than previous generations. Together, a recession
brought on by the financial sector and a massive expansion in student loans

drive their wealth slump. This generation's borrowers still earn more than those who did not borrow, but the payout of taking out loans has reduced significantly from the previous cohort. Consequently, 20 percent of this cohort had no wealth in their early thirties.

From Shared Growth to Diverging Destinies

We now turn to the wealth distribution among retiring households. Similar to Figure 6.5, Figure 6.7 shows the net worth at the 95th, 90th, 75th, 50th, 25th, and 10th percentiles for those born between 1929 and 1952 when they were 60–64 years old. We see a broad-based increase in wealth for the first three retiring cohorts. The wealth at the 95th percentile expanded from $1.1 million for those born 1929–1934 to $2.3 million for those born 1941–1946, and even the wealth at the 10th percentile grew (from $4,400 to $6,000). This growth reflects a multitude of developments during the economic boom that began after World War II and lasted for almost three decades. Rural farmers migrated to towns and cities with better-paying jobs. A growing share of women participated in the labor force. Workers became more educated and productive. And, perhaps most importantly, strong labor unions ensured that economic growth was distributed equitably. This era has been heralded as a period of shared prosperity, although not everyone benefited equally.

Notably, upper and middle families in the 1935–1946 cohorts accumulated their wealth during the long bull markets of the 1980s and 1990s. In the 20 years between January 1980 and December 2000, the S&P 500 index grew more than tenfold, rising from 114.16 to 1,366.01, with an annualized return of 12 percent (adjusting for inflation). Families who invested in the stock market rode a golden escalator—their wealth doubled every six years. Tax cuts enacted from the late 1970s onward allowed them to retain more wealth. As a result, equity became a more significant component of these families' wealth. Figure 6.8a documents the rise of stock ownership across birth cohorts. It shows that stocks constituted only 8 percent of wealth for those born in 1929–1934 at the 75th percentile but expanded to more than 22 percent among subsequent cohorts. As a result, these families' financial security was more and more dependent on the performance of the stock market.

Broad-based wealth growth ended for the cohort born between 1947 and 1952, who joined the workforce at the close of shared prosperity and the dawn of financialization. While the net worth of households at the upper end remained on par with the previous cohorts, wealth fell significantly for those in the middle and lower half. The median net worth dropped from $196,000

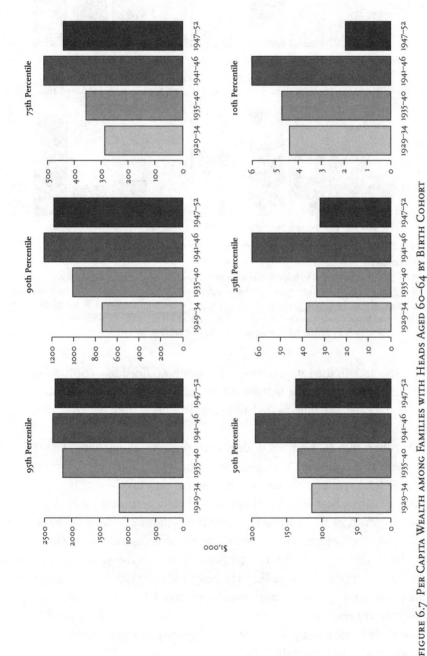

FIGURE 6.7 PER CAPITA WEALTH AMONG FAMILIES WITH HEADS AGED 60–64 BY BIRTH COHORT

NOTE: The sample is restricted to households with heads aged 60–64. All amounts are inflation-adjusted to the 2016 dollar. To account for the delay of marriage and the increase in divorce, the net worth of married couples is divided by two. SOURCE: Survey of Consumer Finance 1989–2016, Federal Reserve.

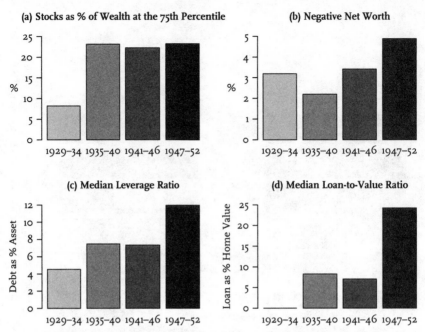

(a) Stocks as % of Wealth at the 75th Percentile

(b) Negative Net Worth

(c) Median Leverage Ratio

(d) Median Loan-to-Value Ratio

FIGURE 6.8 WEALTH CHARACTERISTICS, FAMILIES WITH HEADS AGED 60–64 BY BIRTH COHORT

NOTE: The sample is restricted to households with heads aged 60–64. Stocks include both directly and indirectly held equity. Leverage ratio is calculated as the total value of debt divided by total assets. (Combined) loan-to-value ratio is calculated as the total value of debt secured by the primary residence divided by the total value of primary residence and among homeowners only. SOURCE: Survey of Consumer Finance 1989–2016, Federal Reserve.

to $138,000 and, in the 10th percentile, net worth declined from $6,000 to $2,000 (Figure 6.7). As the bottom fell out, the share of households that were "underwater" as they neared retirement jumped from 3.4 to almost 5 percent (Figure 6.8b).

This cohort also took up more debt than previous generations. Figure 6.8C presents the median leverage ratio, calculated as a household's total debts over total assets. It shows that the median ratio was less than 5 percent for the cohort born 1929–1934 but more than 12 percent for those born 1947–1952. Much of this borrowing came in the form of additional loans on mortgages, in which families used their homes as collateral. Figure 6.8D shows that the majority of homeowners born 1929–1934 had paid off their mortgages by the time they reached their early sixties. In contrast, homeowners born 1947–1952 still carried a substantial amount of debt tied to their primary residence in this stage of their lives. Half owed a quarter or more of their home's value when counting mortgages, home equity loans, and home equity lines of credit.

In sum, the wealth of retiring families has expanded over time. Individuals born before 1946 were likely to accumulate more wealth than their parents had by the same ages. Much of this expansion was driven by the postwar economic boom and, for upper- and middle-class families, the high-return stock market. Yet the bottom began to fall out for those who were born in 1947 or later. This cohort was more likely than their predecessors to exit prime working age without sufficient savings. Additionally, debt gained prominence among this cohort. The debt-to-asset and loan-to-home-value ratios both increased dramatically compared to previous cohorts. As such, the wealth of these families had become more sensitive to changing interest rates.

Summary

In the era of big finance, the proliferation of financial investment vehicles has revolutionized how households manage their wealth, and this has entrenched social class inequality over time. In this chapter, we examined how inequality among families has been exacerbated by a symbiotic relationship between two primary beneficiaries of financialization: affluent families who amass fortunes in the stock market and the investment managers who invest their riches. Access to the stock market is restricted to the extremely wealthy, highly paid workers, and baby boomers with retirement accounts. Thus, the tension between capital and labor has surfaced as a new and growing tension between privileged and marginal workers, between older and younger generations.

The uneven distribution of US wealth has widened over the last 45 years. Compared to the era of shared prosperity immediately after World War II, fewer American families today have sufficient means to accumulate wealth. The concentration of capital among the top has created a two-tiered society with a pronounced fault line between the richest and the rest. The systemic inequality underpinning American capitalism ensures that affluent families have better life outcomes in education, marriage, and even health. Wealth endures because it is transferable: parents and grandparents can pass it down to their children and grandchildren. If the playing field is, indeed, level, then these children are born on first or second base. Wealth inequality not only all but guarantees success for those at the top, it minimizes the chances of upward mobility for the other 90 percent. Unlike incomes, which may leap and fall from year to year, wealth inequality is actually a stable divide that reproduces social class inequality from one generation to the next.

We have also seen that the booming stock market and global financial order provide unprecedented opportunities for the wealthy to grow their fortunes and stash them abroad. Instead of investing in real estate and other tangible assets, today's rich accumulate a diverse portfolio of financial assets and exploit tax loopholes to preserve their wealth for future generations. This drives profits into the coffers of financial and law firms, who manage the rich's fortunes and chart tax laws to retain elites' wealth through both legal and criminal tax avoidance. Meanwhile, middle-class families have turned to the stock market, but to a far lesser extent, and the bulk of Americans have little or no exposure to the risks and potential rewards of the stock market. If they have assets, they are in the form of primary residences and transportation. To them, financial security is a luxury, not a right.

Make no mistake; the notion of an inclusive stock market is a fiction. From 1989 to 2016, the top decile of affluent families owned about 80 percent of the equity market, and their share has increased over time. The racial wealth gap has also widened, partly because white families invest more of their assets in the stock market than black families, even after accounting for overall wealth. Rather than serving as the great leveler, the stock market rewards the haves and the financial professionals who serve them. Financial firms garner high profits from wealth management, capitalizing on the divide between the rich and the poor.

Finally, we have shown that these developments cannot be explained by life stages but are clearly tied to financialization. Wealth among young households grew steadily across birth cohorts born before the mid-1970s, then fell for those who were born around 1980. These early millennials have fewer assets and greater debts than their predecessors, and this is largely due to the finance-driven recession and mushrooming student debt. The generations who came of age during the post–World War II period of shared prosperity had larger fortunes upon retirement than previous generations—but also more than any *subsequent* generations. Among those who were born in 1947 or later (including many baby boomers), a large proportion is about to exit the workforce without adequate savings.

Wealth inequality has increased for all cohorts—the only consistency we found was across these generations. The riches garnered from owning financial capital have widened economic gaps among older and younger generations. This trend appears to be getting worse. In the next chapter, we explore the consequences of the Great Recession, the major event determining how millennials embarked on their financial lives.

CHAPTER 7 | The Aftermath

THE 2008 FINANCIAL CRISIS brought the greatest economic losses to hit American families since the Great Depression. By 2011, 26 million Americans were still out of the labor force, 4 million families had lost their homes, and households had forfeited $11 trillion in wealth (Financial Crisis Inquiry Commission 2011). Most visible in the Occupy Wall Street movement, which famously demanded attention to the divide between the high salaries and lavish lifestyles of the 1 percent and the struggles of the 99 percent, public sentiment toward Wall Street soured as the recession unfolded. The financial services industry became the poster child of a society enabling excessive greed and corruption alongside poverty and hunger.

Protests were not the only way public scrutiny turned toward the financial sector. The government interventions required to right the tilting ship challenged the status quo. The Troubled Asset Relief Program (TARP), introduced in the final months of the Bush administration, attempted to restore liquidity in financial markets, while giving state officials more monitoring power over the institutions that had become so deeply entangled in a web of debt. In addition to two large stimulus packages boosting the economy during the crisis, Barack Obama signed the Dodd-Frank Wall Street Reform and Consumer Protection Act of 2010 to curb high salaries for executives and strengthen regulation in the financial sector. Both initiatives aimed to smooth the sector's functioning to minimize systemic risks, especially those posed by the key firms deemed "too big to fail"—the ones whose failure could very well topple the American economy all together, but whose recklessness had led directly to the financial crisis. Tapping into the public's anger toward Wall Street, federal and state prosecutors began cracking down on all sorts of financial wrongdoings. For a moment, it seemed the era of big finance had come to an end.

Despite these interventions, the policies implemented since the Great Recession have neither altered the path of widening economic inequality nor made inroads toward the definancialization of the economy. This *should* come as a shock. The decades following the Great Depression played out in a strikingly different way. In the 1930s and 1940s, a substantial reduction in wealth among the rich, combined with a series of high-level reforms, led to a period of declining inequality. This has been referred to as the "Great Compression" (Goldin and Margo 1992; Grusky, Western, and Wimer 2011). The New Deal stimulus package, the implementation of a federal minimum wage, the enactment of Social Security, and support for unionization and other labor reforms provided new protections to the rights and livelihood of many American workers.

The Great Recession and its aftermath, by contrast, have exacerbated both income and wealth inequality. Inequality has increased since 2007. Incomes remained steady for top earners but dropped for the bottom 60 percent of earners (Grusky and Kricheli-Katz 2012). The mortgage crisis signaled a collapse in wealth for middle- and working-class families. These families tend to invest a large portion, if not all, of their wealth in housing and have higher debt burdens. They are more vulnerable to liquidity crunches, such as those brought about by losing a job or experiencing a medical emergency (and its attendant costs, including loss of income).

So *why* did the Great Recession exacerbate rather than mitigate inequality? Some scholars and commentators have attributed this phenomenon to a weakened labor movement and fewer worker protections, alongside a more radicalized political right wing (Grusky et al. 2011). But this account misses the power of finance to rebound and overlooks its fundamental role in *generating* economic disparities. In this chapter, we trace the major developments since the financial crisis, showing how most regulatory and legal responses were designed to boost liquidity, reduce systematic risk, and penalize fraudulent activities in financial markets. While working toward these goals, these policies also facilitated the further concentration of financial market power and intensified the intertwinement of Wall Street and Pennsylvania Avenue, the private intermediation of public services, and the dominance of finance in corporate governance. In the end, these policies have done more to *restore* than *reform* the financial order.

The next section briefly recounts the collapse of financial markets and the immediate responses to the shortage of credit. This is followed by a discussion of policy efforts to reform the financial sector after the crisis was partially contained. We see that these efforts, while promoting a more robust financial system, did little to reduce dependency on the financial sector. As safeguards set in place to prevent another crisis and protect consumers come under attack from the Trump administration, we conclude in a somber place: an analysis of how economic inequality has intensified in the aftermath of the recession.

The Liquidity Crisis

The financial crisis began in 2007 when a massive number of American households defaulted on their mortgages. This tipping point would later be traced to a variety of precursors, including the securitization of mortgages, increasing number of subprime and home equity loans, and rampant fraud among mortgage lenders. While mortgage issuers used to hold issued mortgages on their balance sheets and receive payments from borrowers, securitization allowed loan originators to sell mortgages to securities firms to acquire a new round of funding. In theory, securitization should minimize the consequence of individual loan defaults by spreading the risk throughout the global financial system. In practice, it meant that when defaults become systematic, the consequences are far-reaching, hard to trace, and difficult to contain.

In the mid-1990s, US housing prices began to rise. This unprecedented upward trend was largely fueled by securitization. Wholesale mortgage originators saw "issue and sell" as a lucrative business model, in which they could charge borrowers high fees and turn that into a selling point for potential buyers of bundled mortgages. These loans' high and adjustable interest rates made them look like cash cows. Quantity-over-quality practices were adopted to maximize the volume of adjustable-rate subprime mortgages issued. When bankers ran out of borrowers who could meet loan standards, they lowered the standards. The most aggressive of these mortgage originators was Ameriquest, which specialized in subprime loans and generated large profits by deceiving borrowers about future payments and falsifying documents. Other lenders, such as Countrywide and New Century, joined the race to the bottom, steering black and Hispanic borrowers toward high-cost loans and lending to families with little disposable income. Borrowers were assured that their homes would quickly accrue value in the bullish housing market, and surely their incomes would rise, so they need not worry about being able to make rising payments. Instead, many of these loans were ticking time bombs that would easily go off when the interest rate went up, the home's value dropped, or the payment ballooned.

Securities firms on Wall Street packaged these mortgages into tradable securities and sold them to banks and institutional investors all around the world, who were eager to find investment options that guaranteed handsome returns. The popularity of these securities grew in global, particularly European, capital markets, as the major rating agencies labeled parts of them "prime" investments and the faith in dollar remained strong. Little did the investors know or care that the ratings were generated through an automated process and little careful investigation of the underlying mortgages. These ratings became increasingly unreliable as securities firms began to mix toxic mortgages into bundles of highly rated securities. There was just such high demand to buy them on the global market.

In the mid 2000s, a handful of hedge funds realized that reckless lending practices were prevalent in the mortgage market and many borrowers would not be able to fulfill their obligations. To take advantage of this development, they asked securities firms to create derivatives for mortgage-backed securities—essentially, insurance policies that would pay out if and when borrowers defaulted on their mortgages. Even though these hedge funds were not motivated to insure these mortgage-backed securities against future losses but rather to profit from their failure, Wall Street bankers were happy to oblige. Their analysts believed that these securities were extremely safe, so they could take in risk-free insurance premiums from hedge fund fools without having to pay out (Lewis 2010).

The bankers' faith was rooted in the impression that the US housing market was, overall, robust. This was true when finance was driven by housing demand, but not when housing demand was driven by the financial sector's desire to peddle mortgages. In short, they did not realize that their practices had brought the system to the brink of collapse. Later, some banks, like Goldman Sachs, began to agree with these hedge fund managers: the collapse of the mortgage market was imminent. Instead of writing down these deals, they sold these insurance policies to institutional clients as if they were prime-grade securities.

By late 2006, the primary and secondary mortgage markets were beginning to crumble. More and more homeowners struggled to meet their minimum payments, and mortgage delinquency started its unusual (but, in retrospect, unavoidable) upward trajectory. There had been a 15-year-long decline in defaults, but by 2010, at the height of the housing collapse, more than 11 percent of homeowners were unable to pay their mortgages on time. *Thousands* were foreclosed upon, forced to abandon their homes. Those mortgage originators who still held loans that were too toxic to sell were the first to go down. New Century filed for bankruptcy in April 2007. Ameriquest was sold to Citigroup in August 2007, and Countrywide was taken over by Bank of America four months later. But the fault lines shaken by this collapse ran deeper and wider than the mortgage market.

As more people defaulted on their debt, foreign and domestic holders of mortgage-backed securities faced significant losses. Investment funds in the United States and Europe began to fail. Wall Street banks, which had issued a massive quantity of derivatives for these securities at a very low premium, and the investors who held these policies, now had to pay out on these insurance plans. The overstretched circle of credit snapped. International banks found themselves unable to repay the large amount of debt they had incurred to operate. The panic was exacerbated when Bear Stearns, Lehman Brothers, and Washington Mutual collapsed, in quick succession, over six months. As panicked investors pulled their money out of the markets, a number of high-profile financial fraud cases, including Bernie Madoff's infamous Ponzi scheme, were revealed. Any remaining confidence in the stability of financial markets and the credibility of the people running them was effectively squelched. Businesses and households relying on regular credit were suddenly unable to sustain their payment schedules.

With a complete collapse of the financial system looming large and drawing near, the federal government took action. It had to. The transatlantic liquidity crisis could not be allowed to deepen. So the Treasury Department facilitated the acquisition of failing institutions by larger banks. Notably, JPMorgan Chase obtained Bear Stearns and Washington Mutual, Bank of America subsumed Merrill Lynch, Barclays acquired Lehman Brothers, and Wells Fargo annexed Wachovia. The intention was to stop the dominos from falling, which these acquisitions did, but the stopgap measure also meant an even more concentrated banking sector (Figure 3.2).

The government itself took over sponsored enterprises such as Fannie Mae and Freddie Mac, both of which had followed the lead of private lenders and were loaded with toxic mortgage-backed securities. It extended large bailouts to struggling firms with insufficient cash flow. For example, the insurance giant American International Group (AIG) accepted $85 billion in federal money to cover unexpected obligations. Most of this money went straight to large banks such as Goldman Sachs, Merrill Lynch, and Bank of America. And the government outsourced the management of the toxic assets to behemoth money manager BlackRock, who oversaw the $130 billion the US government assumed during the Bear Stearns and AIG takeovers, the $5 trillion balance sheets of Fannie Mae and Freddie Mac, and the New York Fed's $1.2 trillion in mortgage securities (Andrews 2010). With some calling BlackRock "a shadow government," the private intermediation of public policy continued. For a more legitimate solution in a democratic society, the Treasury Department and the Federal Reserve urged Congress to pass TARP in September 2008, funneling $700 billion to rescue failing banks and corporations.

In addition to the rescue packages, extraordinary monetary policies were implemented by the Federal Reserve to inject liquidity into banks, regardless of their nationalities. The federal funds rate was pushed to zero to encourage banks to borrow. Three rounds of quantitative easing flooded money into financial markets through the purchase of large sums of government bonds and mortgage-backed securities. By 2014, the Federal Reserve held $4.5 trillion in mortgage-backed securities, bank debt, and Treasury securities on its balance sheet, hoping that cash infusion would grease the corroded economic wheels and reverse the downward spiral.

As the dust settled, it remained unclear whether these extraordinary monetary maneuvers were sufficient to save the economy. Although catastrophic fallout was avoided, the recovery came slowly, if at all, for most Americans. The housing crisis continued; the residential mortgage delinquency rate did not reach its peak of 11.53 percent until the first quarter of 2010 (Figure 7.1). The rate remained above 10 percent in the following two years and showed no sign of decline until 2013. By 2016, the delinquency rate was still above 4 percent, higher than levels in the 1990s. The unemployment rate doubled from 5 percent in April 2008 to 10 percent in October 2009 (Figure 7.2).

In the end, it took a total of 77 months for employment to return to its prerecession level, a staggeringly long period compared to the median of 22 months following the 10 previous recessions.[1] This supposed "recovery," however, concealed the discouraged workers who dropped out of the labor force. The share of the population who are not employed rose from 37 percent in 2007 to 42 percent through 2014. The economic harm brought by the crisis was long-lasting and rivaled only by the Great Depression that began in 1929 and led to the rise of fascism worldwide. If the 1990s saw serious intellectuals on the left beginning to acknowledge the efficiency of the market, the late 2000s saw intellectuals on the right contemplating the self-destructive nature of free markets.

Reform or Restore

While aggressive measures were used to resuscitate the economy, it was clear that boosting liquidity did nothing to address the underlying causes of the crisis. To prevent another financial disaster, the Obama administration proposed a series of bills that eventually led to the Dodd-Frank Wall Street

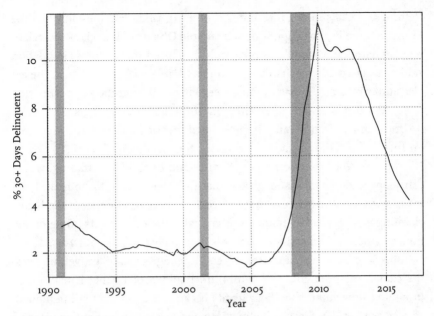

FIGURE 7.1 DELINQUENCY RATE ON SINGLE-FAMILY RESIDENTIAL MORTGAGES

NOTE: Federal Reserve Charge-Off and Delinquency Rates on Loans and Leases at Commercial Banks release. Seasonally adjusted. Delinquent loans and leases are those past due 30 days or more and still accruing interest as well as those in nonaccrual status. SOURCE: Federal Reserve Bank of St. Louis, Federal Reserve Economic Data.

FIGURE 7.2 PROPORTIONS OF LABOR FORCE AND POPULATION NOT EMPLOYED, 2005–2017

NOTE: The lighter line is referenced to the right axis and the darker line is referenced to the left axis. Both series (UNRATE and EMRATIO) are for noninstitutional civilian population aged 16 and older based on the Current Population Survey. The population series is calculated as 100-EMRATIO. SOURCE: Federal Reserve Bank of St. Louis, Federal Reserve Economic Data.

Reform and Consumer Protection Act of 2010. Dodd-Frank established the Financial Stability Oversight Council and the Office of Financial Research to regulate large and complex banks and introduced the Orderly Liquidation Authority as an exit mechanism for nonbank financial institutions. The act also authorized the Bureau of Consumer Financial Protection to ensure that fewer Americans would fall victim to harmful financial products.

Importantly, Dodd-Frank implemented restrictions and requirements on financial activities that could threaten the stability of financial markets. Notably, the Volcker Rule prohibits banks from speculative trading, which can jeopardize savings and give banks the opportunity to both deal the cards and place their bets. The rule faced strong opposition from big banks claiming that proprietary trading was crucial to their profits. Its implementation, originally scheduled for 2010, was repeatedly delayed until 2015.

Internationally, regulators from 27 countries agreed to collectively increase the capital requirements and minimum liquidity of financial institutions in light of how vulnerable these giants became as soon as credit tightened. Known as Basel III, these guidelines demanded banks hold more equity and liquid assets, which could buffer unexpected losses and reduce bankruptcy risk. The Federal Reserve Board announced in 2011 that it would follow these guidelines to avoid another massive bailout. Regulators in the United States mandated annual stress tests to ensure that financial institutions could weather harsh economic conditions. All these efforts shared the objective of minimizing the systematic risks and conflicting interests revealed to be so pervasive in the financial sector.

Although Dodd-Frank represents the most comprehensive financial regulation since Glass-Steagall, it remains unclear whether the act is adequate in reducing systematic risks. Former representative Barney Frank, who authored the bill, has identified how the regulation remains fragmented, with little communication between agencies (Valladares 2015). Frank has publicly voiced concern that the law imposes too-stringent requirements on small banks, while doing little to regulate private equity and hedge funds (Neidig 2016). Another unforeseen consequence of this reform is the expansion of the hedge fund industry, as capital has flown from the newly and more heavily regulated investment banks into less transparent sectors of financial services (International Monetary Fund 2014). In an era of zero interest rates, pension funds and other institutional investors began turning to these alternative, and often riskier, investments for higher yields. In response, the assets managed by hedge funds rebounded from $1.5 trillion in 2008 to more than $3.5 trillion in 2018, a figure above and beyond the industry's precrisis numbers.[2]

In addition to regulatory reforms, authorities took legal action against the main culprits of the crisis. The antagonism directed toward Wall Street was apparent in the Goldman Sachs hearings of 2010. The Securities and Exchange Commission accused the firm's sales team of dumping toxic mortgage securities on its clients, and senators from both sides of the aisle took turns castigating Goldman Sachs for causing the greatest economic disaster in modern history, receiving massive government bailouts, and failing to use bailout funds for the lending needed to reinvigorate the economy (Chan and Story 2010). Despite this bipartisan attack, the Goldman Sachs officials insisted that they had not misled or defrauded their investors (Story 2010), yet a series of Department of Justice investigations would eventually show this testimony to be false. In 2016, Goldman Sachs agreed to pay more than $5 billion in both penalties and settlements. These sorts of settlements rarely entail the acknowledgment of guilt, but in this case, the company was forced to admit that it made false and misleading representations to prospective clients of their mortgage-backed financial products (Petroff 2016). Bank of America, JPMorgan, and Citigroup also settled with the Department of Justice. By the end of 2016, the largest banks had been ordered to pay a combined total of nearly $60 billion in fines in response to charges of fraud, abuse, wrongful foreclosures, and manipulating interest and exchange rates.

Who paid for this $60 billion? Bank shareholders, not executives. In fact, Jamie Dimon, the CEO of JPMorgan Chase, received a 74 percent *raise* after settling with the Department of Justice in 2014 (Cohan 2015), bringing his salary back up to $20 million. Over 1,000 bankers were prosecuted and more were jailed than in the savings-and-loan crisis of the 1980s, yet only one executive, Credit Suisse's Egyptian-born Kareem Serageldin, was sent to prison for overvaluing mortgage securities in the early 2000s. None of the executives at the big banks or subprime lenders have been convicted, despite the fact that their offenses had graver consequences for homeowners and society as a whole.

Some have accused the government of being too lenient on Wall Street executives, while federal prosecutors maintain that these cases are too difficult to prove (Cohan 2015; Eisinger 2014). The lack of convictions may simply reflect a broader trend in declining prosecutions for white-collar crime. Whereas in the 1990s, these cases accounted for an average of 17.6 percent of all federal cases, they declined to 9.4 percent in 2012. The Justice Department used to go after "bad apples" and make examples of them. Now, it goes after institutions, forcing law enforcement to weigh the economic consequences of their legal actions. While shifting the onus to institutions may seem like a logical way to target systemic malpractice, the aftermath of the financial crisis exposed the shortcomings of this approach (Eisinger 2017). Institutions cannot be imprisoned for wrongdoing, only fined. And when dealing with exceedingly wealthy institutions, fines—even in the billions—may not be enough to deter crime or promote institutional change.

Dodd-Frank's passage signaled that the regulatory pendulum had swung away from laissez-faire practices, but since that time, the pendulum appears to have swung back. In 2017, the Trump administration proposed significant rollbacks to Dodd-Frank via the Financial CHOICE Act, which passed in the House along party lines in June (House Committee on Financial Services 2017; Rappeport 2017). The bill's key revisions including replacing the Consumer Financial Protection Bureau (CFPB) with the Consumer Law Enforcement Agency, making it an executive branch and giving the president power over its personnel decisions. The legislation would also reduce the bureau's regulatory authority, particularly in the areas of payday lending and arbitration agreements. In addition, the bill would repeal the exit mechanisms set in place for "too big to fail" financial institutions, making federal bailouts likely when large banks fail (thus removing consequences for overreaching risks). Importantly, the CHOICE Act sought to revoke the Volcker Rule, allowing banks to continue the business of speculative trading.

The looming threat of bigger and more powerful banks sparked bipartisan support for another bill, the Economic Growth, Regulatory Relief, and Consumer Protection Act, that amended Dodd-Frank in 2018. This second bill aimed to bolster smaller banks rather than restrict big banks. Even as Democrats and Republicans alike voiced concerns about the behemoth institutions that grew by acquiring failing banks during the crash, the aftermath spawned an even *more* concentrated banking sector with fewer, larger institutions. The goal of repealing restrictions, rather than increasing the might of regulatory power, prompted Congress to find rare common ground—perhaps also a sign of the political bulwark posed by the Trump administration and its supporters.

Backers of the bill cited the need to support small and medium-sized banks against the might of large banks, and, indeed, the legislation eased oversight for hundreds of smaller institutions. Smaller banks—those with under $100 billion in total assets—can, for example, bypass the stress test requirement designed to measure a lender's ability to withstand a financial crisis (Quarles 2018). The bill also raised the "too big to fail" threshold from $50 billion in assets to $250 billion. Barney Frank himself has also called the threshold too low, but he believes it could be safely raised to $100 or $125 billion—well under $250 billion (Berman 2018). In addition, banks with less than $10 billion in assets, designated as community banks, now bypass the

Volcker Rule (Rappeport 2018). Small lenders are no longer be subject to certain disclosure requirements under the Home Mortgage Disclosure Act, and the regulatory burden of midsize banks was reduced. The sole focus on the size of financial institutions ignores that mid-level financial conglomerates such as American Express, Charles Schwab, and Suntrust Banks are still big and tightly linked to larger institutions in both visible and invisible ways. If a few of these smaller banks fail, they are likely to bring down the giants with them. Still, with rare bipartisan support, the bill passed in the Senate with a vote of 67 to 31 and then in the House, 258 to 159.

In addition to the rollback of Dodd-Frank, real ground has been gained by the financial sector. Most notably, Senate Republicans, along with a tiebreaking vote from Vice President Mike Pence, blocked a proposal from the CFPB to ban banks and other institutions from inserting arbitration clauses in their contracts. This would have restored consumers' right to pool their resources into class-action lawsuits, an important provision since few individual consumers can go head to head with large corporations such as Wells Fargo and Equifax in court. In effect, the vote practically protected banks from civil lawsuit. Mick Mulvaney, a longtime opponent of the CFPB, was later appointed its acting director with the ability to weaken the bureau's capacity from within. Mulvaney quickly suspended all new investigations, dropped cases against payday lenders, and folded the Office for Students and Young Consumers into the Office of Financial Education, eliminating the only federal agency mandated to protect student loan borrowers.

Perhaps the most significant policy change that had benefited banks, fund managers, and shareholders in the wake of the Great Recession was the tax reform of 2017. The $1.5 trillion tax bill represented the first legislative victory for Republicans since Trump entered office. The bill not only brings disproportional benefits for the wealthy by cutting income and estate taxes but also by permanently reducing the social responsibility of American corporations. The corporate tax rate was slashed from 35 to 21 percent, and the rate for overseas subsidiaries was dropped to a measly 10.5 percent (Kaplan and Rappeport 2017; Kitroeff 2018). The bill's proponents claimed that all that cash would be used to raise wages, increase hiring, lower prices, and promote innovation, in the long run benefiting workers and consumers and stimulating the economy. Trickle-down economics was suddenly and inexplicably in vogue on Capitol Hill.

Investors and bankers know better than that. In response to the tax plan released in September 2017, analysts at Goldman Sachs and other institutions adjusted their forecasts upward. They predicted that the tax cut package would lead to a 10 percent gain in corporate earnings and greater return to shareholders. Indeed, the tax cuts set off another rally in the stock market, increasing total stock market capitalization by $2.7 trillion in merely three months. Many corporations used their retained earnings to reward shareholders and top executives. One investment research company, TrimTabs, estimated that an average of $4.8 billion was spent *per day* to buy back shares in the first quarter of 2018.[3]

At this point, it is perhaps safe to say that the crisis was a missed opportunity for change. With some exceptions, the policies implemented in its aftermath worked to restore our financialized economy, rather than address how it perpetuates and deepens inequality. The most severe blow for the financial sector since the Great Depression did not lead to a reckoning, but a regrouping. In the following section, we revisit inequality trends after the recession. We show that the policies deployed to rescue the financial sector revived its profits, which surged sharply amidst the recession and continued to grow in the decade after. In the meantime, capital's share of income grew, the wage and wealth gaps continued to expand, household wealth shrank, and debt piled up.

Inequality: A Decade After

The tightening of financial regulation since the financial crisis was initially resisted with the arguments that added restrictions would destabilize the financial sector and reduce the services it could provide in a vulnerable economy. This claim has not stood the test of time. Figure 7.3 documents the growth of profits in the financial and nonfinancial sectors relative to their 2007 levels. While the crisis did wipe out almost three-quarters of total financial profits, the comeback was startling. Before the end of recession, the financial sector had brought in a quarter more income than 2007. Profits continued to grow in the following years. In 2017, the sector made 80 percent more than before the financial crisis. Profit growth was much slower in the nonfinancial sector, which recovered in 2010 and grew 38 percent in 2017.

Financial sector or not, rising profits do not mean that the economy, as a whole, has recovered. In fact, profit gains are partially attributable to losses in wages and employment. Figure 7.4 shows labor's and capital's share of national income—that is, how much income goes to those doing work and those owning capital. While we would expect labor's share to decrease during a recession, it is abnormal that the share would remain low during a period of fast economic growth. This signals that American

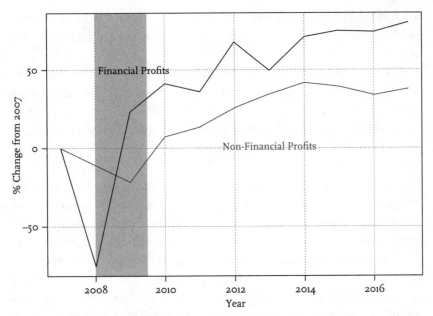

FIGURE 7.3 FINANCIAL AND NONFINANCIAL PROFITS SINCE THE GREAT RECESSION

NOTE: Corporate profits with inventory valuation adjustment. Financial sector includes the Federal Reserve banks and industries such as credit intermediation and related activities; securities, commodity contracts, and other financial investments and related activities; insurance carriers and related activities; funds, trusts, and other financial vehicles; and bank and other holding companies. SOURCE: Bureau of Economic Analysis, National Economic Account, Table 6.16.

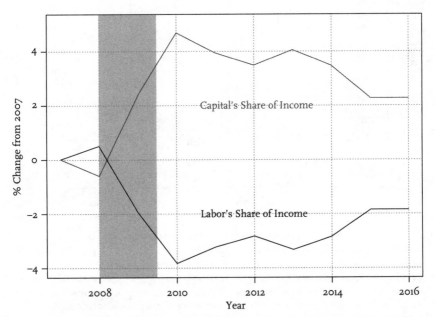

FIGURE 7.4 LABOR'S AND CAPITAL'S SHARE OF INCOME SINCE THE GREAT RECESSION

NOTE: Calculated as private-sector gross operating surplus over the sum of compensation and private-sector gross operating surplus. SOURCE: Bureau of Economic Analysis, National Economic Account, GDP by Industry Series.

workers may never truly recover from the recession. The pendulum continues to swing toward capital, and its velocity only increases with massive automation.

By this point, it would be naive to believe the massive losses would be equitably shared among workers. Chapter 2 showed a great divergence in wages since 1980. This trend was unaltered by the financial crisis or its aftermath. Top earners were affected by the recession, but their wages quickly recovered in 2010 (Figure 7.5). In recent years, wages at the 95th percentile rose more than 12 percent compared to their precrisis level. The median wage, however, did not recover until 2015. The economic upswing in the years since has only brought an increase between 1 and 2.5 percent. Similar to wages, wealth gaps yawned open in the aftermath of the recession. Thanks to the monetary policies that focused on financial markets, wealthy households were barely hurt by the Great Recession. At its worst, their net worth was reduced by about 10 percent compared to 2007 levels and fully recovered by 2016. The wealth of middle-class Americans, on the other hand, went into a free fall: the median net worth

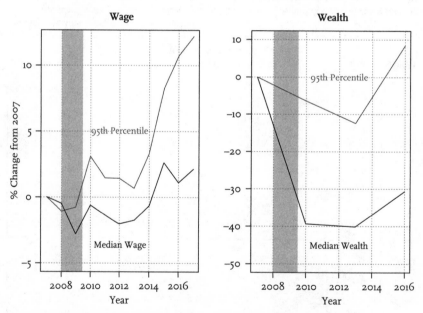

FIGURE 7.5 TOP AND MEDIAN WAGE/WEALTH SINCE THE GREAT RECESSION

NOTE: Estimates include all private sector employees aged 25–65. Wage is calculated as annual earnings divided by the product of usual work hours per week and the number of weeks worked and inflation adjusted by the consumer price index published by the Bureau of Labor Statistics. SOURCE: Bureau of Labor Statistics, Current Population Survey Annual Social and Economic Supplement, Survey of Consumer Finance 2007–2016, Federal Reserve.

dropped about 40 percent from 2007 to 2010 and stayed low until very recently.

The unequal recovery of wealth manifested across different racial groups. Figure 7.6 shows that, while the racial wealth divide was already astonishing before the recession (Oliver and Shapiro 2006; Shapiro 2004), it has worsened further in the decade following. Even though the median household wealth of white, black, and Hispanic households all dropped around 25 percent after the burst of real estate bubble, white households recovered at a much faster pace than their minority counterparts. The difference was most salient between 2010 and 2013, during which period white households stabilized their wealth but minority households continued in a downward spiral. By 2016, black households had lost about 30 percent of their wealth, compared to 14 percent for white families.

The lack of wealth recovery among black households is, in part, due to the accumulation of nonmortgage debt since the recession (Figure 7.7). Following a 16 percent decline in debt during the recession, median black debt surged, more than doubling its 2007 level by 2016. A large portion comes from student loans: in 2007, student loans constituted around

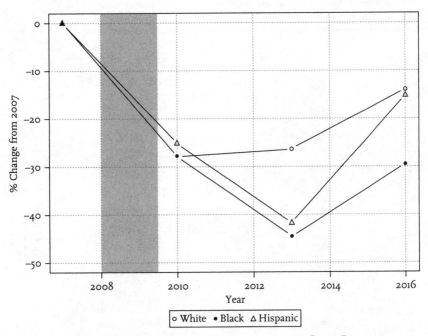

FIGURE 7.6 MEDIAN HOUSEHOLD WEALTH BY RACE SINCE THE GREAT RECESSION
NOTE: The racial status of a household is determined by the racial status of the household head. SOURCE: Survey of Consumer Finance 2007–2016, Federal Reserve.

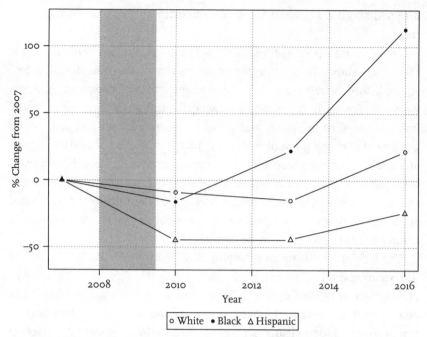

FIGURE 7.7 MEDIAN HOUSEHOLD NONMORTGAGE DEBT BY RACE SINCE THE GREAT RECESSION

NOTE: The racial status of a household is determined by the racial status of the household head. SOURCE: Survey of Consumer Finance 2007–2016, Federal Reserve.

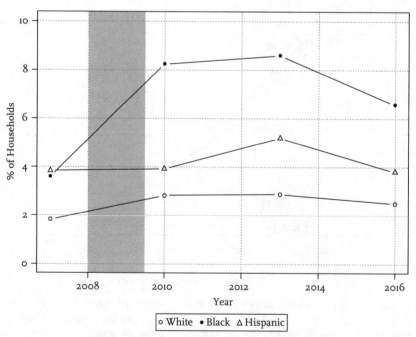

FIGURE 7.8 PAYDAY LOAN USAGE BY RACE SINCE THE GREAT RECESSION

NOTE: The numbers indicate the proportion of households that had a payday loan within the past year. SOURCE: Survey of Consumer Finance 2007–2016, Federal Reserve.

23 percent of all consumer debt among black households (Seamster and Charron-Chénier 2017). The number jumped to more than 50 percent in 2016. White and Hispanic households also carried more student loan debt in 2016 than before (with the share increasing from 13 to 21 percent and from 10 to 32 percent, respectively). Ideally, these loans would lead into a meaningful increase in future income and perhaps even wealth-building. However, if the promise of mobility is not delivered, the racial wealth divide is likely to intensify in the decades to come.

As much as median wealth and debt help us understand how the recession destroyed wealth and worsened racial divides among typical households, they provide little insight into the hardships faced by the severely disadvantaged, excluded from mainstream finance altogether. Figure 7.8 examines the prevalence of payday loans since 2007. In 2007, black and Hispanic households were twice as likely to take on payday loans as white households. While the share of households that used payday loans increased across all racial groups during the recession, the growth was most dramatic among black families, likely due to racial biases in lending that limit black people's access to credit with better terms. The proportion of payday borrowers increased from 3.6 percent in 2007 to 8.2 percent in 2010. Loosening regulations around high-interest lending would disproportionately affect minority households—they would have more access to credit, but pay a higher price, with consequences that will compound for generations to come.

Summary

It took massive economic devastation before either ordinary American citizens or the federal government realized that finance had become the quintessential—and most vulnerable—feature of the US economy. As the damage broadened, shock turned into hostility toward Wall Street. Protestors congregated. Officials assured investors. Pundits reprimanded executives clutching their bonuses. Congress proposed bills. For a moment, it seemed the crisis would mark the end, or at least the beginning of the end, of financialization.

Yet even though the crisis eventually led to a recession that was comparable only to the Great Depression, the outcome could not be more different. Instead of seeking to preserve the livelihood of American families and overhaul the financial system, much of the response since the Great Recession has served to restore the status quo. A decade later, an observer could safely conclude that the financial crisis was a missed opportunity to transform a flawed system. Rising inequality has kept rising. The dominance of finance in the US economy has only been cemented.

The response to the crisis came mainly on two fronts, both of which reinstated the prior financial order. As the subprime mortgage market collapsed and the suppliers of credit lost their confidence, the first priority was to rescue overleveraged financial institutions, then use them to inject liquidity into the economy. However, the extreme monetary measures were ineffective in stimulating economic growth; banks consolidated, financial profits resurged, and bonuses rebounded. The housing and unemployment crises continued for years.

The second priority for those charged with reviving the US economy after the financial crisis was to prevent another crisis. That meant reducing the systematic risks inherent to an opaque and complex financial sector and punishing those who were responsible for the crash. While many believed the solution was to break up banks that were too big to fail, the reform eventually focused on padding large financial institutions with more capital. Despite some effort to integrate oversight, regulatory agencies remained fragmented. Moreover, prosecutors at the state and federal levels both sought to hold banks and other lenders accountable, and yet, in the end, only one Egyptian banker was jailed. Companies paid fines, while top employees pocketed bonuses.

Only political deadlock prevented the Trump administration from completely eliminating Dodd-Frank, at least the parts that target giant financial institutions. However, a series of executive decisions have already loosened regulation, and more legislative action is expected to unwind the regulatory regime configured after the financial crisis. The 2018 tax overhaul was another massive giveaway from the federal government to finance, with significant corporate tax cuts transferring more resources to fund managers and shareholders.

Economic inequality now receives less attention than it did during the Great Recession, but its major indicators have only worsened a decade later. Benefiting from favorable monetary policies, financial profits rebounded in the midst of recession and continued to grow in the Dodd-Frank era. While proponents of these policies would applaud these profits as signs of success, the profits have not trickled down as promised. Labor's share of income dropped and may never return to its 2007 level. Earnings further diverged, with the wages of top earners increasing much more rapidly than those of median workers. The racial wealth divide expanded during the recovery, partially driven by black households taking on more nonmortgage debt. New consumer protection policies did not curb payday lending, which grew from extreme employment insecurity. And the most pressing public issue exposed by the financial crisis has gone unaddressed: inequality remains deeply entrenched.

Conclusion

IN 1965, SOCIAL PSYCHOLOGIST Melvin Lerner (1965) published a study in the *Journal of Personality and Social Psychology*. He had conducted an experiment with 22 college students at the University of Kentucky, in which each student was asked to observe two workers collaborating on a word game and then evaluate each worker's contribution. The students were told that, due to limited research funding, only one of the two workers would be paid, and, specifically, the selection was entirely *by chance*. Lerner then left the room and played a tape to the students without telling them it was prerecorded. The tape began with Lerner interviewing the two workers, followed by the interaction between the workers while they were performing an anagram task, and ended with the random selection of the payee. Afterward, Learner asked the students to rate each worker's contribution.

Since all students observed identical processes, one would expect them to have similar opinions regarding who contributed more to the task. This was not the case. Lerner found that the students' evaluations were highly contingent on which worker was paid at the end. They tended to rate the worker who was paid as performing better than the one who was unpaid, despite knowing full well that the selection of payee had nothing to do with performance or effort. In other words, the students seemed to justify an arbitrary outcome by believing that the rewarded worker was indeed more deserving than the one deprived.

A year later, Lerner and his colleague Carolyn Simmons (1966) published another experimental study. This time, they asked 72 students, under different conditions, to observe an innocent student receiving painful electric shocks for a fictitious human learning study. Lerner and Simmons found that, when given the option, most students decided to replace electric shocks with positive reinforcement. They did not like seeing the "object" suffer. Yet when the option was not present and when the students knew the suffering would continue, they reacted by devaluing the victim, rating the person as unlikeable and socially inept. A similar negative assessment was not observed among students informed that the suffering was concluded or for those with the option to terminate it.

From these two experiments and subsequent studies, Lerner developed the Just World Hypothesis. He argued that, to gain a basic sense of control, people needed to believe that the world (or at least the environment relevant to themselves) is fundamentally just. That is, the idea that people normally receive what they deserve—more often than not, good behaviors are rewarded and bad behaviors punished. This belief is crucial in helping individuals pursue long-term plans that have few immediate rewards, as well as in regulating quotidian altruistic behaviors. In the meantime, the belief in the association between behavior and outcome could be so strong that people use the outcome to infer the behavior, even when they are aware the outcome may be accidental. Indeed, Lerner and Simmons observed that students who perceived the experiment to be "interesting" or "enjoyable" were much more likely to devalue the victim than those who thought of it as "senseless" or "cruel."

The lesson from these studies, obviously, is not about whether the world we live in is just or unjust, but that, as humans, we have a tendency or need to believe the world is just. We are rationalizing animals who think "Everything happens for a reason" or "There is no such thing as coincidence." We look for and sometimes make up explanations for every reward or punishment. It helps us gain a sense of control. Where there is no clear explanation, we still believe it must be *something* about the recipients that generates these outcomes. This tendency is particularly strong when we do not question whether the rules are unfair or believe there is nothing we can do about the way the game is set up.

The main purpose of this book is to resist this tempting heuristic. We must scrutinize the rules of the game, especially considering the tremendous surge of economic inequality in the United States. The growing divide is not simply an adjustment to market-based supply and demand. Challenging our instinct to think society is fair and just, we have questioned whether those who are rewarded financially are necessarily making proportional contributions to society and whether those who are deprived have some fatal deficiency.

The central thesis of this book is that the rise of finance is a fundamental *cause* of the growing economic inequality in the United States. Financialization is not simply about the (relative) growth of finance in the economy, but a wide-ranging reversal of the role of finance from a secondary, supportive activity to the principal driver of the economy. The most damaging outcome of the current financial system is perhaps not another financial crisis but a social crisis, which may not be as acute but equally detrimental. Financialization is fundamental, not only because finance directly allocates resources across the economy, but also in that it provides motives, worldviews, logics, rhetoric, and technologies to other inequality-generating trends such as union decline, changing politics, new work arrangements, technological advancements, and globalized economies.

This book illustrates how financialization has widened inequality in three principal and interconnected ways. First, the concentration of market power, the increase in political influence, and the intermediation of public policies have allowed the financial sector to extract economic resources from the productive sector and households without providing commensurate economic benefits. Second, the financialization of nonfinancial firms has undermined the accord between capital and labor by reorienting management toward financial markets and undermining capital's dependence on labor. Third, the deinstitutionalization of traditional risk-pooling units such as states or companies has created an atomized risk regime that transfers economic uncertainties to individuals, increasing the regressive consumption of financial services.

Figure 8.1 summarizes the historical and distributional processes through which financialization has intensified economic inequality. We began with the historical conditions that empowered the US financial sector to garner enormous profits. Empirically, this phenomenon is perhaps most apparent in the last quarter of the 20th century, when incomes spiked in the financial sector. Yet the antecedents are found much earlier. We identified the aftermath of World War II and the inception of the Bretton Woods system as a key historical moment that established a new international monetary order. By designating the dollar as the global reserve currency, this transnational system placed the United States at the center of the capitalist world.

This historical context influenced three US policies that would set the stage for its financial system to proliferate and prosper, accumulating profits and controlling assets previously held by other parts of the economy. First, the government intentionally maintained a trade deficit with postwar allies to export dollars and rebuild the country's capitalist economy. Even after the Bretton Woods system collapsed, the primacy of the dollar in global currency exchanges remained (and has been actively maintained). Second, a countermovement to the progressive mobilizations of the 1960s emerged within the corporate and financial sectors, which pressured

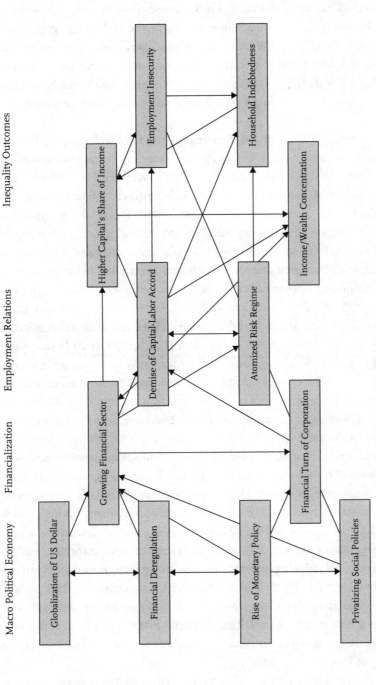

Macro Political Economy   Financialization   Employment Relations   Inequality Outcomes

FIGURE 8.1 DISTRIBUTIONAL REGIME OF FINANCIALIZED AMERICA

Capitol Hill to deregulate Wall Street. Third, in the face of economic stagnation and the high inflation of the 1970s, the Federal Reserve prioritized monetary policy over stimulating employment, as in previous recessions. When Reagan took over the White House in the 1980s, the policy and economic context supported the rise of neoliberal over Keynesian economics. As a result, the financial restrictions—and welfare protections—set in place during the Great Depression were rolled back steadily over the next 20 years. Money poured into Wall Street on an unprecedented and risky scale.

The ensuing policy agenda of adjusting interest rates and attracting foreign investments created incentives that spurred three major transformations in the economy with tremendous consequences for workers. First, the financial sector expanded in leaps and bounds. Financial firms consolidated into mega-institutions with unprecedented size and might. Before, banks provided simple lending services and deposit accounts. Following the gradual repeal of Glass-Steagall in the 1990s, banks came to offer asset and wealth management, stock market trading, corporate and investment banking, venture capital, insurance business, risk management, real estate, and government finance products. With these expanded services came high profits and compensation for financial elites, and the financial sector has flexed increasing political might, demonstrated by escalating campaign contributions and lobbying efforts to devise regulation and tax law to favor of industry interests. The government now relies on financial institutions to enact economic, social, and foreign policies. Public goods such as bankruptcy mediation, student loans, and fiscal stimulus policy have been transferred to stewards in the financial sector.

Second, a revolution has occurred in how executives manage corporations. Today, executives strive to increase value for shareholders rather than reinvest to broaden their market share—the prior gold standard for corporate management. To maximize returns for shareholders, firms have cut costs by automating and downsizing jobs, moving factories overseas, outsourcing entire production units, and channeling resources into financial ventures. Downsizing and reducing benefits have become the new norm—they cut the cost of employing domestic workers. Financial firms champion these as best practices and garner high fees from mergers and acquisitions, spinoffs, and other corporate restructurings. This changing institutional context inspired nonfinancial firms to focus on financial markets and financial firms to create a variety of investment products.

Finally, these developments led to a collapse of the unspoken agreement that had, for so long, tied corporations to their employees and local communities. Instead, firms became beholden to the interest of their investors. With this, working- and middle-class pay stagnated, unions collapsed, and employee benefits disappeared. The social contract between an employer and employee during the post–World War II era disappeared, and with it went promotion opportunities, incremental raises, health insurance, pension plans, and other benefits. Risks formerly assumed by the government and corporations have since been transferred to workers, who are now expected to work flexible and contingent hours. The greatest burden has been placed on those most vulnerable: the declining middle class, the struggling working class, and the barely surviving poor.

We are now in the regressive distribution regime of the financialized era, where finance's share of profits has skyrocketed and labor's share of income plummeted. Top earners gained tremendously—especially executives and those in financial services—giving them an edge in navigating the risks associated with work in this new economic era. Low and middle incomes have stagnated, placing an ever-greater financial toll on these workers. This has resulted in an atomized inequality regime in which those with high incomes are able to grow and invest their money in financial products that stabilize their class position and boost profits in financial services. Meanwhile, the majority of US households struggle to generate meaningful wealth. For many, debt rather than income fuels their livelihoods. This household debt comes in the form of credit cards, auto loans, home mortgages, and healthcare debts and serves to stimulate artificial growth and plentiful bounty for the financial sector. Lenders are inspired to devise new credit products touted as liberatory, but actually further indebted the middle and working class. The cycle of inequality continues.

Beyond the United States

While this book focuses on the United States, similar trends have unfolded in Europe, Asia, and other countries. Studies of inequality on the Organization for Economic Cooperation and Development's member countries have repeatedly identified increased financial activity as a significant factor in widening inequality (Assa 2012; Kus 2012; Kwon and Roberts 2015), especially in the concentration of income at the top (Kwon, Roberts, and Zingula 2017). Sociologist Olivier Godechot (2016a), particularly, found that in OECD countries finance's share of GDP is associated with 20 to 40 percent of increasing inequality from 1980 to 2007. He points to the increased volume of stocks traded and bank assets as key explanations for inequality.

In addition to widening the economic divide in general, financialization has reshaped economic institutions and regulatory structures, leading to an increase in the top income share in France (Godechot 2012) and among 14 OECD countries between 1990 and 2010 (Flaherty 2015). Labor's share of income tends to be lower in more financialized economies (Dünhaupt 2016; Hein 2015). The connection between financialization and inequality appears more pronounced in the United States, the United Kingdom, and other liberal market economies (Dore 2008; Roberts and Kwon 2017), and a study of 18 affluent capitalist democracies identifies credit expansion—along with financial sector employment and financial crises—as a primary factor of heightened inequality (Hyde, Vachon, and Wallace 2018).

The fact that executives today manage corporations to increase shareholder dividends has broken the accord between capital and labor and transferred resources into the global financial services industry. Changes in corporate governance, such as stock market capitalization and dividend payments of nonfinancial corporations, have been identified as main drivers of inequality worldwide (Dünhaupt 2012). Another analysis of 18 advanced industrial democracies since 1960 finds that stock market capitalization plays a significant role in widening income inequality, while union density and mobilization curb these trends (Huber, Huo, and Stephens 2017). These studies all point out how a finance-driven economy and the pre-eminence of the shareholder-value model have undermined workers' collective bargaining power, increased flexible employment, and increased the importance of stock markets to corporate finance (Darcillon 2015; Vachon, Wallace, and Hyde 2016).

Indeed, research on specific countries supports these claims, while also revealing variations in how executives respond to an emerging global norm that promotes the interests of shareholders. In France, the dominance of the shareholder model has inspired corporate executives at nonfinancial firms to develop financial products much like those at Sears and General Electric in the United States. This development is associated with increasing dependence on financial channels and weakened labor bargaining power, both of which contribute to depressed wages (Alvarez 2015). Meanwhile, research by sociologist Jiwook Jung and Eunmi Mun (2016) in Japan finds that corporate dividends have increased in response to direct and indirect pressure from both domestic and foreign investors, reaching a level on par with what we have seen in the United States. Despite widespread evidence of pressure to adapt to the shareholder norm, some Japanese executives resisted, recommitting to the previous stakeholder model, called *keiretsu*. They have largely avoided downsizing—a key strategy employed to cut costs and increase shareholder dividends (Jung and Mun 2017). It appears that when the shareholder model is introduced to a new country, it adapts according to the institutional context.

We have also shown that the credit-centered policy model in the United States has dampened political efforts to address finance-driven inequality. This is consistent with other research across OECD nations. In a study of 20 OECD countries from 1995 to 2007, sociologist Basak Kus (2013) finds that consumption driven by credit and cheap imports (specifically from China) suppresses public frustration with rising inequality and reduces the pressure on governments to redistribute resources (see also Kus and Fan 2015). As in the United States, credit has become a safety net abroad, indebting—and eventually immiserating—the potential beneficiaries of redistribution. And when the social safety net is cobbled together from credit, the destitute and the poor are often excluded. To the extent these groups gain access to credit, it is likely to be high-interest loans of last resort.

All these comparative studies underscore that the links between financialization and inequality are not unique to the United States. Contemporary financialization is, in every sense, a global phenomenon. As credit ferociously circulates around the world, the collapse of the US real estate market *could* quickly escalate into a worldwide crisis. When multinational firms seek to maximize profits, their cost-cutting strategies *could* reverberate through international supply chains to shape the employment conditions of workers far away. The lending of one country is the borrowing of another. Because the nation remains the dominant unit in how we think about the world and how we measure economy and define society, existing studies are often like blindfolded men seeking to learn about the shape of an elephant. This book is certainly guilty of this myopia. More studies are much needed to understand how financialization and inequality are connected at the global level.

So We Beat On

> Consequently two view-points are always tenable. The one, how can you improve human nature until you have changed the system? The other, what is the use of changing the system before you have improved human nature?
>
> —GEORGE ORWELL, on Charles Dickens

We began this book without expecting to make specific policy recommendations. The book, after all, is about what happened, not what will happen. Many historical developments are irreversible, the past is invariably romanticized, and the future is rarely intended. The Glass-Steagall era has passed, and its restrictions are no longer sensible a century later. More progressive redistribution or basic income is always an option for addressing market inequality. Yet the separation between work and income challenges certain fundamental, but perhaps unwarranted, beliefs in American society, and therefore is likely to face severe pushback, even from people who would otherwise benefit from these programs. We also do not intend to evangelize certain European models, as this approach ignores the social infrastructure in which such models emerge and trivializes the problems they entail.

That said, we believe progress can still be made through inventive and carefully considered policies. This is nowhere more evident than in the financial reform that followed the 2008 financial crisis. Appropriate regulation, enhanced oversight, and strict enforcement did deter hubris and stabilize finance, at least temporarily. Tough scrutiny of financial products, often post hoc, did prevent more borrowers from being trapped in debt spirals and investors from purchasing bogus securities. Without sustaining caution, it is equally certain that new loopholes will be identified and exploited, and the regulation will loosen up when the pressure fades. The cat-and-mouse game continues.

This book, however, also makes it clear that the problems of finance go well beyond wrongdoing in the financial sector. So much of the malfeasance on Wall Street may seem trivial in comparison to the consequences of a "well-functioning" financial system. Finance is at the heart of contemporary inequality. "Financial reform" should not be limited to stabilizing the financial sector but expanded to recognize that finance has fundamentally reorganized the distribution of economic resources. We should seek to prioritize the interest of society over that of finance.

From this perspective, financial conglomerates' market power not only creates systematic risk but also appropriates economic rent from the rest of the economy. More regulation is unlikely to solve this problem, as it largely preserves existing financial institutions. Thus, the real question is how regulation can be refigured to moderate existing financial institutions' dominance. In certain places, rules should be *eliminated*. That would facilitate competition between incumbents and newcomers, many of which have emerged from Silicon Valley. A more numerous and diverse set of financial institutions, even if imperfect, would cut back both systemic risk and rent-seeking power, as well as the likelihood of fraudulent activities, antitrust violations, and conflicts of interest, all of which are still commonplace. If financial markets are occupied by a greater number of firms, the incentive to preserve one's reputation may outweigh the incentive to create short-term profits.

Regulatory capture is always a risk, perhaps nowhere more so than in an industry dominated by a handful of conglomerates. Accordingly, regulatory dependency on the information and knowledge provided by firms should be reduced; appropriate policies should be based on independent studies that attend to the needs of customers, not the preferences of firms. This may require substantially more research capacity than currently exists in regulatory agencies, so many of which are being gutted even as we write.

These regulatory changes, of course, would not be effective without instituting a new culture in high finance, where currently the dollar is the sole unit that measures individual success. This distinction may explain why similarly bad behaviors are less frequent in industries that also feature an oligarchy. The success of financial institutions would, more appropriately, be measured by the *output* metric of how well they meet customers' needs, rather than the *input* metric of how much money they make. Good actors should be valorized and bad actors disgraced, penalized, or even debarred. Such change is most likely when regulators intervene not only with legal authority but also through efforts aimed at community building. More regulation will not distill compliance into ethics, nor will castigating all financial professionals as "greedy" or "immoral" motivate them to pursue public good.

As money continues to be channeled from New York City to Washington in order to influence the government's decisions regarding the future of finance and the US economy as a whole, perhaps real economic reform requires political reform. This might fruitfully start with organized countervailing forces (Galbraith [1952] 1993) that restrain Wall Street and promote the interests of the citizens. There is a role for other large actors, such as state pension systems and nonfinancial firms, to bring pressure on Capitol Hill to foster the independence of regulators and reduce the power of the largest financial firms. The mobilization of these large actors is critical in constraining the power of Wall Street. It is perhaps equally important to make clear that, though finance claims to benefit the public, in its current form, it mostly serves the interests of its own professionals and the country's wealthiest citizens. Middle-class and working-class families do not benefit much from the rising tide; instead, much of their income has been transferred away through fees and borrowing.

Besides reforming the financial sector, policies should aim to structurally weaken the private intermediation of public policies. The direct student loans developed during the Bush and Clinton administrations show that a "public option" may be feasible for providing financial services to households in need. Some have advocated for public bank accounts or even a "central bank for all" (Baradaran 2015; Ricks, Crawford, and Menand 2018), while others believe that the Postal Service might be leveraged as a replacement for the relief currently provided by payday lenders. Such public options could be set up as revenue-neutral, or even profitable without being predatory. Private entities, with their supposedly greater efficiency, might then compete to offer lower prices and better services. In any case, the interests of Main Street, not Wall Street, should determine the practicality of public options.

Not all solutions need to come from government. A new wave of socially responsible investing (SRI) products has emerged to address the negative consequences of the shareholder-value model. Also called impact, sustainable, or green investing, these products seek to generate both profits and positive impacts. SRIs are a response to the recognition that public corporations often inflict social and environmental harms that are not factored into their balance sheets. Their main goal is to generate profits that reduce negative and promote positive externalities, and they have gained legitimacy and popularity in the past 10 years. A 2016 estimate indicated that a fifth of professionally managed assets, or $8.72 trillion, were guided by social purposes in addition to profit motives (Bernasek 2014; Colby 2016). The concept is particularly welcomed by pension funds, foundations, college endowments, and religious mutual funds that face public scrutiny of their investment decisions or have goals other than maximizing returns (Peifer 2011). University endowments at Harvard, Columbia, Georgetown, and other campuses have made concrete efforts to address climate change, promote prison reform, and undertake other prosocial causes by divesting from companies deemed unsustainable and unethical (Cirillo 2017; Milman 2017; Steyer 2017). Large family and state pension funds have changed course as well. Notably, the Rockefeller Family Fund and Rockefeller Brothers Fund (RBF) have both decided to divest from all fossil fuel assets in recent years. Stephen Heintz, RBF's chief operating officer, described the move as morally aligned with the fund's mission to promote social change, citing the deleterious effects on the environment and on people's health. On behalf of the fund, he said, "For us, it's not just a moral imperative, but it makes good financial sense" (Heintz 2016).

There is perhaps no more forceful advocate for SRIs than Laurence Fink, the chief executive of BlackRock. He founded the world's largest asset management company and oversees more than $6 trillion in investments. In his 2018 letter to CEOs, titled "A Sense of Purpose," Fink stated, "To prosper over time, every company must not only deliver financial performance, but also show how it makes a positive contribution to society. Companies must benefit all of their stakeholders, including shareholders, employees, customers, and the communities in which they operate." He demanded companies step in where governments fail, building a new, cooperative relationship with shareholders that focuses on addressing societal challenges and achieving long-term growth.

Idealistic, sure, but efforts like these help to set bar just a bit higher when it comes to norms for investment and corporate governance. Furthermore, for BlackRock and other mega-institutional investors, sustainable growth ultimately best serves their business interests. The sheer size of their assets, along with large quantities of index funds and retirement savings they control, means that these institutional investors count on long-term economic growth and societal stability more than many smaller, actively managed funds. Unlike hedge funds or private equity firms that can exploit information asymmetry to bet on winners, bet against anticipated losers, or extract resources from companies without considering the consequences, these mega-investors *are* the market. Their business models rely on corporations creating actual value.

Leading investment firms in this market have introduced funds that emphasize environmental sustainability, promote gender and racial equality, curb executive compensation, or protect human rights. For example, TIAA-CREF Social Choice Bond Fund allocates 70 percent of its assets to bonds issued by established corporations that have the best ratings. The remaining 30 percent is used to finance projects or companies that generate measurable and positive impacts. Vanguard FTSE Social Index, among other requirements, mandates its listed companies have at least one woman on their board of directors and an equal-opportunity policy in place. The S&P 500 Environmental & Socially Responsible Index filters out businesses with significant activities in fossil fuels, tobacco, or military armament industries. And the AFL-CIO's Housing Investment Trust aims to create quality union construction jobs as well as to build affordable and energy-efficient housing.

Most notably, Just Capital, a nonprofit organization that aims to promote socially beneficial business practices, teamed up with Goldman Sachs to create the JUST 500 Exchange-Traded Fund in 2018. The fund picks the top 500 companies from the 1,000 largest corporations in the United States, using rankings produced by Just Capital. The fund scores companies based on how they treat their workers and customers, the quality of their products, the impact on environment, the support for communities, job creation, and corporate governance. The importance of each dimension is weighted according to extensive surveys of Americans to reflect society-wide values. In theory, the effort will encourage corporations to compete with one another on social performance.

All these investment vehicles still pursue returns, while jointly illustrating that there *is* more than one shareholder value. Sociologist Emily Barman (2016) argues that the classic shareholder-value model has become less hegemonic over time, as value entrepreneurs construct and institutionalize new social values and performance metrics in the organizational field. These norms and measures are then used to regulate and promote the provision of social goods from supposedly for-profit entities. In certain cases, Barman argues, corporations could be more successful in producing social changes than nonprofits and governments, due to their economic self-sufficiency and greater scale of delivery. Following this logic, strategies such as public campaigns and shareholder resolutions, commonly used to extract more payouts from the companies, can also be used to pressure the provision of social goods.

The proponents and, of course, the merchants of SRI claim that the pursuit of social responsibility does not necessarily mean lower financial returns. They cite numbers showing that these types of investment vehicles are comparable to, and even outperform, the market as a whole. The S&P 500 Environmental & Socially Responsible Index had annualized returns of 14.91 percent between 2012 and 2016, compared to 14.78 percent of S&P 500 (S&P Global 2017). Similarly, Russell's FTSE4Good US 100 had 107.8 percent compound five-year returns compared to 107.1 percent for the benchmark index (FTSE Russell 2017). Some studies find that the pursuit of social good could lead to higher profits. For example, there is evidence linking employee satisfaction to shareholder returns (Edmans 2011). Workforce diversity is also believed to enhance a firm's performance (Herring 2009), though the connection may be more tenuous than its advocates prefer (Stojmenovska, Bol, and Leopold 2017).

There are good reasons to be skeptical about these claims. In theory, fund managers unconstrained by such preferences are able to exploit alternative preferences and invest in high-profit firms avoided by more socially conscious investors. The strong performance of SRI indices in the past years might simply reflect the bull market and the 2014 collapse of crude oil prices rather than any superiority of more ethical firms. Moreover, the relationship between social and financial performance is likely endogenous: companies with greater resources are more able or highly pressured to pursue social goods.

Social and environmental activists also question whether SRI actually delivers the outcomes it promises. Their foremost concern regards how the measures of environmental and social sustainability are constructed and tracked. While the indices claim to monitor the companies over time, it is unclear how much is invested in tracking the actual practices of these firms. Studies have even found that ethics controversies are more likely to occur in companies who have adopted environmental, social, and governance policies (Garvey et al. 2016). This is perhaps more indicative of greater scrutiny than greater malfeasance, but it begs the question of whether SRIs are more about reputation management rather than the substance of business practices.

No matter how effective SRI currently is, it offers a potential "market" solution. Financial products could be better designed to reflect the values of household savers and investors rather than the dogma of fund managers, corporate executives, and academics. The business of business does not have to be *only* business. These financial products should be made more accessible to the public and included as an option for all retirement plans. Of course, the success of SRI eventually depends on how corporate executives, who benefit much from the finance-driven governance model, respond to the new mandates. Nevertheless, it is a step in the right direction.

In the long run, education, housing, and welfare policies should replace credit as the solution to inequality. A century of experimentation has proven that providing more credit inadequately addresses the issue of inequality and worsens it permanently. Not only is the cost of credit regressive, the *supply* of credit is limited for those people who most need it at the times they most need it. A real safety net comprising policies that facilitate stability and upward mobility would address the roots of social problems in ways the democratization of credit or the promotion of financial literacy and inclusion truly cannot.

Where will the money for these policies come from? Instead of raising taxes or issuing more bonds, the federal government could issue new types of governmental securities that pay dividends according to the federal tax revenue (see also Baradaran 2015; Kay 2015; Shiller 1994). The capital raised through these securities might then be designated to funding health, education, housing, and infrastructure policies to promote long-term economic growth, broaden the tax base, and benefit generations to come. Like governmental bonds, such new securities would be an attractive alternative to investors, since the risk of bankruptcy is minimal. Because the dividends are based on tax revenue, their returns also would be much less volatile than even indexed funds. As such, these securities could potentially decouple retirement and financial markets, and protect retirees from unexpected downturns. They would also serve as a countervailing force to balance decades of regressive tax cuts and deficit spending, which would help to reduce inequality. Investors would literally have a stake in the growth of US economy.

For too long, American society has been deprived of shared prosperity. We suspect that there are many answers to the social question through which economic institutions could be organized and conducted so that all members of society more justly share their benefits. These answers must be imagined.

ACKNOWLEDGMENTS

ACKNOWLEDGMENTS TEND TO BE an afterthought, yet from the very beginning our endeavor in writing *Divested* has only been possible with the tremendous support of our colleagues, friends, and families. This book originated at the University of Massachusetts at Amherst with a series of articles written between 2009 and 2014 by Ken-Hou Lin and Donald Tomaskovic-Devey, who played a crucial role in working through ideas and provided tireless guidance toward this venture. At the University of Texas at Austin, Christine Williams advised Megan Tobias Neely's dissertation on social inequality in the hedge fund industry and supplied invaluable insights into the relationship between the financial services industry and inequality more broadly.

We are greatly in debt to Don, as well as Harel Shapira, Nancy Folbre, James Galbraith, Gerald Epstein, and other reviewers who read our full manuscript and gave us generous comments. We also thank David Stein, a former fund manager and current financial advisor, for ensuring that we accurately grasped the inner workings of finance throughout. Colleagues at the University of Massachusetts, University of Texas, Stanford University, and Sciences Po supported the development of this book, and we extend particular thanks to the members of the Inequality Working Group, Family Demography Group, and Fem(me) Sem working group at the University of Texas for their engagement with our articles and book chapters as we developed *Divested*. Feedback from our colleagues at the Max-Po Center on Coping with Instability in Market Societies sharpened our ideas, and considerable support from the Clayman Institute for Gender Research at Stanford and the Institute for New Economic Thinking allowed us to fully pursue this research on finance and inequality.

We thank Jennifer Glass, Kelly Raley, Joya Misra, Andrew Papachristos, Arindrajit Dube, David Pedulla, Olivier Godechot, Adam Cobb, Dustin Avent-Holt, Becky Pettit, Sharmila Rudrappa, Angelina Grigoryeva, and Daniel Fridman. These scholars' insight, encouragement, and friendship helped us travel this long journey. There are more names to be named. But we think the best acknowledgment is to simply highlight their scholarship throughout this book.

We thank our editor, James Cook, for his advice and patience, the editorial team at Oxford University Press for their enthusiasm, and Letta Page for exerting her transformative power of tidying up our writing (so much so, we asked her to edit this acknowledgment as well).

Personally, Megan Tobias Neely thanks her supportive family—especially her favorite community banker, Cajer Neely, who lent his expertise to the manuscript—and her instructive former colleagues at BlackRock who gave her a crash course in Finance 101. And Ken-Hou Lin would like to express gratitude to his parents for their love, J. J. for the enduring support, and A. J. for providing assurance that things can always be different.

NOTES

Introduction

1. See Wells, Matt, "Occupy Wall Street Live: March on Times Square," *The Guardian*, October 15, 2011, and Silver, Nate, "The Geography of Occupying Wall Street (and Everywhere Else)," *FiveThirtyEight*, October 17, 2011. For scholarly work on the Occupy movement, refer to Todd Gitlin's (2012) *Occupy Nation*, Noam Chomsky's (2012) *Occupy*, and David Graeber's (2013) *The Democracy Project*.

2. For more information on the relationship between technological advancement and inequality, refer to Fligstein and Shin 2007. The following research investigates how globalization drives inequality: Duménil and Lévy 2001; Milberg 2008; Milberg and Winkler 2010.

Chapter 1

1. Stock repurchase is commonly accounted as a business expense in corporate finance and thus is not technically a component of profits, which consist of dividends and retained earnings.

2. This is achieved, in part, through Profit Center Accounting, which involves evaluating the performance of an organization's subunits, allocating resources to each unit accordingly, and encouraging competition among units.

Chapter 2

1. Valeria Kogan, "The Salaries of Famous Scientists." https://www.adzuna.co.uk/blog/2016/04/13/how-much-would-famous-scientists-earn-today/.

2. Overall, this research finds that problems commonly associated with living in poverty are worse in societies with more extreme income inequality. For details on how the authors respond to critiques, see also https://www.equalitytrust.org.uk/authors-respond-questions-about-spirit-levels-analysis. An independent report by the Joseph Rowntree Foundation confirmed the authors' findings.

3. When examining inequality, it is important to distinguish between the level of inequality before and after taxes and transfers. The former is commonly referred to as "market-based" inequality, meaning the unequal distribution generated by the

supply and demand in labor and capital markets. The latter is often referred to as "state-mediated" or "disposable income" inequality: the distribution of income after accounting for direct state interventions. The contrast between market and state in this terminology is perhaps misleading since the state plays an essential role in conditioning market activities and therefore shapes the level of inequality before taxes and transfers. Yet the distinction is significant because each measure has its strength and weakness. State-mediated inequality better reflects the unequal distribution of spending power and individuals' well-being. Market-based inequality presents a more accurate picture of the consequences of economic transformations for inequality. Thus, we focus on the latter instead of the former in this book.

4. http://kff.org/health-costs/issue-brief/snapshots-wages-benefits-a-long-term-view/.

5. This measure differs from the conventional accounting, which has national income as the denominator and assigns part of capital's income as labor's income. Instead of distinguishing between two factors of production, labor and capital, our measure focuses on the divide by class (e.g., self-employed and employed).

6. In 2017, 10.7 percent of wage and salary workers were members of unions. For comparison, this is nearly half the 20.1 percent rate in 1983, which amounted to 17.7 million union workers. "Union Members Survey," *Bureau of Labor Statistics*, January 18, 2018.

7. In general, age, education, and income are the primary factors associated with taking up a retirement plan. Access to higher-paying jobs with better retirement benefits increases with age as workers develop their expertise and experience: "Retirement Plan Access and Participation Across Generations," *The Pew Charitable Trusts*, February 2017.

Chapter 3

1. The list is often based on the Harris Poll, an annual survey of the public's perception of 100 high-profile companies that uses six measures of reputation to create a corporate reputation ranking scale: http://www.theharrispoll.com/reputation-quotient. Bank of America, Goldman Sachs, and Wells Fargo fall in the bottom 15, with Wells Fargo placing 97th, right below Monsanto and the Trump Organization and just above Harvey Weinstein's Weinstein Company.

Chapter 4

1. Corkery, Michael and Jessica Silver-Greenberg, "Profits From Store-Branded Credit Cards Hide Depth of Retailers' Troubles," *New York Times*, May 11, 2017.

2. https://gregip.wordpress.com/2002/06/10/credit-window-alternative-lenders-buoy-the-economy-but-also-pose-risk/.

3. For details on GE's day-to-day inner workings during the Welch era, see Bloomberg News, "How Jack Welch Runs GE," June 7, 1998.

4. Under Welch's leadership, the company made it a practice to sell assets to close any gaps in the industrial arm's profits, even though Welch would later criticize an approach to corporate management overly focused on short-term profits. "Losing Its Magic Touch," *The Economist*, March 19, 2009.

5. A swap (also called floating) is a trade in which one party exchanges the market price of an asset while the second party agrees to exchange a fixed price. Both parties

agree to make the transaction at a given point in the future. Meanwhile, an option is a contract in which a buyer secures the right to buy or sell a given security, but is not obligated to do so. A futures contract requires the buyer to buy or sell an asset at a specified price and date in the future. To demonstrate how Enron or another company establishes a fixed price in the future, let us use the example of an airline company that, fearing a rise in fuel costs, wants to lock in the price of oil. This airline could purchase a stock option on the price of oil, giving the airline the right (but not the obligation) to buy the barrel at the specified price at the specified point in the future. Thus if the price of a barrel were, in April 2017, $49, the airline might buy a stock option in which it would agree to pay $50 a barrel in April 2018. If, by that date, the price per barrel had risen to $100, the airline would want to exercise its right to buy the barrel for $50 and stabilize its operating costs. If the price had dropped to $40, however, the airline would not be required to pay $50; it could purchase oil at the market price of $40. In short, financial derivatives like options allow actors in a turbulent market to minimize exposure to future risks.

6. The Financial Accounting Standards Board guideline at the time required only 3 percent of the company to be owned by outside investors. The low threshold made it easy for Enron to create subsidiaries that were nominally independent.

7. For details, see Lu, Wei and Anders Melin, "Ranking Where to Work to Be a Rich CEO or Richer than Neighbors," *Bloomberg News*, November, 16, 2016. Cross-national comparison is inherently difficult because nonmonetary corporate perks are difficult to track; thus, the compensation gap is greater when US CEOs receive a higher share of their total compensation from corporate perks and lower when they receive a lower share.

8. A study conducted by the US Government Accountability Office found that even among households over age 55, about half have no savings for retirement and 29 percent have neither a retirement savings account nor a defined benefit plan: http://www.gao.gov/products/GAO-15-419. Among this group, 41 percent did not own a home.

Chapter 5

1. The amount of debt a family carries relative to their income after paying taxes.

2. Predatory lending refers to the practice of targeting high-interest loans to those lacking access to alternative forms of credit.

3. Franklin D. Roosevelt: "Statement on Signing the Home Owners Loan Act Is Signed," June 13, 1933. Online by Gerhard Peters and John T. Woolley, *The American Presidency Project*. https://www.presidency.ucsb.edu/documents/statement-signing-the-home-owners-loan-act-signed

4. Because younger and older households tend to have lower income, these households would have been classified as poor in our analysis even when they have greater earnings potential or large amount of wealth.

5. Residential debt includes mortgage and home equity loans, educational loans include both deferment and repayment period, and vehicle loans include installment plans for all types of vehicles.

6. Meanwhile, many state universities have shifted financial aid from need-based to merit-based awards, which has further put education resources into the hands

of those better off. This is because merit is often determined based on SAT scores and high school grades, which are associated with higher-income families. As a result, one in five students from high-income households receives merit-based aid. For more information refer to Rampell, Catherine, "Freebies for the Rich," *New York Times Magazine,* September 24, 2013.

7. Pew Research Center finds that racial wealth gaps have widened in the years following the Great Recession. In 2013, the median net worth of white households was 13 and 10 times greater than that of black and Hispanic households, respectively. Kochhar, Rakesh, and Richard Fry, "Wealth Inequality Has Widened Along Racial, Ethnic Lines Since End of Great Recession," *Pew Research Center,* December, 12, 2014.

Chapter 6

1. The literature consistently finds that family wealth in childhood is strongly associated with the opportunities one has throughout life. For a review of the research on intergenerational wealth mobility, refer to Keister and Moller 2000; Killewald, Pfeffer, and Schachner 2017; Schneider, Hastings, and LaBriola 2018; Spilerman 2000.

2. Here we are following the scholarly convention, though we acknowledge that studies have shown that men tend to have greater control over family wealth than women in a variety of cases (Bessière 2013; Pahl 1983).

3. Nation Center for Educational Statistics, Digest of Education Statistics, Table 330.10. Average undergraduate tuition and fees and room and board rates charged for full-time students in degree-granting postsecondary institutions, by level and control of institution: 1963–1964 through 2015–2016 (https://nces.ed.gov/programs/digest/d16/tables/dt16_330.10.asp).

Chapter 7

1. For reference, the 10 previous recessions post-1946 ranged in duration from six to 16 months, averaging about 10.5 months. At 18 months, the 2007–2009 recession was the longest recession since 1946. https://www.minneapolisfed.org/publications/special-studies/recession-in-perspective.

2. In 2018, hedge fund assets under management hit an all-time high of $3.6 trillion, with 7 percent growth over the previous year. Refer to Preqin, "Q2 2018 Hedge fund Asset Flows" (http://docs.preqin.com/reports/Preqin-Hedge-Fund-Asset-Flows-Q2-2018.pdf).

3. The rate of buybacks doubled that of the previous year before Congress cut taxes in December 2017. JPMorgan also predicted that share repurchases would set a new record of about $800 billion in 2018. Steward, Emily, "Corporate Stock Buybacks Are Booming, Thanks to the Republican Tax Cuts," *Vox,* March 22, 2018, and Cox, Jeff, "Companies Are Putting Tax Savings in the Pockets of Shareholders," *CNBC,* March 12, 2018.

REFERENCES

Abramson, Larry. 2007. "Report: JPMorgan Chase Paid Student-Aid Officers." *National Public Radio*, May 10.

Acemoglu, Daron, David Dorn, Gordon H. Hanson, and Brendan Price. 2014. *Import Competition and the Great US Employment Sag of the 2000s*. National Bureau of Economic Research.

Addo, Fenaba R. 2014. "Debt, Cohabitation, and Marriage in Young Adulthood." *Demography* 51(5): 1677–701.

Addo, Fenaba R., Jason N. Houle, and Daniel Simon. 2016. "Young, Black, and (Still) in the Red: Parental Wealth, Race, and Student Loan Debt." *Race and Social Problems* 8(1): 64–76.

Akard, Patrick J. 1992. "Corporate Mobilization and Political Power: The Transformation of U.S. Economic Policy in the 1970s." *American Sociological Review* 57(5): 597–615.

Akerlof, George A., Paul M. Romer, Robert E. Hall, and N. Gregory Mankiw. 1993. "Looting: The Economic Underworld of Bankruptcy for Profit." *Brookings Papers on Economic Activity* 1993(2): 1–73.

Alderson, Arthur S., and Tally Katz-Gerro. 2016. "Compared to Whom? Inequality, Social Comparison, and Happiness in the United States." *Social Forces* 95(1): 25–53.

Alderson, Arthur S., and Francois Nielsen. 2002. "Globalization and the Great U-Turn: Income Inequality Trends in 16 OECD Countries." *American Journal of Sociology* 107(5): 1244–99.

Alstadsæter, Annette, Niels Johannesen, and Gabriel Zucman. 2018. "Who Owns the Wealth in Tax Havens? Macro Evidence and Implications for Global Inequality." *Journal of Public Economics* 162: 89–100.

Alvarez, Ignacio. 2015. "Financialization, Non-financial Corporations and Income Inequality: The Case of France." *Socio-Economic Review* 13(3): 449–75.

Amel, Dean F., and Michael J. Jacowski. 1989. "Trends in Banking Structure since the Mid-1970s." *Federal Reserve Bulletin* 75: 120–133.

Anderson, Elisabeth, Bruce G. Carruthers, and Timothy W. Guinnane. 2015. "An Unlikely Alliance: How Experts and Industry Transformed Consumer Credit

Policy in the Early Twentieth Century United States." *Social Science History* 39(4): 581–612.

Andrews, Dan, and Andrew Leigh. 2009. "More Inequality, Less Social Mobility." *Applied Economics Letters* 16(15): 1489–92.

Andrews, Suzanna. 2010. "Larry Fink's $12 Trillion Shadow." *Vanity Fair*, March 2.

Appelbaum, Eileen, and Rosemary Batt. 2014. *Private Equity at Work: When Wall Street Manages Main Street.* New York: Russell Sage Foundation.

Arendt, Hannah. 1973. *The Origins of Totalitarianism.* New York: Houghton Mifflin Harcourt.

Arrighi, Giovanni. 1994. *The Long Twentieth Century: Money, Power and the Origins of Our Times.* London: Verso.

Assa, Jacob. 2012. "Financialization and Its Consequences: The OECD Experience." *Finance Research* 1(1): 35–39.

Autor, David H. 2003. "Outsourcing at Will: The Contribution of Unjust Dismissal Doctrine to the Growth of Employment Outsourcing." *Journal of Labor Economics* 21(1): 1–42.

Autor, David H. 2014. "Skills, Education, and the Rise of Earnings Inequality among the 'Other 99 Percent.'" *Science* 344(6186): 843–51.

Autor, David H., David Dorn, and Gordon H. Hanson. 2013. "The China Syndrome: Local Labor Market Effects of Import Competition in the United States." *American Economic Review* 103(6): 2121–68.

Autor, David H., Frank Levy, and Richard J. Murnane. 2003. "The Skill Content of Recent Technological Change: An Empirical Exploration." *Quarterly Journal of Economics* 118(4): 1279–333.

Autor, David H., and Brendan Price. 2013. "The Changing Task Composition of the US Labor Market: An Update of Autor, Levy, and Murnane (2003)." Unpublished manuscript.

Avent-Holt, Dustin. 2012. "The Political Dynamics of Market Organization: Cultural Framing, Neoliberalism, and the Case of Airline Deregulation." *Sociological Theory* 30(4): 283–302.

Avent-Holt, Dustin. 2017. "The Class Dynamics of Income Shares: Effects of the Declining Power of Unions in the US Airline Industry, 1977–2005." *Socio-Economic Review.* mwx048, https://doi-org.ezproxy.lib.utexas.edu/10.1093/ser/mwx048

Banerjee, Abhijit V., and Esther Duflo. 2003. "Inequality and Growth: What Can the Data Say?" *Journal of Economic Growth* 8(3): 267–99.

Baradaran, Mehrsa. 2015. *How the Other Half Banks: Exclusion, Exploitation, and the Threat to Democracy.* Cambridge, MA: Harvard University Press.

Baradaran, Mehrsa. 2017. *The Color of Money: Black Banks and the Racial Wealth Gap.* Cambridge, MA: Harvard University Press.

Barman, Emily. 2016. *Caring Capitalism: The Meaning and Measure of Social Value.* New York: Cambridge University Press.

Baum, Sandy, Jennifer Ma, Matea Pender, and Meredith Welch. 2017. *Total Federal and Nonfederal Loans over Time.* College Board.

Benabou, Roland. 1996. "Inequality and Growth." Pp. 11–92 in *NBER Macroeconomics Annual 1996, vol. 11.* Cambridge, MA: MIT Press.

Benard, Stephen, and Shelley J. Correll. 2010. "Normative Discrimination and the Motherhood Penalty." *Gender & Society* 24(5): 616–46.

Benton, Richard A., and Lisa A. Keister. 2017. "The Lasting Effect of Intergenerational Wealth Transfers: Human Capital, Family Formation, and Wealth." *Social Science Research* 68: 1–14.

Berman, Russell. 2018. "Heidi Heitkamp Takes On Elizabeth Warren over the Senate Banking Bill." *The Atlantic*, March 14.

Bernasek, Anna. 2014. "The Surge in Investing by Conscience." *New York Times*, May 31.

Bessière, Céline. 2013. *Au tribunal des couples: Enquête sur des affaires familiales.* Paris: Éditions Odile Jacob.

Bielby, William T. 2012. "Minority Vulnerability in Privileged Occupations: Why do African American Financial Advisers Earn less than Whites in a Large Financial Services Firm?" *The ANNALS of the American Academy of Political and Social Science* 639(1): 13–32.

Binder, Amy, Davis, Daniel, and Bloom, Nick. 2016. "Career Funneling: How Elite Students Learn To Define and Desire 'Prestigious' Jobs." *Sociology of Education* 89: 20–39.

Black, William K. 2013. *The Best Way to Rob a Bank Is to Own One: How Corporate Executives and Politicians Looted the S&L Industry.* Austin: University of Texas Press.

Blair-Loy, Mary, and Amy S. Wharton. 2004. "Mothers in Finance: Surviving and Thriving." *Annals of the American Academy of Political and Social Science* 596(1): 151–71.

Blanchflower, David G., Phillip B. Levine, and David J. Zimmerman. 2003. "Discrimination in the Small-Business Credit Market." *Review of Economics and Statistics* 85(4): 930–43.

Bowles, Samuel, David M. Gordon, and Thomas E. Weisskopf. 1986. "Power and Profits: The Social Structure of Accumulation and the Profitability of the Postwar U.S. Economy." *Review of Radical Political Economics* 18(1–2): 132–67.

Bowles, Samuel, David M. Gordon, and Thomas E. Weisskopf. 2015. *After the Waste Land: Democratic Economics for the Year 2000.* New York: Routledge.

Bowley, Graham. 2010. https://dealbook.nytimes.com/2010/07/16/with-settlement-blankfein-keeps-his-grip/?searchResultPosition=1

Boyer, Robert. 2000. "Is a Finance-Led Growth Regime a Viable Alternative to Fordism? A Preliminary Analysis." *Economy and Society* 29(1): 111–45. doi:10.1080/030851400360587

Braucher, Jean, Dov Cohen, and Robert M. Lawless. 2012. "Race, Attorney Influence, and Bankruptcy Chapter Choice." *Journal of Empirical Legal Studies* 9(3): 393–429.

Brick, Ivan E., Oded Palmon, and John K. Wald. 2006. "CEO Compensation, Director Compensation, and Firm Performance: Evidence of Cronyism?" *Journal of Corporate Finance* 12(3): 403–23.

Briscoe, Forrest, and Chad Murphy. 2012. "Sleight of Hand? Practice Opacity, Third-Party Responses, and the Interorganizational Diffusion of Controversial Practices." *Administrative Science Quarterly* 57(4): 553–84.

Bureau of Labor Statistics. 2018. *Union Members Summary.* Washington, DC.

Burhouse, Susan, Karyen Chu, Ryan Goodstein, Joyce Northwood, Yazmin Osaki, and Dhruv Sharma. 2013. *2013 FDIC National Survey of Unbanked and Underbanked Households*. Federal Deposit Insurance Corporation.

Burke, Edmund, III. 2009. "Islam at the Center: Technological Complexes and the Roots of Modernity." *Journal of World History* 20(2): 165–86.

Calder, Lendol. 2001. *Financing the American Dream: A Cultural History of Consumer Credit*. Princeton, NJ: Princeton University Press.

Cappelli, Peter H. 2012. *Why Good People Can't Get Jobs: The Skills Gap and What Companies Can Do About It*. Philadelphia: Wharton Digital Press.

Cappelli, Peter H., and J. R. Keller. 2013. "A Study of the Extent and Potential Causes of Alternative Employment Arrangements." *Industrial & Labor Relations Review* 66(4): 874–901.

Cappiello, Brendan. 2013. "'The Price of Inequality' and the 2005 Bankruptcy Abuse Prevention and Consumer Protection Act." *North Carolina Banking Institute* 401(17): 401–34.

Cardao-Pito, Tiago. 2017. "Classes in Maximizing Shareholders' Wealth: Irving Fisher's Theory of the Economic Organization in Corporate Financial Economics Textbooks." *Contemporary Economics* 11(4): 369–81.

Castilla, Emilio J. 2008. "Gender, Race, and Meritocracy in Organizational Careers." *American Journal of Sociology* 113(6): 1479–526.

Castilla, Emilio J., and Benard Stephen. 2010. "The Paradox of Meritocracy in Organizations." *Administrative Science Quarterly* 55(4): 543–76.

Catalyst. 2015. "Catalyst Quick Take: Women's Earnings and Income." *New York: Catalyst*. Retrieved August 13, 2015.

Chan, Sewell, and Louise Story. 2010. "Goldman Pays $550 Million to Settle Fraud Case." *New York Times*, July 15.

Charles, Kerwin Kofi, and Erik Hurst. 2002. "The Transition to Home Ownership and the Black-White Wealth Gap." *Review of Economics and Statistics* 84(2): 281–97.

Chen, Clara Xiaoling, and Tatiana Sandino. 2012. "Can Wages Buy Honesty? The Relationship between Relative Wages and Employee Theft." *Journal of Accounting Research* 50(4): 967–1000.

Cherian, Madhavi. 2014. "Race in the Mortgage Market: An Empirical Investigation Using HMDA Data." *Race, Gender & Class; New Orleans* 21(1–2): 48–63.

Cherlin, Andrew J. 2014. *Labor's Love Lost: The Rise and Fall of the Working-Class Family in America*. New York: Russell Sage Foundation.

Chetty, Raj, David Grusky, Maximilian Hell, Nathaniel Hendren, Robert Manduca, and Jimmy Narang. 2017. "The Fading American Dream: Trends in Absolute Income Mobility since 1940." *Science* 356(6336): 398–406.

Cingano, Federico. 2014. "Trends in Income Inequality and its Impact on Economic Growth." No 163, OECD Social, Employment and Migration Working Papers. Paris: OECD Publishing.

Cirillo, Jeff. 2017. "Georgetown to Avoid Investing in Private Prisons." *The Hoya*, October 6.

Cobb, J. Adam. 2015. "Risky Business: Firms' Shifting of Retirement Risk and the Decline of Defined Benefit Pension Plans." *Organizational Science* 26(5): 1332–50.

Cobb, J. Adam, and Ken-Hou Lin. 2017. "Growing Apart: The Changing Firm-Size Wage Effect and Its Inequality Consequences." *Organization Science*. https://doi.org/10.1287/orsc.2017.1125

Cochrane, Debbie, and Diane Cheng. 2016. *Student Debt and the Class of 2015*. Washington, DC: Institute for College Access & Success.

Cockburn, Andrew. 2016. "Down the Tube." *Harper's Magazine*, April.

Cohan, William D. 2015. "How Wall Street's Bankers Stayed Out of Jail." *The Atlantic*, September.

Colby, Laura. 2016. "Sustainable Investments Surged by Third to $8.7 Trillion in 2016." *Bloomberg*, November 14.

Coleman-Jensen, Alisha, Matthew P. Rabbitt, Christian A. Gregory, and Anita Singh. 2016. *Household Food Security in the United States in 2015*. Economic Research Report 215. United States Department of Agriculture.

Conley, Dalton. 2010. *Being Black, Living in the Red: Race, Wealth, and Social Policy in America*. Berkeley: University of California Press.

Cooper, Michael J., Huseyin Gulen, and Alexei V. Ovtchinnikov. 2010. "Corporate Political Contributions and Stock Returns." *Journal of Finance* 65(2): 687–724.

Cooper, Michael J., Huseyin Gulen, and P. Raghavendra Rau. 2016. "Performance for Pay? The Relation between CEO Incentive Compensation and Future Stock Price Performance." SSRN Scholarly Paper. ID 1572085. Rochester, NY: Social Science Research Network.

Corak, Miles. 2013. "Income Inequality, Equality of Opportunity, and Intergenerational Mobility." *Journal of Economic Perspectives* 27(3): 79–102.

Core, John E., Robert W. Holthausen, and David F. Larcker. 1999. "Corporate Governance, Chief Executive Officer Compensation, and Firm Performance." *Journal of Financial Economics* 51(3): 371–406.

Correll, Shelley J., Stephen Benard, and In Paik. 2007. "Getting a Job: Is There a Motherhood Penalty?" *American Journal of Sociology* 112(5): 1297–339.

Costa, D. L., and M. E. Kahn. 2003. "Understanding the American Decline in Social Capital, 1952–1998." *Kyklos* 56(1): 17–46.

Cowley, Stacy, and Jessica Silver-Greenberg. 2017. "Loans 'Designed to Fail': States Say Navient Preyed on Students." *New York Times*, April 9.

Crotty, James. 2003. "The Neoliberal Paradox: The Impact of Destructive Product Market Competition and Impatient Finance on Nonfinancial Corporations in the Neoliberal Era." *Review of Radical Political Economics* 35(3): 271–79.

Darcillon, Thibault. 2015. "How Does Finance Affect Labor Market Institutions? An Empirical Analysis in 16 OECD Countries." *Socio-Economic Review* 13(3): 477–504.

Dash, Eric, and Jennifer Bayot. 2005. "Bankruptcy Law Is Criticized for Creditors' Role in Counseling." *New York Times*, October 14.

Davis, Gerald F. 2009. *Managed by the Markets: How Finance Re-shaped America*. New York: Oxford University Press.

Davis, Gerald F. 2010. "The Twilight of the Berle and Means Corporation." *Seattle University Law Review* 34: 1121–38.

Davis, Gerald F. 2016. *The Vanishing American Corporation: Navigating the Hazards of a New Economy*. 1 edition. Oakland, CA: Berrett-Koehler Publishers.

De Figueiredo, Rui J. P., and Geoff Edwards. 2007. "Does Private Money Buy Public Policy? Campaign Contributions and Regulatory Outcomes in Telecommunications." *Journal of Economics & Management Strategy* 16(3): 547–76.

Deery, Stephen J., and Andrea Mahony. 1994. "Temporal Flexibility: Management Strategies and Employee Preferences in the Retail Industry." *Journal of Industrial Relations* 36(3): 332–52.

Dewey, Scott. 1998. "Working for the Environment: Organized Labor and the Origins of Environmentalism in the United States, 1948–1970." *Environmental History* 3(1): 45–63.

Dobbin, Frank, and Jiwook Jung. 2010. "The Misapplication of Mr. Michael Jensen: How Agency Theory Brought Down the Economy and Why It Might Again." *Research in the Sociology of Organizations* 30(B): 29–64.

Dore, Ronald. 2008. "Financialization of the Global Economy." *Industrial and Corporate Change* 17(6): 1097–112.

Doren, Catherine, and Eric Grodsky. 2016. "What Skills Can Buy: Transmission of Advantage through Cognitive and Noncognitive Skills." *Sociology of Education* 89(4): 321–42.

Duménil, Gérard, and Dominique Lévy. 2001. "Costs and Benefits of Neoliberalism: A Class Analysis." *Review of International Political Economy* 8(4): 578–607.

Dünhaupt, Petra. 2012. "Financialization and the Rentier Income Share: Evidence from the USA and Germany." *International Review of Applied Economics* 26(4): 465–87.

Dünhaupt, Petra. 2016. "Determinants of Labour's Income Share in the Era of Financialisation." *Cambridge Journal of Economics* 41(1): 283–306.

Dunlap, Riley E., and Angela G. Mertig. 1991. "The Evolution of the U.S. Environmental Movement from 1970 to 1990: An Overview." *Society & Natural Resources* 4(3): 209–18.

Dynan, Karen E., Jonathan Skinner, and Stephen P. Zeldes. 2004. "Do the Rich Save More?" *Journal of Political Economy* 112(2): 397–444.

Eberhardt, Pia, and Cecilia Olivet. 2012. *Profiting from Injustice: How Law Firms, Arbitrators and Financiers Are Fuelling an Investment Arbitration Boom.* Brussels: Corporate Europe Observatory and the Transnational Institute.

Edmans, Alex. 2011. "Does the Stock Market Fully Value Intangibles? Employee Satisfaction and Equity Prices." *Journal of Financial Economics* 101(3): 621–40.

Eichengreen, Barry. 2010. *Exorbitant Privilege: The Rise and Fall of the Dollar and the Future of the International Monetary System.* New York: Oxford University Press.

Eisinger, Jesse. 2012. https://dealbook.nytimes.com/2012/07/18/behind-credit-default-swaps-market-a-cartel-left-open-to-collusion/?searchResultPosition=1

Eisinger, Jesse. 2014. "Why Only One Top Banker Went to Jail for the Financial Crisis." *New York Times*, April 30.

Eisinger, Jesse. 2017. *The Chickenshit Club: Why the Justice Department Fails to Prosecute Executives.* New York: Simon & Schuster.

Epstein, Gerald A., and Arjun Jayadev. 2005. "The Rise of Rentier Incomes in OECD Countries: Financialization, Central Bank Policy and Labor Solidarity." Pp. 46–74 in *Financialization and the World Economy*, edited by G. A. Epstein. Northampton, MA: Edward Elgar.

Fama, Eugene F., and Michael C. Jensen. 1983. "Separation of Ownership and Control." *Journal of Law and Economics* 26(2): 301–25.

Farber, David R. 2002. *Sloan Rules: Alfred P. Sloan and the Triumph of General Motors.* Chicago: University of Chicago Press.

Fellowes, Matthew C., and Patrick J. Wolf. 2004. "Funding Mechanisms and Policy Instruments: How Business Campaign Contributions Influence Congressional Votes." *Political Research Quarterly* 57(2): 315–24.

Financial Crisis Inquiry Commission. 2011. *The Financial Crisis Inquiry Report.* New York: PublicAffairs.

Firebaugh, Glenn, and Matthew B. Schroeder. 2009. "Does Your Neighbor's Income Affect Your Happiness?" *American Journal of Sociology* 115(3): 805–31.

Fitch, Catherine A., and Steven Ruggles. 2000. "Historical Trends in Marriage Formation: The United States 1850–1990." Pp. 59–88 in *The Ties That Bind: Perspectives on Marriage and Cohabitation*, edited by Linda J. Waite, Christine Bachrach, Michelle J. Hindin, Elizabeth Thomson, and Arland Thronton. Hawthorne, NY: Walter de Gruyter, Inc.

Flaherty, Eoin. 2015. "Top Incomes under Finance-Driven Capitalism, 1990–2010: Power Resources and Regulatory Orders." *Socio-Economic Review* 13(3): 417–47.

Fligstein, Neil. 1993. *The Transformation of Corporate Control.* Reprint ed. Cambridge, MA: Harvard University Press.

Fligstein, Neil. 2001. *The Architecture of Markets: An Economic Sociology of Twenty-First-Century Capitalist Societies.* Princeton, NJ: Princeton University Press.

Fligstein, Neil, Jonah Stuart Brundage, and Michael Schultz. 2017. "Seeing Like the Fed: Culture, Cognition, and Framing in the Failure to Anticipate the Financial Crisis of 2008." *American Sociological Review* 82(5): 879–909.

Fligstein, Neil, and Adam Goldstein. 2015. "The Emergence of a Finance Culture in American Households, 1989–2007." *Socio-Economic Review* 13(3): 575–601.

Fligstein, Neil, and Taekjin Shin. 2007. "Shareholder Value and the Transformation of the U.S. Economy, 1984–2000." *Sociological Forum* 22(4): 399–424.

Folbre, Nancy. 2001. *The Invisible Heart: Economics and Family Values.* New York: New Press.

Forbes, Kristin J. 2000. "A Reassessment of the Relationship between Inequality and Growth." *American Economic Review* 90(4): 869–87.

Freeman, Richard B., and James L. Medoff. 1992. *What Do Unions Do?* New York: Basic Books.

Freeman, Richard B. 2010. "It's financialization!." *International Labour Review* 149(2): 163–83.

Fridman, Daniel. 2016. *Freedom from Work: Embracing Financial Self-Help in the United States and Argentina.* Stanford, CA: Stanford University Press.

Friedline, Terri, Rainier D. Masa, and Gina A. N. Chowa. 2015. "Transforming Wealth: Using the Inverse Hyperbolic Sine (IHS) and Splines to Predict Youth's Math Achievement." *Social Science Research* 49: 264–87.

Frontain, Michael. 2010. "Enron Corporation." *Handbook of Texas Online.*

FTSE Russell. 2017. *FTSE4Good Index Series. Factsheet.*

Galbraith, James K. 2012. *Inequality and Instability: A Study of the World Economy Just before the Great Crisis*. New York: Oxford University Press.

Galbraith, John Kenneth. 1993. *American Capitalism: The Concept of Countervailing Power*. New ed. New Brunswick, NJ: Transaction Publishers.

Garvey, Gerald T., Joshua Kazdin, Joanna Nash, Ryan LaFond, and Hussein Safa. 2016. "A Pitfall in Ethical Investing: ESG Disclosures Reveal Vulnerabilities, Not Virtues." SSRN Scholarly Paper. ID 2840629. Rochester, NY: Social Science Research Network.

Gilens, Martin. 2005. "Inequality and Democratic Responsiveness." *Public Opinion Quarterly* 69(5): 778–96.

Godechot, Olivier. 2012. "Is Finance Responsible for the Rise in Wage Inequality in France?" *Socio-Economic Review* 10(3): 447–70.

Godechot, Olivier. 2016a. "Financialization Is Marketization! A Study of the Respective Impacts of Various Dimensions of Financialization on the Increase in Global Inequality." *Sociological Science* 3: 495–519.

Godechot, Olivier. 2016b. *Wages, Bonuses and Appropriation of Profit in the Financial Industry: The Working Rich*. London: Taylor & Francis Group.

Goetzmann, William N. 2016. *Money Changes Everything: How Finance Made Civilization Possible*. Princeton, NJ: Princeton University Press.

Golden, Lonnie. 2015. "Irregular Work Scheduling and Its Consequences." SSRN Scholarly Paper. ID 2597172. Rochester, NY: Social Science Research Network.

Goldin, Claudia, and Lawrence F. Katz. 2009. *The Race between Education and Technology*. Cambridge, MA: Harvard University Press.

Goldin, Claudia, and Robert A. Margo. 1992. "The Great Compression: The Wage Structure in the United States at Mid-Century." *Quarterly Journal of Economics* 107(1): 1–34.

Goldstein, Adam. 2012. "Revenge of the Managers: Labor Cost-Cutting and the Paradoxical Resurgence of Managerialism in the Shareholder Value Era, 1984 to 2001." *American Sociological Review* 77(2): 268–94.

Goldstein, Joshua R., and Catherine T. Kenney. 2001. "Marriage Delayed or Marriage Forgone? New Cohort Forecasts of First Marriage for US Women." *American Sociological Review* 66(4): 506–19.

Gordon, David. 2002. "From the Drive System to the Capital-Labor Accord: Econometric Tests for the Transition between Productivity Regimes." *Industrial Relations* 36(2): 125–59.

Gordon, David M. 1996. *Fat and Mean: The Corporate Squeeze of Working Americans and the Myth of Managerial "Downsizing."* New York: Free Press.

Gottlieb, Robert. 2005. *Forcing the Spring: The Transformation of the American Environmental Movement*. Revised. Washington, DC: Island Press.

Gourevitch, Peter Alexis, and James Shinn. 2007. *Political Power and Corporate Control: The New Global Politics of Corporate Governance*. Princeton, NJ: Princeton University Press.

Greider, William. 2001. "The Right and US Trade Law: Invalidating the 20th Century." *The Nation*, November 17.

Grusky, David B., Bruce Western, and Christopher Wimer. 2011. *The Great Recession*. New York: Russell Sage Foundation.

Grusky, David B., and Tamar Kricheli-Katz, eds. 2012. *The New Gilded Age: The Critical Inequality Debates of Our Time*. Stanford, CA: Stanford University Press.

Gutiérrez, Germán, and Thomas Philippon. 2017. *Declining Competition and Investment in the US*. National Bureau of Economic Research.

Gutter, Michael, and Angela Fontes. 2006. "Racial Differences in Risky Asset Ownership: A Two-Stage Model of the Investment Decision-Making Process." *Journal of Financial Counseling and Planning* 17(2).

Hacker, Jacob S., and Paul Pierson. 2011. *Winner-Take-All Politics: How Washington Made the Rich Richer—and Turned Its Back on the Middle Class*. New York: Simon & Schuster.

Hamilton, James D. 2013. "Off-Balance-Sheet Federal Liabilities." Working Paper 19253. National Bureau of Economic Research.

Hanley, Caroline. 2014. "Putting the Bias in Skill-Biased Technological Change? A Relational Perspective on White-Collar Automation at General Electric." *American Behavioral Scientist* 58(3): 400–15.

Harkness, Sarah K. 2016. "Discrimination in Lending Markets: Status and the Intersections of Gender and Race." *Social Psychology Quarterly* 79(1): 81–93.

Harrington, Brooke. 2008. *Pop Finance: Investment Clubs and the New Investor Populism*. Princeton, NJ: Princeton University Press.

Harrington, Brooke. 2016. *Capital without Borders: Wealth Managers and the One Percent*. Cambridge, MA: Harvard University Press.

Hein, Eckhard. 2015. "Finance-Dominated Capitalism and Re-distribution of Income: A Kaleckian Perspective." *Cambridge Journal of Economics* 39(3): 907–34.

Heintz, Stephen. 2016. "Rockefeller Fund CEO: We're Getting Out of Fossil Fuels Investments." *CNN*, April 22.

Henriques, Diana B. 2001. "Enron's Collapse: The Derivatives; Market That Deals in Risks Faces a Novel One." *New York Times*, November 29.

Henry, David. 2013. "JPMorgan to Stop Making Student Loans: Company Memo." *Reuters*, September 5.

Herring, Cedric. 2009. "Does Diversity Pay? Race, Gender, and the Business Case for Diversity." *American Sociological Review* 74(2): 208–24.

Hester, Donald D. 2008. *The Evolution of Monetary Policy and Banking in the US*. Berlin, Heidelberg: Springer.

Heywood, John S., and Daniel Parent. 2012. "Performance Pay and the White-Black Wage Gap." *Journal of Labor Economics* 30(2): 249–90.

Hill, Mary S., Thomas J. Lopez, and Austin L. Reitenga. 2016. "CEO Excess Compensation: The Impact of Firm Size and Managerial Power." *Advances in Accounting* 33(Supplement C): 35–46.

Hillman, Nicholas W. 2016. http://wiscape.wisc.edu/docs/WebDispenser/wiscapedocuments/wp018.pdf?sfvrsn=12

Ho, Catherine. 2013. "Trade Deal Draws Lobbying from Businesses, Unions." *Washington Post*. https: //www.washingtonpost.com/business/capitalbusiness/trade-deal-draws-lobbying-from-businesses-unions/2013/05/24/19704276-c262-11e2-914f-a7aba60512a7_story.html.

Ho, Karen. 2009. *Liquidated: An Ethnography of Wall Street*. Durham, NC: Duke University Press.

Holland, Kelley. 2015. "Looking for the Next Crisis? Try Student Debt." *USA Today*, June 24.

Hong, Harrison, Jeffrey D. Kubik, and Jeremy C. Stein. 2004. "Social Interaction and Stock-Market Participation." *Journal of Finance* 59(1): 137–63.

Houle, Jason N. 2014. "A Generation Indebted: Young Adult Debt across Three Cohorts." *Social Problems* 61(3): 448–65.

Houpt, James V. 1999. "International Activities of US Banks and in US Banking Markets." *Federal Reserve Bulletin* 85: 599–615.

House Committee on Financial Services. 2017. *H.R. 10 Financial CHOICE Act of 2017*. Washington, DC.

Hout, Michael. 2016. "Money and Morale Growing Inequality Affects How Americans View Themselves and Others." *The Annals of the American Academy of Political and Social Science* 663(1): 204–28.

Howerth, Ira W. 1906. "The Social Question of Today." *American Journal of Sociology* 12(2): 254–68.

Huber, Evelyne, Jingjing Huo, and John D. Stephens. 2017. "Power, Policy, and Top Income Shares." *Socio-Economic Review*. mwx027, https://doi-org.ezproxy.lib.utexas.edu/10.1093/ser/mwx027

Humphrey, David B., and Lawrence B. Pulley. 1997. "Banks' Responses to Deregulation: Profits, Technology, and Efficiency." *Journal of Money, Credit and Banking* 29(1): 73–93.

Hyde, Allen, Todd Vachon, and Michael Wallace. 2018. "Financialization, Income Inequality, and Redistribution in 18 Affluent Democracies, 1981–2011." *Social Currents* 5(2): 193–211.

Hyman, Louis. 2012. *Debtor Nation: The History of America in Red Ink*. Reprint ed. Princeton, NJ: Princeton University Press.

Igan, Deniz, Prachi Mishra, and Thierry Tressel. 2012. "A Fistful of Dollars: Lobbying and the Financial Crisis." *NBER Macroeconomics Annual* 26(1): 195–230.

Imrohoroglu, Ayse, Antonio Merlo, and Peter Rupert. 2001. "What Accounts for the Decline in Crime?" SSRN Scholarly Paper. ID 267784. Rochester, NY: Social Science Research Network.

Indiviglio, Daniel. 2010. "How Americans' Love Affair with Debt Has Grown." *The Atlantic*, September 26.

International Monetary Fund. 2014. *Global Financial Stability Report: Risk Taking, Liquidity, and Shadow Banking Curbing Excess While Promoting Growth*. World Economic and Financial Surveys.

Jayaratne, Jith, and Philip E. Strahan. 1996. "The Finance-Growth Nexus: Evidence from Bank Branch Deregulation." *Quarterly Journal of Economics* 111(3): 639–70.

Jayaratne, Jith, and Philip E. Strahan. 1997. "The Benefits of Branching Deregulation." *Economic Policy Review* 3(4).

Jay-Z. 2017. "The Story of O.J." Roc Nation.

Jerrim, John, and Lindsey Macmillan. 2015. "Income Inequality, Intergenerational Mobility, and the Great Gatsby Curve: Is Education the Key?" *Social Forces* 94(2): 505–33.

Jez, Su Jin. 2014. "The Differential Impact of Wealth versus Income in the College-Going Process." *Research in Higher Education* 55(7): 710–34.

Johnson, Christian A., and George G. Kaufman. 2007. "A Bank by any Other Name . . . " *Economic Perspectives* 31(4).

Jung, Jiwook. 2015. "Shareholder Value and Workforce Downsizing, 1981–2006." *Social Forces* 93(4): 1335–68.

Jung, Jiwook. 2016. "Through the Contested Terrain: Implementation of Downsizing Announcements by Large U.S. Firms, 1984 to 2005." *American Sociological Review* 81(2): 347–73.

Jung, Jiwook, and Eunmi Mun. 2016. "Bending but Not Breaking? Foreign Investor Pressure and Dividend Payouts by Japanese Firms." *Sociological Forum* 31(3): 663–84.

Jung, Jiwook, and Eunmi Mun. 2017. "Does Diffusion Make an Institutionally Contested Practice Legitimate? Shareholder Responses to Downsizing in Japan, 1973–2005." *Organization Studies* 38(10): 1347–72.

Kalleberg, Arne L. 2011. *Good Jobs, Bad Jobs: The Rise of Polarized and Precarious Employment Systems in the United States, 1970s–2000s*. New York: Russell Sage Foundation.

Kamenetz, Anya. 2016. "Good News on Student Loans . . . for Some." *NPR*, July 26.

Kang, Songman. 2015. "Inequality and Crime Revisited: Effects of Local Inequality and Economic Segregation on Crime." *Journal of Population Economics* 29(2): 593–626.

Kaplan, Thomas, and Alan Rappeport. 2017. "Republican Tax Bill Passes Senate in 51–48 Vote." *New York Times*, December 19.

Katznelson, Ira. 2005. *When Affirmative Action Was White: An Untold History of Racial Inequality in Twentieth-Century America*. New York: Norton.

Kay, John. 2015. *Other People's Money: The Real Business of Finance*. New York: PublicAffairs.

Keister, Lisa A. 2000a. "Race and Wealth Inequality: The Impact of Racial Differences in Asset Ownership on the Distribution of Household Wealth." *Social Science Research* 29(4): 477–502.

Keister, Lisa A. 2000b. *Wealth in America: Trends in Wealth Inequality*. New York: Cambridge University Press.

Keister, Lisa A. 2004. "Race, Family Structure, and Wealth: The Effect of Childhood Family on Adult Asset Ownership." *Sociological Perspectives* 47(2): 161–87.

Keister, Lisa A., and Stephanie Moller. 2000. "Wealth Inequality in the United States." *Annual Review of Sociology* 26(1): 63–81.

Kelly, Kate. 2017. "Investing in the Pain of Student Debt Is a Tough but Tempting Play." *New York Times*, February 9.

Kennedy, Allan A. 2001. *The End of Shareholder Value: Corporations at the Crossroads*. Cambridge, MA: Basic Books.

Kennedy, Edward. 1998. *Congressional Record*. 105th Congress.

Keynes, John Maynard. 1936. *General Theory of Employment, Interest and Money*. Cambridge: Macmillan Cambridge University Press, for Royal Economic Society.

Kiel, Paul. 2008. "Banks' Favorite (Toothless) Regulator." *ProPublica*. Retrieved March 19, 2017 (http://www.propublica.org/article/banks-favorite-toothless-regulator-1125).

Kiel, Paul, and Annie Waldman. 2015. "The Color of Debt: How Collection Suits Squeeze Black Neighborhoods." *Pro Publica*, October 8.

Killewald, Alexandra. 2013. "Return to Being Black, Living in the Red: A Race Gap in Wealth That Goes beyond Social Origins." *Demography* 50(4): 1177–95.

Killewald, Alexandra, Fabian T. Pfeffer, and Jared N. Schachner. 2017. "Wealth Inequality and Accumulation." *Annual Review of Sociology* 43(1): 379–404.

King, Robert G., and Ross Levine. 1993. "Finance and Growth: Schumpeter Might Be Right." *Quarterly Journal of Economics* 108(3): 717–37.

Kitroeff, Natalie. 2018. "Tax Law May Send Factories and Jobs Abroad, Critics Say." *New York Times*, January 8.

Kornrich, Sabino. 2016. "Inequalities in Parental Spending on Young Children: 1972 to 2010." *AERA Open* 2(2): 1–12.

Kornrich, Sabino, and Frank Furstenberg. 2013. "Investing in Children: Changes in Parental Spending on Children, 1972–2007." *Demography* 50(1): 1–23.

Krippner, Greta R. 2011. *Capitalizing on Crisis: The Political Origins of the Rise of Finance.* Cambridge, MA: Harvard University Press.

Kristal, Tali. 2013. "The Capitalist Machine: Computerization, Workers' Power, and the Decline in Labor's Share within U.S. Industries." *American Sociological Review* 78(3): 361–89.

Krueger, Alan. 2012. "The Rise and Consequences of Inequality." Presentation Made to the Center for American Progress, January 12th. Available at www. Americanprogress. Org/Events/2012/01/12/17181/the-Rise-and-Consequences-of-Inequality.

Kunz, Diane B. 1997. "The Marshall Plan Reconsidered: A Complex of Motives." *Foreign Affairs* 76(3): 162–70.

Kus, Basak. 2012. "Financialisation and Income Inequality in OECD Nations: 1995–2007." *Economic and Social Review* 43(4): 477–95.

Kus, Basak. 2013. "Consumption and Redistributive Politics: The Effect of Credit and China." *International Journal of Comparative Sociology* 54(3): 187–204.

Kus, Basak, and Wen Fan. 2015. "Income Inequality, Credit and Public Support for Redistribution." *Intereconomics—Review of European Economic Policy* 2015(4): 198–205.

Kwon, Roy, and Anthony Roberts. 2015. "Financialization and Income Inequality in the New Economy." *Sociology of Development* 1(4): 442–62.

Kwon, Roy, Anthony Roberts, and Karissa Zingula. 2017. "Whither the Middle Class? Financialization, Labor Institutions, and the Gap between Top- and Middle-Income Earners in Advanced Industrial Societies." *Sociology of Development* 3(4): 377–402.

Lambert, Susan J. 2008. "Passing the Buck: Labor Flexibility Practices That Transfer Risk onto Hourly Workers." *Human Relations* 61(9): 1203–27.

Lamont, Michèle. 2002. *The Dignity of Working Men: Morality and the Boundaries of Race, Class, and Immigration.* Cambridge, MA: Harvard University Press.

Langley, Paul. 2008. *The Everyday Life of Global Finance: Saving and Borrowing in Anglo-America.* New York: Oxford University Press.

Lattman, Peter. 2013. https://dealbook.nytimes.com/2013/04/12/ex-credit-suisse-executive-pleads-guilty-to-inflating-value-of-mortgage-bonds/?searchResultPosition=1

Lazonick, William, and Mary O'Sullivan. 2000. "Maximizing Shareholder Value: A New Ideology for Corporate Governance." *Economy and Society* 29(1): 13–35.

Lee, Cheol-Sung, Francois Nielsen, and Arthur S. Alderson. 2007. "Income Inequality, Global Economy and the State." *Social Forces* 86(1): 77–112.

Leicht, Kevin T. 1989. "On the Estimation of Union Threat Effects." *American Sociological Review* 54(6): 1035–47.

Leicht, Kevin T., and Scott T. Fitzgerald. 2006. *Postindustrial Peasants: The Illusion of Middle-Class Prosperity.* New York: Macmillan.

Lerner, Melvin J. 1965. "Evaluation of Performance as a Function of Performer's Reward and Attractiveness." *Journal of Personality and Social Psychology* 1(4): 355.

Lerner, Melvin J., and Carolyn H. Simmons. 1966. "Observer's Reaction to the 'Innocent Victim': Compassion or Rejection?" *Journal of Personality and Social Psychology* 4(2): 203–10.

Lewis, Michael. 2010. *The Big Short: Inside the Doomsday Machine.* New York: Norton.

Lin, J. T., C. Bumcrot, T. Ulicny, A. Lusardi, G. Mottola, C. Kieffer, and G. Walsh. 2016. "Financial Capability in the United States 2016." Finra Investor Education Foundation.

Lin, Ken-Hou. 2015. "The Financial Premium in the US Labor Market: A Distributional Analysis." *Social Forces* 94(1): 1–30.

Lin, Ken-Hou. 2016. "The Rise of Finance and Firm Employment Dynamics." *Organization Science* 27(4): 972–88.

Lin, Ken-Hou, Samuel Bondurant, and Andrew Messamore. 2018. "Union, Premium Cost, and the Provision of Employment-Based Health Insurance." *Socius.* doi:10.1177/2378023118798502

Lin, Ken-Hou, and Megan Tobias Neely. 2017. "Gender, Parental Status, and the Wage Premium in Finance." *Social Currents* 4(6): 535–55.

Lin, Ken-Hou, and Donald Tomaskovic-Devey. 2013. "Financialization and U.S. Income Inequality, 1970–2008." *American Journal of Sociology* 118(5): 1284–329.

Lovenheim, Michael F., and C. Lockwood Reynolds. 2013. "The Effect of Housing Wealth on College Choice: Evidence from the Housing Boom." *Journal of Human Resources* 48(1): 1–35.

Madden, Janice Fanning. 2012. "Performance-Support Bias and the Gender Pay Gap among Stockbrokers." *Gender & Society* 26(3): 488–518.

Madden, Janice Fanning, and Alexander Vekker. 2008. *Evaluating Whether Employment Outcomes for Brokers and Broker Trainees at Merrill Lynch Are Racially Neutral.* http://www.merrillclassaction.com/pdfs/DrsMaddenVekkerExpRebuttalRep.pdf

Magdoff, Harry, and Paul M. Sweezy. 1987. *Stagnation and the Financial Explosion.* New York: New York University Press.

Mankiw, N. Gregory. 2013. "Defending the One Percent." *Journal of Economic Perspectives* 27(3): 21–34.

Marmot, M. G., G. Rose, M. Shipley, and P. J. Hamilton. 1978. "Employment Grade and Coronary Heart Disease in British Civil Servants." *Journal of Epidemiology and Community Health* 32(4): 244–49.

Massey, Douglas, and Nancy Denton. 1993. *American Apartheid: Segregation and the Making of the Underclass.* Cambridge, MA: Harvard University Press.

Mayer, Susan E. 2001. "How Did the Increase in Economic Inequality between 1970 and 1990 Affect Children's Educational Attainment?" *American Journal of Sociology* 107(1): 1–32.

McCarthy, Justin. 2015. "Little Change in Percentage of Americans Who Own Stocks." *Gallup.com*. Retrieved April 13, 2017 (http://www.gallup.com/poll/182816/little-change-percentage-americans-invested-market.aspx).

McGuire, Gail M. 2000. "Gender, Race, Ethnicity, and Networks the Factors Affecting the Status of Employees' Network Members." *Work and Occupations* 27(4): 501–24.

McGuire, Gail M. 2002. "Gender, Race, and the Shadow Structure: A Study of Informal Networks and Inequality in a Work Organization." *Gender & Society* 16(3): 303–22.

McLean, Bethany, and Peter Elkind. 2004. *The Smartest Guys in the Room: The Amazing Rise and Scandalous Fall of Enron*. New York: Portfolio Trade.

McMenamin, Terence M. 2007. "A Time to Work: Recent Trends in Shift Work and Flexible Schedules." *Monthly Labor Review* 130: 3–15.

Meyer, Brett. 2017. "Financialization, Technological Change, and Trade Union Decline." *Socio-Economic Review*. mwx022, https://doi-org.ezproxy.lib.utexas.edu/10.1093/ser/mwx022

Milberg, William. 2008. "Shifting Sources and Uses of Profits: Sustaining US Financialization with Global Value Chains." *Economy and Society* 37(3): 420–51.

Milberg, William, and Deborah Winkler. 2010. "Financialisation and the Dynamics of Offshoring in the USA." *Cambridge Journal of Economics* 34(2): 275–93.

Miller, Seymour M., and Donald Tomaskovic-Devey. 1983. *Recapitalizing America: Alternatives to the Corporate Distortion of National Policy*. Boston: Routledge & Kegan Paul.

Mills, Melinda. 2004. "Demand for Flexibility or Generation of Insecurity? The Individualization of Risk, Irregular Work Shifts and Canadian Youth." *Journal of Youth Studies* 7(2): 115–39.

Milman, Oliver. 2017. "Harvard 'Pausing' Investments in Some Fossil Fuels." *The Guardian*, April 27.

Mishel, Lawrence, and Jessica Schieder. 2016. *Stock Market Headwinds Meant Less Generous Year for Some CEOs: CEO Pay Remains up 46.5% since 2009*. 109799. Washington, DC: Economic Policy Institute.

Moosa, Imad A. 2017. "Does Financialization Retard Growth? Time Series and Cross-Sectional Evidence." *Applied Economics* 50(31): 3405–15.

Morduch, Jonathan, and Rachel Schneider. 2017. *The Financial Diaries: How American Families Cope in a World of Uncertainty*. Princeton, NJ: Princeton University Press.

Morrissey, Monique. 2016. *The State of American Retirement: How 401(k)s Have Failed Most American Workers*. Washington, DC: Economic Policy Institute.

Munnell, Alicia H., Geoffrey M. B. Tootell, Lynn E. Browne, and James McEneaney. 1996. "Mortgage Lending in Boston: Interpreting HMDA Data." *American Economic Review* 86(1): 25–53.

Murphy, Kevin J. 2002. "Explaining Executive Compensation: Managerial Power versus the Perceived Cost of Stock Options." *University of Chicago Law Review* 69(3): 847–69.

Nadler, Jerrold. 1998. *Congressional Record*. 105th Congress.

Nau, Michael. 2013. "Economic Elites, Investments, and Income Inequality." *Social Forces* 92(3): 437–61.

Nau, Michael, Rachel E. Dwyer, and Randy Hodson. 2015. "Can't Afford a Baby? Debt and Young Americans." *Research in Social Stratification and Mobility* 42: 114–22.

Neckerman, Kathryn M., and Florencia Torche. 2007. "Inequality: Causes and Consequences." *Annual Review of Sociology* 33(1): 335–57.

Neely, Megan Tobias. 2018. "Fit to Be King: How Patrimonialism on Wall Street Leads to Inequality." *Socio-Economic Review* 16(2): 365–85.

Neidig, Harper. 2016. "Barney Frank Admits 'Mistake' in Dodd-Frank." *The Hill*, November 20.

Neustadtl, Alan, and Dan Clawson. 1988. "Corporate Political Groupings: Does Ideology Unify Business Political Behavior?" *American Sociological Review* 53(2): 172–90.

Noble, Safiya. 2018. *Algorithms of Oppression: How Search Engines Reinforce Racism.* New York: New York University Press.

Nocera, Joe. 2013. https://www.nytimes.com/2013/03/10/opinion/sunday/nocera-rigging-the-ipo-game.html?searchResultPosition=1

Norris, Floyd. 2002. "Market Place; New Set of Rules Is in the Works for Accounting." *New York Times*, October 22.

Oakley, Diane, and Kelly Kenneally. 2015. *Retirement Security 2015: Roadmap for Policy Makers.* National Institute on Retirement Security.

OECD. 2011. *Divided We Stand: Why Inequality Keeps Rising.* Paris: Organization for Economic Cooperation and Development.

OECD. 2014. *Society at a Glance: OECD Social Indicators: 2014.* Revised ed. Paris: Organization for Economic Cooperation and Development.

Oishi, Shigehiro, and Selin Kesebir. 2015. "Income Inequality Explains Why Economic Growth Does Not Always Translate to an Increase in Happiness." *Psychological Science* 26(10): 1630–38.

Oliver, Melvin, and Thomas M. Shapiro, eds. 2006. *Black Wealth/White Wealth: A New Perspective on Racial Inequality.* 2nd ed. New York: Routledge.

Oppel, Richard A. 2001. "Employees' Retirement Plan Is a Victim as Enron Tumbles." *New York Times*, November 22.

Oreopoulos, Philip, Till von Wachter, and Andrew Heisz. 2012. "The Short- and Long-Term Career Effects of Graduating in a Recession." *American Economic Journal: Applied Economics* 4(1): 1–29.

Orhangazi, Özgür. 2008. *Financialization and the US Economy.* Northampton, MA: Edward Elgar Publishing.

Ostry, Jonathan David, Andrew Berg, and Charalambos G. Tsangarides. 2014. *Redistribution, Inequality, and Growth.* International Monetary Fund. https://www.imf.org/external/pubs/ft/sdn/2014/sdn1402.pdf

Pahl, Jan. 1983. "The Allocation of Money and the Structuring of Inequality within Marriage." *Sociological Review* 31(2): 237–62.

Palan, Ronen, Richard Murphy, and Christian Chavagneux. 2013. *Tax Havens: How Globalization Really Works.* Ithaca, NY: Cornell University Press.

Partnoy, Frank. 2006. "A Revisionist View of Enron and the Sudden Death of 'May.'" Pp. 54–89 in *Enron and World Finance*, edited by P. Dembinski, C. Lager, A. Cornford, and J. Bonvin. New York: Palgrave Macmillan.

Peifer, Jared L. 2011. "Morality in the Financial Market? A Look at Religiously Affiliated Mutual Funds in the USA." *Socio-Economic Review* 9(2): 235–59.

Pernell, Kim, Jiwook Jung, and Frank Dobbin. 2017. "The Hazards of Expert Control: Chief Risk Officers and Risky Derivatives." *American Sociological Review* 82(3): 511–41.

Petroff, Alanna. 2016. "DoJ vs Big Banks: $60 Billion in Fines for Toxic Mortgages." *CNN*, December 23.

Philippon, Thomas. 2015. "Has the US Finance Industry Become Less Efficient? On the Theory and Measurement of Financial Intermediation." *American Economic Review* 105(4): 1408–38.

Philippon, Thomas, and Ariell Reshef. 2012. "Wages and Human Capital in the U.S. Finance Industry: 1909–2006." *Quarterly Journal of Economics* 127(4): 1551–609.

Picchi, Aimee. 2016. "Congrats, Class of 2016: You're the Most Indebted Yet." *CBS*, May 4.

Piketty, Thomas. 2014. *Capital in the Twenty-First Century.* Cambridge, MA: Belknap Press of Harvard University Press.

Piketty, Thomas, and Emmanuel Saez. 2006. "The Evolution of Top Incomes: A Historical and International Perspective." *American Economic Review* 96(2): 200–205.

Piketty, Thomas, Emmanuel Saez, and Gabriel Zucman. 2017. "Distributional National Accounts: Methods and Estimates for the United States." *Quarterly Journal of Economics* 133(2): 553–609.

Polanyi, Karl. 2001. *The Great Transformation: The Political and Economic Origins of Our Time.* 2nd ed. Boston: Rinehart & Company.

Pope, Devin G., and Justin R. Sydnor. 2011. "What's in a Picture? Evidence of Discrimination from Prosper.Com." *Journal of Human Resources* 46(1): 53–92.

Powell, Lewis F. 1971. "Confidential Memorandum: Attack of American Free Enterprise System." https://scholarlycommons.law.wlu.edu/powellmemo/

Prasad, Monica. 2012. *The Land of Too Much: American Abundance and the Paradox of Poverty.* Cambridge, MA: Harvard University Press.

Quarles, Randal K. 2018. "Implementation of the Economic Growth, Regulatory Relief, and Consumer Protection Act." Board of Governor's for the Federal Reserve System, October 2.

Rampell, Catherine. 2011. "Out of Harvard, and into Finance." *Economix Blog.* Retrieved April 18, 2013 (http: //economix.blogs.nytimes.com/2011/12/21/out-of-harvard-and-into-finance/).

Rappeport, Alan. 2017. "Bill to Erase Some Dodd-Frank Banking Rules Passes in House." *New York Times*, June 8.

Rappeport, Alan. 2018. "Senate Passes Bill Loosening Banking Rules, but Hurdles Remain in the House." *New York Times*, March 14.

Ricks, Morgan, John Crawford, and Lev Menand. 2018. "A Public Option for Bank Accounts (Or Central Banking for All)." SSRN Scholarly Paper. ID 3192162. Rochester, NY: Social Science Research Network.

Rivera, Lauren A. 2015. *Pedigree: How Elite Students Get Elite Jobs.* Princeton, NJ: Princeton University Press.

Roberts, Adrienne. 2013. "Financing Social Reproduction: The Gendered Relations of Debt and Mortgage Finance in Twenty-First-Century America." *New Political Economy* 18(1): 21–42.

Roberts, Anthony, and Roy Kwon. 2017. "Finance, Inequality and the Varieties of Capitalism in Post-industrial Democracies." *Socio-Economic Review* 15(3): 511–38.

Rosenfeld, Jake. 2014. *What Unions No Longer Do.* Cambridge, MA: Harvard University Press.

Rosenfeld, Jake, and Patrick Denice. 2015. "The Power of Transparency: Evidence from a British Workplace Survey." *American Sociological Review* 80(5): 1045–68.

Rosenfeld, Jake, and Meredith Kleykamp. 2009. "Hispanics and Organized Labor in the United States, 1973 to 2007." *American Sociological Review* 74(6): 916–37.

Rosenfeld, Jake, and Meredith Kleykamp. 2012. "Organized Labor and Racial Wage Inequality in the United States." *American Journal of Sociology* 117(5): 1460–502.

Ross, Stephen L., and John Yinger. 2002. *The Color of Credit: Mortgage Discrimination, Research Methodology, and Fair-Lending Enforcement.* Cambridge, MA: MIT Press.

Roth, Louise Marie. 2006. *Selling Women Short: Gender and Money on Wall Street.* Princeton, NJ: Princeton University Press.

Rugh, Jacob S., and Douglas S. Massey. 2010. "Racial Segregation and the American Foreclosure Crisis." *American Sociological Review* 75(5): 629–51.

Saez, Emmanuel, and Gabriel Zucman. 2016. "Wealth Inequality in the United States since 1913: Evidence from Capitalized Income Tax Data." *Quarterly Journal of Economics* 131(2): 519–78.

Salter, Malcom. 2008. *Innovation Corrupted: The Origins and Legacy of Enron's Collapse.* Cambridge, MA: Harvard University Press.

Sanders, Jeffrey S. 2011. "The Path to Becoming A Fortune 500 CEO." Retrieved April 13, 2017 (https://www.forbes.com/sites/ciocentral/2011/12/05/the-path-to-becoming-a-fortune-500-ceo/#2b37b8fb709b).

Scheer, Robert. 2010. *The Great American Stickup: How Reagan Republicans and Clinton Democrats Enriched Wall Street While Mugging Main Street.* New York: Bold Type Books.

Schneider, Daniel, Orestes P. Hastings, and Joe LaBriola. 2018. "Income Inequality and Class Divides in Parental Investments." *American Sociological Review* 83(3): 475–507.

Scott-Clayton, Judith E. 2018. "The Looming Student Loan Crisis Is Worse Than We Thought." Community College Research Center. Evidence Speaks, Vol. 2, No. 34. Brookings Institution. https://academiccommons.columbia.edu/doi/10.7916/D8WT05QV

Seamster, Louise, and Raphaël Charron-Chénier. 2017. "Predatory Inclusion and Education Debt: Rethinking the Racial Wealth Gap." *Social Currents* 4(3): 199–207.

Seelye, Katharine Q. 1998. "Panel to Vote on Measure to Tighten Bankruptcy Law." *New York Times*, May 14.

Shapiro, Thomas M. 2004. *The Hidden Cost of Being African American: How Wealth Perpetuates Inequality.* New York: Oxford University Press.

Shiller, Robert J. 1994. *Macro Markets: Creating Institutions for Managing Society's Largest Economic Risks.* New York: Oxford University Press.

Shin, Taekjin. 2012. "CEO Compensation and Shareholder Value Orientation among Large US Firms." *Economic and Social Review* 43(4): 535–59.

Shin, Taekjin. 2014. "Explaining Pay Disparities between Top Executives and Nonexecutive Employees: A Relative Bargaining Power Approach." *Social Forces* 92(4): 1339–72.

Shin, Taekjin, and Jihae You. 2017. "Pay for Talk: How the Use of Shareholder-Value Language Affects CEO Compensation." *Journal of Management Studies* 54(1): 88–117.

Siegel, Robert. 2007. "2005 Law Made Student Loans More Lucrative." *NPR*, April 24.

Silver-Greenberg, Jessica. 2012. https://www.nytimes.com/2012/07/14/business/mastercard-and-visa-settle-antitrust-suit.html?searchResultPosition=1

Smith, Adam. 1950 [1776]. *An Inquiry into the Nature and Causes of the Wealth of Nations.* Methuen.

Song, Jae, David J. Price, Fatih Guvenen, and Nicholas Bloom. 2015. "Firming Up Inequality." *The Quarterly Journal of Economics* 134(1): 1–50.

S&P Global. 2017. *S&P 500 Environmental & Socially Responsible Index. Strategy.*

Sparshott, Jeffrey. 2015. "Congratulations, Class of 2015: You're the Most Indebted Ever (for Now)." *WSJ Blogs—Real Time Economics.* Retrieved October 2, 2015 (http: //blogs.wsj.com/economics/2015/05/08/congratulations-class-of-2015-youre-the-most-indebted-ever-for-now/).

Spilerman, Seymour. 2000. "Wealth and Stratification Processes." *Annual Review of Sociology* 26(1): 497–524.

Stein, Judith. 2010. *Pivotal Decade: How the United States Traded Factories for Finance in the Seventies.* New Haven: Yale University Press.

Stein, Judith. 2011. *Pivotal Decade: How the United States Traded Factories for Finance in the Seventies.* August 14 ed. New Haven: Yale University Press.

Stevenson, Thomas H., and D. Anthony Plath. 2002. "Marketing Financial Services to the African-American Consumer: A Comparative Analysis of Investment Portfolio Composition." *California Management Review* 44(4): 39–64.

Steyer, Robert. 2017. "Columbia University to Divest from Some Coal Companies." *Pensions & Investments.* Retrieved October 20, 2017 (http://www.pionline.com/article/20170315/ONLINE/170319903/columbia-university-to-divest-from-some-coal-companies).

Stojmenovska, Dragana, Thijs Bol, and Thomas Leopold. 2017. "Does Diversity Pay? A Replication of Herring (2009)." *American Sociological Review* 82(4): 857–67.

Story, Louise. 2010. "Goldman on the Defensive before Senate Panel." *New York Times*, April 27.

Subramanian, S. V., and Ichiro Kawachi. 2006. "Whose Health Is Affected by Income Inequality? A Multilevel Interaction Analysis of Contemporaneous and Lagged Effects of State Income Inequality on Individual Self-Rated Health in the United States." *Health & Place* 12(2): 141–56.

Sullivan, Teresa A., Elizabeth Warren, and Jay Lawrence Westbrook. 1997. "Consumer Bankruptcy in the United States: A Study of Alleged Abuse and of Local Legal Culture." *Journal of Consumer Policy* 20(2): 223–68.

Tabb, Charles. 2006. "Consumer Bankruptcy Filings: Trends and Indicators." *University of Illinois Law and Economics Working Papers.*

Taibbi, Matt. 2012. https://www.rollingstone.com/politics/politics-news/the-scam-wall-street-learned-from-the-mafia-190232/

Tamborini, Christopher R., and ChangHwan Kim. 2017. "Education and Contributory Pensions at Work: Disadvantages of the Less Educated." *Social Forces* 95(4): 1577–606.

Thomas, C. William. 2002. "The Rise and Fall of Enron." *Journal of Accountancy* 193(4): 41.

Tichy, Noel, and Ram Charan. 1989. "Speed, Simplicity, Self-Confidence: An Interview with Jack Welch." *Harvard Business Review* 67(5): 112–20.

Tomaskovic-Devey, Donald, and Dustin Avent-Holt. 2019. *Relational Inequalities: An Organizational Approach.* New York: Oxford University Press.

Tomaskovic-Devey, Donald, and Ken-Hou Lin. 2011. "Income Dynamics, Economic Rents, and the Financialization of the U.S. Economy." *American Sociological Review* 76(4): 538–59.

Tomaskovic-Devey, Donald, Ken-Hou Lin, and Nathan Meyers. 2015. "Did Financialization Reduce Economic Growth?" *Socio-Economic Review* 13(3): 525–48.

Tooze, Adam. 2018. *Crashed: How a Decade of Financial Crises Changed the World.* New York: Viking.

Townsend, Peter. 1979. *Poverty in the United Kingdom: A Survey of Household Resources and Standards of Living.* Berkeley: University of California Press.

Trumbull, Gunnar. 2014. *Consumer Lending in France and America: Credit and Welfare.* New York: Cambridge University Press.

Turco, Catherine J. 2010. "Cultural Foundations of Tokenism Evidence from the Leveraged Buyout Industry." *American Sociological Review* 75(6): 894–913.

Turner, Adair. 2015. *Between Debt and the Devil: Money, Credit, and Fixing Global Finance.* Princeton, NJ: Princeton University Press.

Useem, Michael. 1993. *Executive Defense: Shareholder Power and Corporate Reorganization.* Cambridge, MA: Harvard University Press.

Vachon, Todd E., Michael Wallace, and Allen Hyde. 2016. "Union Decline in a Neoliberal Age: Globalization, Financialization, European Integration, and Union Density in 18 Affluent Democracies." *Socius* 2: 2378023116656847.

Valenti, Catherine. 2006. "A Year after Enron, What's Changed?" *ABC News,* January 6.

Valladares, Mayra Rodríguez. 2015. "Despite Regulatory Advances, Experts Say Risk Remains a Danger to Large Banks." *New York Times,* March 23.

Vielkind, Jimmy. 2010. "Lobbyist Lazio Got Millions." *Times Union,* February 21.

Warren, Elizabeth. 2002. "The Market for Data: The Changing Role of Social Sciences in Shaping the Law." SSRN Scholarly Paper. ID 332162. Rochester, NY: Social Science Research Network.

Warren, Elizabeth. 2003. "Financial Collapse and Class Status: Who Goes Bankrupt?" *Osgoode Hall Law Journal* 41(1): 115–46.

Welch, Jack, and John A. Byrne. 2003. *Jack: Straight from the Gut.* New York: Grand Central Publishing.

Western, Bruce, Deirdre Bloome, and Christine Percheski. 2008. "Inequality among American Families with Children, 1975 to 2005." *American Sociological Review* 73(6): 903–20.

Western, Bruce, and Jake Rosenfeld. 2011. "Unions, Norms, and the Rise in U.S. Wage Inequality." *American Sociological Review* 76(4): 513–37.

Whoriskey, Peter. 2018. "'A Way of Monetizing Poor People': How Private Equity Firms Make Money Offering Loans to Cash-Strapped Americans." *Washington Post*, July 1.

Wilkinson, Richard G. 2005. *The Impact of Inequality: How to Make Sick Societies Healthier*. New York: New Press.

Wilkinson, Richard G., and Kate Pickett. 2011. *The Spirit Level: Why Greater Equality Makes Societies Stronger*. Reprint ed. London: Bloomsbury Press.

Williams, Richard, Reynold Nesiba, and Eileen Diaz McConnell. 2005. "The Changing Face of Inequality in Home Mortgage Lending." *Social Problems* 52(2): 181–208.

Wilson, George, and Vincent J. Roscigno. 2010. "Race and Downward Mobility from Privileged Occupations: African American/White Dynamics across the Early Work-Career." *Social Science Research* 39(1): 67–77.

Wingfield, Adia Harvey. 2014. "Crossing the Color Line: Black Professional Men's Development of Interracial Social Networks." *Societies* 4: 240–55.

Wolff, Edward N. 2015. "Household Wealth Inequality, Retirement Income Security, and Financial Market Swings 1983 through 2010." Pp. 245–78 in *Inequality, Uncertainty, and Opportunity: The Varied and Growing Role of Finance in Labor Relations, LERA Research Volumes*, edited by C. E. Weller. Ithaca, NY: Cornell University Press.

Wyly, Elvin, Markus Moos, Daniel Hammel, and Emanuel Kabahizi. 2009. "Cartographies of Race and Class: Mapping the Class-Monopoly Rents of American Subprime Mortgage Capital." *International Journal of Urban and Regional Research* 33(2): 332–54.

Yeung, W. Jean, and Dalton Conley. 2008. "Black-White Achievement Gap and Family Wealth." *Child Development* 79(2): 303–24.

Young, Kevin, and Stefano Pagliari. 2017. "Capital United? Business Unity in Regulatory Politics and the Special Place of Finance." *Regulation & Governance* 11(1): 3–23.

Zucman, Gabriel. 2013. "The Missing Wealth of Nations: Are Europe and the U.S. Net Debtors or Net Creditors?" *Quarterly Journal of Economics* 128(3): 1321–64.

INDEX

For the benefit of digital users, indexed terms that span two pages (e.g., 52–53) may, on occasion, appear on only one of those pages.

Figures are indicated by *f* following the page number.

mortgage lending and securitization
regulation, 66
Sallie Mae, 73–74
low-income households
Chapter 13 bankruptcy reform
on, 70–71
credit expansion on, 113
debt, cost of borrowing, 129–30, 129f
debt, delinquency, 131–32, 132f
debt and debt burden, 112–13, 112f,
130–31, 130f
income inequality, 33, 193n2
negative net worth, 132, 133f
US vs. other countries, 31–32

Macy's credit cards, 89–90
managed equity, wealth on, 146–47, 146f
Mankiw, Gregory, "Defending the One
Percent," 29–30, 31
market-based inequality, 193n2
market idealism, 27
marketing, financial products, racism
in, 143–44
market-oriented employment, 41–43
market populism, 146–47
market power, concentrated, 61–64, 62f,
63f, 178
*Marquette National Bank of Minneapolis v.
First of Omaha Service Corporation*, 57
Marshall Plan, 17
mass-market credit cards, 59–60
Maxima Shareholder Valorem, 24
McFadden Act of 1927, 52–53
Meckling, William, 91
mergers and acquisitions, 44, 46, 94,
103, 105, 108
merit-based financial aid, 125, 195–96n6
Mexico, 34–35, 40
middle class
leveraging for, debt, 113
lifestyle, debt financing, 112
in stock market, 137
millennials
student loans, debt burden and
payoff, 150–52, 151f
wealth slump, 146f, 148–52, 149f, 151f

Mishra, Prachi, 66
mobility, social, 30
money market mutual funds, 55
Morris, Arthur, 115
Morris Plan banks, 115
mortgage crisis
delinquency rate, 162, 163f
market collapse (late 2006), 160–61
securitization, 159
wealth collapse, 158
mortgage lending
financial industry lobbying, 66
First Nationwide Financial
Corporation, 87–88, 91
GMAC, 87–88, 91
Home Mortgage Disclosure Act of
1975, 119
redlining, racial, 119, 126–27,
143–44, 195n7
mortgages
adjustable-rate, 59–60
adjustable-rate subprime, 159
subprime, 59–60
Mulvaney, Mick, 167
Mun, Eunmi, 182–83
mutual banks, 53–54
mutual funds, 92–93, 94f
401(k) plans on, 92
definition, 92

NAACP, 118
Nadler, Jerrold, 71
National Credit Club Card Inc., 117
National Highway Traffic Safety
Administration, 134
National Housing Act of 1934, 116
National Welfare Rights Organization,
120
need-based financial aid, 125, 195–96n6
net worth, negative, 132, 133f
New Century, 159, 160–61
New Gilded Age, 4
nonbank banks, 3–4, 58, 87–88,
98, 162–64
nonfinance firms, in financial markets,
9, 12–13, 13f

North American Free Trade Agreement
(NAFTA), 39–40

Obama, Barack, 2008 financial crisis, 3,
25, 99, 121, 157, 162
Occupy Wall Street, 2, 157
off-balance sheet "partners,"
101–2, 195n6
Office of Financial Education, 133
Office of Financial Research, 162–64
Office of the Comptroller of the
Currency, 64, 87
Office of Thrift Supervision (OTS), 64
offshoring, 38, 46
option, 101, 194–95n5
Orderly Liquidation Authority, 162–64
Organization for Economic Cooperation
and Development (OECD) member
nations, 181–83
outsourcing, 32, 40–43, 46, 180
ownership society, 138

Pagliari, Stefano, 65–66
part-time workers, 42, 107
patrimonialism, 79
payday loans, 127–28, 172*f*, 173
pension funds, state and municipal,
92, 94*f*
people's portfolio, 137–56. *See also*
wealth, household, finance on
performance pay, 41–43
Personal Responsibility and Work
Opportunity Act, 122
petroleum dollar (petrodollar)
system, 19–20
Philippon, Thomas, 60, 63–64
Pierson, Paul, 21
Piketty, Tomas, 4, 33–34, 49–50
"poison pill," 94–95
policies, loose monetary (2001+), 67
politics
financial sector involvement,
64–66, 65*f*
Regan era reorientation, 22–25
poor. *See* low-income households
Powell, Lewis, 21

Prasad, Monica, 16
predatory lending, 115, 195n2
Price, Daniel, 40
principal-agent problem, 67–68
private equity, 65*f*, 66, 68, 94, 94*f*, 107,
165, 188
private intermediation, of public
policies, 66–69, 68*f*, 178, 185–86
productivity, income and, 31
product safety, 134
Profit Center Accounting, 193n2
progressive redistribution, 183–84
Public Company Oversight Board, 102–3
public policies. *See also specific types*
private intermediation of, 66–69,
68*f*, 178, 185–86
Pulley, Lawrence, 62–63

quantitative easing, 66–69, 96, 162

race
Chapter 13 bankruptcy reform
on, 70–71
Civil Rights Act, 118
Community Reinvestment Act, 119,
122
compensation in finance, 78–81, 80*f*
contract and temporary staffing, 42
credit and lending disparities, 119,
126–27, 143–44, 195n7
creditworthiness, 119, 127
debt, burden, 130–31, 130*f*
debt, cost of borrowing, 129–30, 129*f*
debt, expansion, ethnic minority
men, 14–15, 15*f*
debt, nonmortgage, since Great
Recession, 171–73, 172*f*
on debt consequences, 48
Equal Credit Opportunity Act, 119
Fair Housing Act, 118, 144
financial products marketing, 143–44
Home Mortgage Disclosure Act,
119, 167
inequality and, 45
NAACP, 118
stock ownership, 143–44, 144*f*